Introduction
to
HEALTH
PLANNING

FOURTH EDITION

Philip N. Reeves
Russell C. Coile, Jr.

INFORMATION RESOURCES PRESS
Arlington, Virginia   1989

Jacket and cover design by
WORDMARQUE DESIGN ASSOCIATES
Fairfax, Virginia.

Available from
Information Resources Press
1110 North Glebe Road
Suite 550
Arlington, Virginia 22201

Library of Congress Catalog Card Number 89-081230
ISBN 0-87815-059-5

CONTENTS

v

FIGURES

TABLES

ACRONYMS

ACLI	American Council of Life Insurance
AIDS	acquired immune deficiency syndrome
CCRC	continuing-care retirement center
CEO	chief executive officer
CFO	chief financial officer
CON	certificate of need
COO	chief operating officer
CS	cohort survival
DHEW	Department of Health, Education, and Welfare
DPI	Decision Process International
DRA	death rate (actual)
DRE	death rate (estimated)
DRG	Diagnostic Related Group
DSS	decision support system
ER	emergency room
GE	General Electric
GIGO	garbage in, garbage out
GM	General Motors
GNP	gross national product
HCFA	Health Care Financing Administration
HCIA	Health Care Investment Analysts
HIAA	Health Insurance Association of America
HMO	health maintenance organization
HSA	Health Systems Agencies
HSP	health system plan

JCAHO	Joint Commission on Accreditation of Healthcare Organizations
LAN	local area network
LRRA	long-range recommended action
MIS	management information system
MRI	magnetic resonance imaging
NCHS	National Center for Health Statistics
NIMH	National Institute of Mental Health
NME	National Medical Enterprises
PMU	program management unit
PPO	Preferred Provider Organization
PPS	prospective payment system
ROI	return on investment
SBU	strategic business unit
SEC	Securities and Exchange Commission
SHPDA	State Health Planning and Development Agency
SRRA	short-range recommended actions
SWOT	strengths, weaknesses, opportunities, threats
TAP	Trend Analysis Program
TPA	third-party administrator
UAW	United Auto Workers
UCLA	University of California, Los Angeles
UDI	Unnecessary Death Index
VALS	values, attitudes, and life-styles

PREFACE

This edition of *Introduction to Health Planning* continues to reflect the authors' confidence in the fundamental principles of systems planning.

In some respects this is idealistic, since our experience shows that most community planning has reverted to the unintegrated, categorical planning that was prevalent before the late 1960s. This outcome of national politics has caused some informed leaders to speculate that the destruction of a federally supported community planning effort was a Pyrrhic victory. We hope, however, that within the foreseeable future, public officials will remove their ideological blinders and recognize that coordination through an officially sanctioned planning process can lead to more effective and efficient delivery of health services to the citizenry. For instance, they may admit that planning services to AIDS victims should be formally integrated with the planning of maternal and child health programs that serve the victims' children, who may themselves be afflicted with this disease.

At this point, we are unable to predict whether this will lead to a repetition of history, beginning with collaboration with private sector programs (such as the activities of business coalitions), or whether the response will be a more direct return to a system mandated and supported by governments.

On the other hand, many organizations have grown to the point that they can plan successfully only if they deal with their diverse enterprises as subsystems within a larger organizational context. More importantly, regardless of their size and complexity, organizations must be able to respond as systems that are embedded in, and dependent on, their social, economic, and political environments.

Organizational planning is, in fact, the catalyst that facilitates effective interaction with the supportive and hostile (competitive) elements in an organization's environment. Our belief, reflected throughout this book, is that the primary responsibility of an organization's chief executive is to ensure that there is a symbiotic relationship between the organization and its environment. In fact, responses to a recent Korn-Ferry survey of CEOs in six countries indicated that strategic vision should be given first priority in selecting organizational leaders for the twenty-first century.

Although we do not treat marketing in great detail, the exchange relationship that is the basic focus of marketing is crucial to the survival and prosperity of any organization. We stress the aspects of planning that make those exchange relationships effective. For instance, corporate strategic planning is clearly oriented toward creating an array of offerings that collectively will benefit the stakeholders of a health services organization. This may mean that some for-profit enterprises are created to ensure that there are sufficient resources to sustain altruistic programs that cannot generate sufficient revenue for survival.

In short, this edition of *Introduction to Health Planning* continues the tradition of offering effective techniques for the management of organizations that exist for the benefit of the communities they serve. We cannot deny that some may use these concepts for personal aggrandizement; however, we hope that those with less selfish motivations will use the ideas and methods that we present as the means to defend their organizations against such aggression and to move their organizations ahead along the path of proactive community service.

Along with the continuity of purpose, this edition offers a change in orientation. In particular, because of the persistent turbulence within the health system of the United States, it seemed important to place greater emphasis on the issues and methods involved in anticipating the future. Russell Coile brings special expertise in this regard. His distinctive insights are reflected throughout the book, but are particularly evident in the later chapters.

Since the present authors are a new team, we wish to acknowledge the many contributions of previous coauthors of this book. Their wisdom and expertise remain a part of the core concepts on which this publication is based.

Finally, we must again recognize the special contributions of the staff of Information Resources Press and particularly Ms. Gene Allen. Our ideas are a necessary condition; the outstanding collaboration of a supportive and highly skilled editorial and publishing team are the sufficient condition for making them available to you.

PHILIP N. REEVES
RUSSELL C. COILE, JR.

CHAPTER 1

AN OVERVIEW OF PLANNING

Planning, a widely used term, is perhaps almost as widely misunderstood and misused. This chapter discusses what planning is, why and where it occurs, by whom and how it is done, and, finally, how this book, with its limited scope, fits into the overall context of planning.

WHAT PLANNING IS NOT

Because planning is often misunderstood and used as a synonym for policymaking, marketing, or regulating, it is important also to indicate what planning is not. Although policymakers, marketers, and regulators may plan and/or use plans, their specific functions are quite different from planning.

Policymaking translates the social principles of a community or organization into guidelines, to ensure that decisions are consistent with those values. Plans should incorporate relevant policies as part of the initial data that influence the decisions made during the plan development process.

Marketing is a much broader activity than planning. It is the management of a specific line function concerned with the exchange relationships between an organization and its environment. This activity should be, and usually is, guided by the organization's strategic and business plans. There also are marketing plans, which will be described later in the discussion of functional planning (pp. 47–51).

Regulation is the control imposed on a system or an organization on the basis of established policies or criteria. As will be shown, a plan may become the foundation for regulatory activities and may be used as the justification for decisions of regulators.

WHAT IS PLANNING?

Planning can best be defined as *making current decisions in the light of their future effects.* This succinct definition encompasses many significant considerations, including the styles, types, and levels of planning.

Styles of Planning

Ackoff[1] provides a useful classification of styles of planning: inactive, reactive, preactive, and interactive. Strategic planning, which is perceived as the sine qua non of health services administration,[2] is an interactive style, defined by Ackoff as an effort to design a desirable future. Jantsch[3] calls strategic planning "futures creative planning" and identifies its three essential characteristics as normative (value directed), integrative (system-wide),[4] and adaptive (cybernetic). Ack-

---

[1] Russell L. Ackoff. *Redesigning the Future.* New York, Wiley, 1974, pp. 22–31.

[2] Carl W. Thieme, Thomas E. Wilson, and Dane M. Long, "Strategic Planning for Hospitals Under Regulation," *Health Care Management Review,* 6(4):35–43, Spring 1981; Peter A. Nottonson, "Master Planning—Key to Survival," *Osteopathic Hospitals,* 25(16):8–11, June 1981; Kenneth M. Jones, Jr., "Long-Range Strategic Financial Planning," *Topics in Health Care Financing,* 7(4):23–29, Summer 1981.

[3] Erich Jantsch, *Technological Planning and Social Futures,* New York, Wiley, 1972, pp. 138–139; for a discussion of the necessity of adaptive systems in the modern environment, see Jay D. Starling, "The Use of System Constructs in Simplifying Organizational Complexity," in: *Organized Social Complexity,* edited by Todd R. LaPorte, Princeton, N.J., Princeton University Press, 1975, pp. 151–172.

[4] The discussion in this book assumes a familiarity with the concepts of general systems theory. The Appendix to this chapter presents a brief review of these concepts and defines related terms as they are used in the remainder of the text.

off points out that there will be occasions when some other style of planning will be more appropriate. The skills and knowledge required for interactive planning, however, should be adequate to allow the competent planner to meet the demands of any style.

In this sense, it is important to note that Ackoff's four styles do not represent types or levels of planning. Types of planning can be most usefully identified by using Parsons's[5] three levels of organizational structure: institutional/community, managerial, and technical. Each of these types should reflect the characteristics enumerated. This can be illustrated by an adaptation of a model originally developed by Lorange and Vancil[6] (Figure 1).

The model depicted in Figure 1 displays *normative* relationships, in that policies (values) have a direct influence on goals and objectives within each level, and higher level policies affect those of

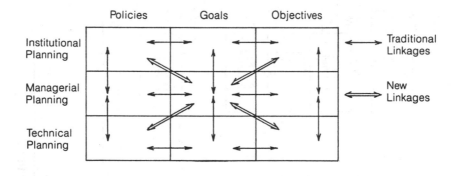

Figure 1 Modified Lorange-Vancil Model of the strategic planning process.

---

[5] Talcott Parsons. *Structure and Process in Modern Societies.* Glencoe, Ill., Free Press, 1970, pp. 59–69.

[6] C. P. McLaughlin, C. M. C. Smythe, P. W. Butler, and A. B. Jones. *Strategic Planning and the Control Processes at Academic Medical Centers.* Washington, D.C., Association of American Medical Colleges, June 1979, p. 27.

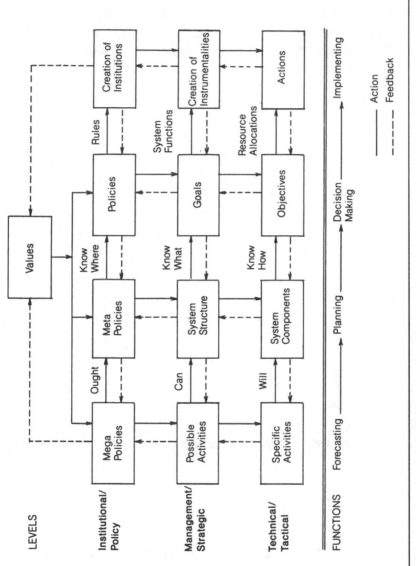

Figure 2   Planning levels and functions.

a lower level. The model is *cybernetic*, in that each stage of the process receives and adapts to information from adjacent stages. It is *integrative*, in that there are both vertical and horizontal flows of influence and feedback. These traditional linkages reflect the situation in a closely linked organization with a clear hierarchy of power. Vancil and Lorange[7] assert that in a decentralized organization with considerable autonomy at each level, the diagonal relationships more accurately describe the plan development process. For instance, the policies of a multihospital system (institutional level) will be strongly influenced by the goals of member hospitals (managerial level).

On several occasions, Jantsch[8] has described the three tiers in greater depth and applied different labels to each level. Figure 2 is an adaptation of Jantsch's models that incorporates Dror's[9] concepts of the components of policy. This figure is the basis for further discussion of each of the three levels of planning.

Note that the model in Figure 2 is actually a two-way matrix that reflects generic functions on the horizontal axis. Other authors suggest different functional sets, but there is general agreement that these generic functions are carried out at all levels of planning.

Types and Levels of Planning

Table 1 presents a complementary analysis of the three levels of planning. It links each of the purposes at the right-hand side of Figure 2 with a recapitulation of the appropriate approach, mode, level of detail, orientation, and supporting disciplines.

---

[7] This sort of arrangement is encouraged by Peters and Waterman. See "Simultaneous Loose-Tight Properties," in: Thomas J. Peters and Robert H. Waterman, Jr., *In Search of Excellence*, New York, Harper & Row, 1982, Chap. 12.

[8] Erich Jantsch, *Technological Planning and Social Futures*, p. 16; _____ "From Forecasting and Planning to Policy Sciences," *Policy Science*, 1(1):31–47, Spring 1970.

[9] Yehezkel Dror. *Design for Policy Sciences*. New York, American Elsevier, 1971.

TABLE 1 Major Characteristics and Predominant Disciplines of Planning Levels

	Planning Levels		
	Policy	*Managerial*	*Technical*
Purpose	Creation of institutions	Development of instrumental systems	Accomplishment of actions
Approach to Goal Attainment	Idealizing Satisficing	Optimizing	Maximizing
Planning Mode	Normative	Allocative	Administrative
Nature of Content	General	Moderately specific	Detailed
Orientation of Decision Makers	General community interest	Health services generalist	Health services specialist
Predominant Disciplines*	Public administration Political science Ecology	Interorganizational behavior Economics Systems analysis Epidemiology engineering	Administrative theory Behavioral science Industrial

*Does not include planning theory, marketing, and information systems, which are of major significance at all three levels.

Policy Planning

The purpose of policy (institutional) planning[10] is to create the social institutions of the future.[11] These new or revised institutions

[10] The term *institutional,* as used by Parsons and Jantsch, refers to social institutions (e.g., educational, religious). Since, however, in health services jargon, *institutional planning* is the term regularly used to denote facility or single organizational planning, the term *policy planning* is used in this book.

[11] The Flexner Report and its impact on the medical system of the United States is a good illustration of social institutional planning. Policy planning in an organizational context is an executive function performed to establish and maintain the corporate value system.

are reflections of society's values. To paraphrase Sir Geoffrey Vickers,[12] policy regulates an institution over time in such a way as to optimize the realization of many conflicting values. Thus, policies are operational statements of society's values. According to Dror,[13] there are three types of policy: *metapolicy*, which is policy on policymaking; *megapolicy*, which expresses broad generic values; and *policy*, which is the focused application of megapolicy. (See pp. 71–80 for further discussion of these concepts. In the United States, for instance, there are

1. Metapolicies, which set out the rules for establishing megapolicy and policy through legislative/regulatory/judicial processes
2. Megapolicies, which espouse free-enterprise capitalism
3. Policies, which govern our health services systems in a fashion that is more or less consistent with the free-enterprise model

The normative nature of planning at this level is obvious. Policy planning is integrative to the extent that it recognizes and attempts to deal with conflicting values between population groups and among policy dimensions (e.g., conflict between economic policy and social policy). The cybernetic aspect of policy planning is reflected in the phases of the policy cycle (Figure 3).

The policy cycle may begin at the point of retrospective policy analysis—an examination of the adequacy and completeness of existing policies. Such an analysis will stimulate policy development to fill identified gaps or correct perceived deficiencies. The proposed policies are then subjected to prospective policy analysis, which provides a basis for choice. Implementability is a crucial factor in choosing among competing policy proposals. Thus, a prospective policy analysis must incorporate the concepts of political science, as well as the cost-benefit analyses (economic, social, political, and the like) that are included in retrospective policy analyses.[14]

---

[12] Sir Geoffrey Vickers. *Freedom in a Rocking Boat: Changing Values in an Unstable Society.* London, Penguin, 1970.

[13] Yehezkel Dror. *Design for Policy Sciences.*

[14] The stages in the policy cycle were developed from ideas presented in Helen Abrams and Cyril Roseman, *State Health Policy Analysis*, Denver, Colo., PACT, 1978.

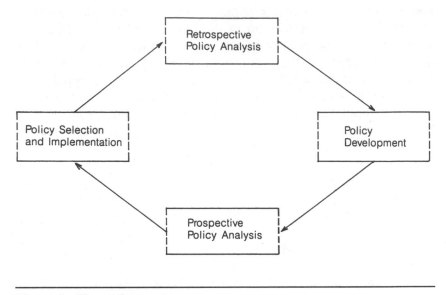

Figure 3   The policy cycle.

It is evident from the preceding description of the policy cycle that all the traditional policy concerns are encompassed within the scope of policy planning. The need to perform this level of planning is demonstrated by the relationship between policy planning and managerial or system planning. Policy planning establishes the nature of the organization, which, in turn, dictates the configuration of the system. For example, health services, as an organization in which the judgment of individual members of one profession is nearly always paramount, cannot accommodate the widespread development of systems similar to an institution such as public education, in which there is considerable standardization and centralization of decision making. In an organization, establishment of the mission is an example of policy planning.

Managerial Planning

Figure 2 indicates that the purpose of managerial (systems) planning is to create the instrumentalities that will perform the functions of the institution. Thus, managerial planning can be thought of as creating systems. Parsons's[15] definition, however, also justifies the use of the term *systems* to indicate a broad perspective with a concern for multiple aspects of the institution's or organization's performance.

Managerial planning is *value-oriented,* in that it responds to the guidance of policy planning, as shown in Figure 2. It is *adaptive,* in that it relies heavily on assessment of the environment for direction, within the constraints set forth by policy. It is *integrative,* in that it seeks to attain an optimum balance among the components of the system. It differs from policy planning, in that policy planning must generally seek to satisfice[16] because of the qualitative nature of many of its analyses, whereas managerial planning has the tools and data that make optimization at least a theoretical possibility. It differs from technical planning, which, because of its narrow focus, seeks to maximize the output of a single component of the system.

To illustrate, in community planning, megapolicy will determine the appropriate scope of health services as an institution. This might range from only medical care to the entire spectrum of health concerns implied by the World Health Organization's definition of health. Megapolicy will also determine the amount of resources that are available for the institution. On the other hand, technical planning tends to be the province of specialists, each of whom is motivated (for good but sometimes self-serving reasons) to provide the public with as much as possible of his/her particular service. Thus, technical planning seeks to acquire as many resources as possible. Managerial planners must bridge the gap between the other levels. They must distribute the allocated resources so as to maximize the system's total output, and they might seek, through the cybernetic process, to obtain a larger allocation of resources for their organizations. If they are not successful, the future instrumentalities that are created will be congenitally malformed. For instance, because of the historical lack of systems planning, health promotion is markedly underdeveloped, whereas medical care might be hypertrophic.

---

[15] Talcott Parsons. *Structure and Process in Modern Societies.*

[16] The term *satisfice* was coined by Herbert Simon to suggest that decision makers will not strive endlessly to reach an optimal position but, rather, will discontinue the search for better solutions after a threshold level of satisfaction has been achieved.

Technical Planning

Technical planning is where the action is. As Mao Tse Tung noted, there is no such thing as a "crossing-the-river" problem; there is a boat problem or a bridge problem. In other words, all of the abstraction of policy planning and managerial planning, no matter how sophisticated and elegant it may be, is of little value unless it leads to specific actions that will move the system, the organization, or the institution toward the realization of its purposes. Fortunately, we understand quite well how to plan in order to accomplish specific tasks. The processes (e.g., budgeting) and techniques (e.g., PERT) have been developed and refined over many years. Unfortunately, much of our technical planning as currently practiced does not meet Jantsch's three criteria: It is often done with little regard for institutional values (e.g., many facilities have established complex, expensive tertiary services in situations where there is little evidence of need and no indication of sufficient demand to ensure that the practitioners can develop and maintain clinical competence). It is seldom based on system-wide analyses (e.g., joint planning between independent acute-care and long-term-care facilities). It is frequently not adaptive (e.g., continued maintenance of obstetric services in the face of declining usage and population projections that predict even fewer fertile females in the service area).

WHY SHOULD WE PLAN?

Ackoff[17] describes a style of planning that attempts to create the future. This is the true reason for planning. It is possible to anticipate what the future will be like if we allow events to follow their natural course (and, of course, if we assume that no unanticipated events will disrupt the pattern of development). Frequently, the predicted situation is not what we might prefer. Planning gives us the option of seeking interventions that will deflect events onto a path leading to circumstances that are better than the results of a laissez-faire approach and that conceivably could lead to the exact outcome we desire. Since efforts to make improvements inevitably involve

---

[17] Russell L. Ackoff. *Redesigning the Future*, pp. 26–31.

reallocation of our finite resources, the goal of a plan must be to ensure that the expected benefits exceed all of the anticipated costs. This makes it imperative that all significant effects of a planning decision be identified and considered. There is no guarantee that our interventions will succeed, but the probability of success can be greatly increased if the interventions are developed through a systematic process based on a careful analysis of the information that is available. This is especially true because planning is done in a time frame that permits thorough, thoughtful decision making, in contrast to the hasty, perhaps frantic, actions that are typical reactions to an unexpected situation.

Systems planning is now regarded as the most effective way to achieve these purposes. Its broader aims make it far more powerful than earlier styles. This can be demonstrated by contrasting it with two types of planning that were prevalent in the days of comprehensive health planning agencies.

The first of these is *problem-oriented planning*. As the name implies, this type of planning deals with specific, recognized problems. It tends to be short term rather than strategic and has a discrete focus, usually based on the assumption that a problem has a single cause and all will be well if this cause is eliminated. This single focus encourages a tendency to apply one solution to the maximum, rather than seeking a suitable balance of resources within the system.

Earlier planning efforts, using the problem-oriented approach, experienced difficulties in keeping pace with the frequently changing focus of activity. Thus, a board of directors could meet monthly, using a "problem-of-the-month" planning process. Clearly, problems are far more persistent than this, and continually shifting the focus from one problem to another means that insufficient time and resources are allocated to deal effectively with any one issue.

At the other extreme are cases in which organizations or individuals are concerned with a single problem and persist in dealing with that issue long after it has ceased being major. This situation is typified by ad hoc groups that somehow become standing committees. Even though such committees make little or no contribution, unfortunately, they still consume their original share of resources and thus prevent newer, more pressing needs from receiving deserved attention.

The second style of planning that has been replaced by systems planning is *resource-oriented*. This method also has a discrete focus, which is particularly damaging because it tends to overlook the fact that resources can be substituted for or can complement one another. This planning style assumes that maximizing resource availability is an end in itself. It does not consider that the demand for resources is in fact a derived demand. For example, people do not want hospitals as such; they want hospitals only because hospitals are a means of producing health services, and they want the good health to which these services contribute.

The resource-oriented plan operates on the assumption that if the availability of some resources in a community can make a contribution to health status by providing services, then more of the same resources will lead to a linear increase in health status. This may be true up to a point, but it is clearly a simplistic assumption, in that it ignores decreasing marginal returns.

In contrast to these outmoded approaches, the *system-oriented planning* process considers all system functions, not merely goal attainment. It also reflects the relationship between resources and output, in which health services are an intermediate output and health status is the final output.

Finally, the health system planning process permits analysis and understanding of interactions within and among subsystems. For instance, many hospitals have failed to achieve the results expected from an expansion of their patient-bed capacity because no consideration was given to the capacity of ancillary services. This can be illustrated at the community level by examining the effects of a decision to change the availability of nursing home beds in a community. If such a decision is made, the question then is, what effects will occur within that subsystem and within related subsystems? If the number of nursing home beds is increased, it is probable that the geographic accessibility of these beds would also be increased, since it is unlikely that all the additional beds would be placed in the same location. This, of course, assumes that accessibility is defined in terms of geographic location. It also assumes that dispersing the beds throughout the community will mean that persons seeking to use these beds will be nearer to them.

These clarifying statements illustrate the need to develop operational definitions for each of the system characteristics to be considered by decision makers. Most people would agree that improved accessibility is desirable, but this apparent consensus might include the views of persons whose frames of reference are dramatically different. For example, it is apparent that the concept of accessibility easily could include spatial, temporal, financial, and cultural dimensions.

Another attribute of the subsystem to be considered here is the efficient use of resources within the system. An increase in the number of nursing home beds would probably affect the level of bed usage, unless one began at a very high level of use and also had a very long waiting list. (In that case, unless the total number of beds was increased substantially, the number of persons on the waiting list might be large enough to maintain the high level of use that prevailed before the bed total was increased.) Furthermore, this probable change in bed use would likely have some effect on the cost of providing nursing home services. If the interactions between the long-term-care subsystem and related subsystems are then examined, one may find that there probably is no connection between the availability of nursing home beds and emergency services. On the other hand, in most communities, it is highly probable that some patients occupy acute-care beds because there are no less-intensive-care beds available. If these persons could be moved into nursing homes, more acute-care beds would become available. The impact this would have on other attributes (e.g., utilization and cost) of the acute-care hospital subsystem could then be studied.

The impact of additional nursing home beds on another component, the mental health facilities subsystem, depends on community policy regarding the location of mental patients. If elderly persons traditionally have been committed to state mental institutions in lieu of alternative-care settings, the availability of nursing home beds may permit these individuals to move back into the community. On the other hand, if elderly persons have been served well by local community noninstitutional organizations, it is not likely that the decision will have any noticeable effect on the use of mental health facilities.

Figure 4 provides a conceptual framework for the analysis of these interactions. The matrix is limited to a small subset of all possible subsystems and to four general attributes. The primary effect of the decision to increase the number of nursing home beds is represented by the X in the cell describing the availability of long-term inpatient-care services. Secondary or ripple effects of this action must also be considered by decision makers. These are most likely to occur in other attributes of the long-term-care subsystem or in the same attribute of other subsystems. Tertiary effects may be important in some cases. For instance, the secondary effect of an increase in the availability of acute-secondary-care services is likely to cause changes in the utilization and cost of these services.

SUBSYSTEM CHARACTERISTICS

	Availability	Accessibility	Utilization	Cost
Acute Inpatient Care	2		3	3
Emergency Service Facilities				
Long-term Inpatient Care	✕	2	2	2
Mental Health Inpatient Care	2			

SUBSYSTEM OF MEDICAL CARE

X = Primary effect
2 = Possible secondary effects
3 = Possible tertiary effects

Figure 4 Interaction analysis related to the increasing availability of beds in nursing homes.

Starling[18] offers three descriptions of system performance that illustrate the types of outcome that may be sought through systems planning. Note that they highlight the importance of an effective control subsystem in today's environment:

1. *Equilibrium-seeking system.* It is assumed that the equilibrium state is efficient and, therefore, that disruptions cause inefficiencies. Consequently, the system seeks to prevent disruptions and, when they do occur, attempts to return to the equilibrium state as quickly as possible. Since the recovery of equilibrium is relatively slow, the system cannot tolerate many disruptions for any period of time, because the cumulative impacts will become so great that the system will disintegrate. In view of this danger, leaders do their best to preserve equilibrium by resisting change and exerting more and more control. This tends to be self-defeating, however, because the system becomes ever more rigid and, thus, less able to cope with the disruptions that will inevitably occur.

2. *Homeostatic system.* Such a system attempts to maintain dynamic processes by responding to feedback messages. It focuses on maintaining an efficient ratio between inputs and outputs. These responses tend to alter the system's components so as to reduce the deviance from preestablished goals. A homeostatic system does not attempt to adapt to the environment by altering its goals.

3. *Adaptive system.* This is an open system that is not disrupted by intrusive events in its environment. In fact, it needs these intrusions so that it can learn how to adapt to the environment. Consequently, some level of deviance among its members is valued as a resource of information and behavior that can be used in the future to make effective adaptations. Because of the high level of interaction with the environment, it is often difficult to determine the precise boundaries of an adaptive system. For instance, because of its involvement in emergency medical services, should a fire department be included in the definition of a medical system?

---

[18] Jay D. Starling. "The Use of System Constructs in Simplifying Organizational Complexity."

WHEN DOES PLANNING OCCUR?

Planning is an endless process. Since it is designed to help the organization cope with a turbulent environment, it follows that the successful planner must constantly seek information about new developments and then incorporate these data into the plan. If this condition were met, there would never be a decision, because each analysis would be subject to revision based on the most recent information. Obviously, this situation is impossible, so a compromise must be made. The usual arrangement is to develop a plan with the intention of revising it on a periodic schedule with the expectation that the plan, although never truly current, will also never be seriously out-of-date. This, of course, assumes that the frequency of the plan revision will be adequate for the rate of change in the environment.

A difficulty often encountered is that the resources required for completely revising the plan are so great that the cost of frequent revisions is more than the organization can afford. There is a related problem concerning the time required to prepare a revision of the entire plan. Charles Breindel[19] has proposed a solution that essentially leads to the continuous development of segments of the plan. This process allows the planners to allocate the available resources according to the relative importance of each segment and thus maximizes the benefits that can be obtained within a limited budget.

WHO PLANS?

Each of us plans to some extent so as to influence the course of our daily lives. For the purposes of this book, however, the question "Who plans?" will focus on the person(s) in an organization who are responsible for planning. There are both practical and theoretical reasons for assigning this responsibility to the organization's leader: The leader has the greatest amount of contact with the organization's environment and, thus, is in the best position to know what the organization will face in the future. Furthermore, because the leader

---

[19] Charles L. Breindel. "Health Planning Processes and Process Documentation." *Hospital and Health Services Administration, 26*(Special II):5–18, 1981.

has the ultimate responsibility for the organization's performance and because planning is designed to enhance the outcome of the organization's efforts, it is reasonable that this individual must be the one to act toward this end. In other words, the leader may delegate the function, but responsibility for the result is not delegable. Consequently, the planning decisions remain the responsibility of the leader regardless of who actually makes them. The leadership role in community planning is typically assumed by a governing body. The members of this body are expected to make decisions based on the best interests of their constituents and of the community as a whole.

This formulation undoubtedly raises questions concerning the role of planners. In simplest terms, the planner performs all the functions delegated by the leader, possibly including decision making if the leader attempts to abdicate his or her responsibilities. Ideally, the role of the planner is that of catalyst or facilitator of the planning process. In this role, the planner should be expected to provide and apply expertise in both the substantive and process aspects of planning.

WHERE DOES PLANNING TAKE PLACE?

Planning activities relate to individuals and organizations of all sizes. In this book, the focus will be on formal planning activities. Such activities require a relatively substantial base of resources to justify their existence (e.g., the average household would not be a candidate for the establishment of a formal planning system). Therefore, planning activities are examined in two settings: large organizations and communities. The objectives of planning in these two settings may differ. Typically, planning in organizations seeks to maximize the results obtained by the activity of a single business entity or a corporate organization, whereas planning activities in communities strive to achieve an optimal balance among the efforts of many organizations within the limits imposed by the resources and values of the community. Nevertheless, the underlying principles and methods are relevant in both cases. Furthermore, because of the increasing interdependence of organizations and their environments, those who practice planning in one setting can succeed only to the extent that they are knowledgeable of and sensitive to the planning activities in the alternate setting.

Organizations

Planning can be done by any organization and by any unit within an organization. The scope and time frame of a plan are determined by the level of authority of those doing the planning and the turbulence of the organization's environment. For instance, a department head in a traditional hospital would prepare plans of limited scope, usually for little more than a year into the future, because a department head has a very limited range of authority and a department's environment is the larger organization, which tends to insulate it from the less-predictable events occurring in the outside world. On the other hand, an organization may use discretion in extending the scope of its activities to whatever range it deems feasible. It also has no buffer between it and the full impact of external events; consequently, it must use a planning horizon that extends far into the future. This will give an organization the time to anticipate events that are currently remote but that will eventually have a major impact on it.

When an organization is part of a larger organization (e.g., a hospital within a vertically integrated corporate structure), however, its planning role will be subject to additional constraints. Specifically, it must operate within the guidelines provided by corporate policies and it must pay close attention to the effects of its decisions on other corporate members. In some organizations that have reorganized internally to create program management units (PMUs),[20] the PMUs may have significant strategic planning responsibilities.

Community

In the public sector, the scope of an organization's plan is usually determined by political jurisdictional boundaries and by a legislative charter. The effective planning horizon does not always reach far into the future, because of the necessity to produce results in time for upcoming elections. Quasi-governmental agencies (such as health systems agencies) and voluntary organizations (such as business

---

[20] Program management unit (PMU) is used interchangeably with strategic business unit (SBU) in this text. The essence of the concept is that the larger organization is subdivided into smaller administrative entities, each having considerable autonomous authority and responsibility.

coalitions) tend to be insulated from political considerations and are thus likely to have more extended planning horizons.

Locations of Planning Levels

Now it is time to consider another division that often appears at the local level: community planning as contrasted to organizational planning.

Parsons[21] made it clear that all three levels or types of activity existed for every organization, but that the locus of a level would vary among organizational types. For instance, policy planning for a private corporation is typically carried out by the board of directors, and the social responsibility of such a firm is internally determined. A public entity, on the other hand, generally has the majority of its community responsibilities and its guiding principles mandated by the legislative and/or executive branches of government.

Within the health services industry, Stuehler's[22] model clearly shows that all levels must exist within organizational plans. Many authors,[23] however, have noted the rapid increase in multi-institutional systems. Zuckerman[24] specifically points out how the loci of many responsibilities (especially policymaking) shift from the individual organizational level to the corporate (system) headquarters.

The intense debate over the continuation of community health planning agencies (health systems agencies [HSAs]) can be attributed largely to disputes over the loci of various levels of planning. There appears to be continuing widespread agreement that system-wide planning is needed at the local level (witness the many "voluntary" planning bodies sponsored by business coalitions that have appeared to fill the vacuums that occurred as HSAs disappeared). Health systems agencies lost much local support because they were com-

---

[21] Talcott Parsons. *Structure and Process in Modern Societies.*

[22] George Stuehler, Jr. "A Model for Planning in Health Institutions." *Hospital and Health Services Administration,* 23(3):6–27, Summer 1978.

[23] For example, M. Orry Jacobs, "Cooperative Planning," *Hospital and Health Services Administration,* 25(4):23–35, Fall 1980.

[24] Howard S. Zuckerman. "Multi-institutional Systems: Promise and Performance." *Inquiry,* 16(4):308–309, Winter 1979.

pelled to emphasize the federally imposed value of cost containment at the expense of the locally espoused values of system improvement. Furthermore, HSAs encountered extreme hostility from providers as it became evident that they were developing narrowly focused technical plans of great specificity to respond to the mandates of federal regulations that emphasized cost containment and to the regulatory requirements imposed by certificate-of-need laws.[25] Parsons's[26] predictions about such invasion of the technical planning turf by those responsible for broad systems planning have proved, unhappily, to be all too true.

Nevertheless, despite the frequent misallocation of responsibility for various levels of planning, it is evident that all three levels are appropriate and necessary in both private and community planning. This confirms Breindel's[27] assessment that the distinctions between micro and macro planning are largely mythical. This is not to say, however, that planning functions are identical in all settings. Rather, it means that the competent planner will be acquainted with both organizational and public sector concerns and techniques (e.g., corporate funds flow analysis and measurement of community tax and debt capacity).

HOW IS PLANNING DONE?

Two Approaches[28]

As noted earlier, planning is a decision-making process. Decision making is frequently characterized as being one of two extremes: synoptic or incremental. *Synoptic* planning, which is the implementation of a rational model of planning, requires a complete analysis of each possible set of alternatives that is available to the organization during the foreseeable future. It emphasizes the avoidance of accepting

---

[25] Gordon D. Brown. "HSAs and Hospitals: Counter-Planning Strategies." *Hospital and Health Services Administration,* 23(4):65–74, Fall 1978.

[26] Talcott Parsons. *Structure and Process in Modern Societies,* p. 64.

[27] Charles L. Breindel. "The Myth of Micro and Macro Health Planning." *Hospital and Health Services Administration,* 25(Special I):38–47, 1980.

[28] See pages 222–225 for additional discussion of the incremental and rational (synoptic) approaches to decision making.

current circumstances as limitations on what the organization seeks to accomplish in the future. *Incremental* decision making focuses on actions that are small deviations from the status quo. The advocates of this approach assert that it is preferable because the conditions required for synoptic planning can never be met. The advantages of incremental planning include the ability to operate from a strong base of information, since the changes are closely related to current experience, and the ability to reverse direction if the results are not satisfactory, since the modest changes that are implemented will not radically alter the situation that supported the status quo.

Clearly, the incremental approach has severe limitations; namely, that modest changes may be insufficient to deal with serious threats posed by the organization's environment and that consideration of only small steps as sequential actions may not allow planners to respond in time to counteract threats or to take advantage of opportunities.

Of course, the synoptic approach is not without problems. These can be summarized by asserting that the decision maker does not have the scope and depth of knowledge that is assumed by the rational model of decision making (which, as its name implies, is based on a rational analysis of current and predicted situations). There is no doubt that this concern is justified, but it does not invalidate the synoptic approach, because the rational model can be approximated despite the lack of perfect information by using techniques such as mixed scanning.

A Compromise

Mixed scanning could be characterized as an incremental alternative to the complete rational approach. It was first suggested by Amitai Etzioni.[29] This model assumes that a system can be viewed in different levels of detail, so that a problem of immediate concern can be examined very closely and with a great deal of specificity. That problem, however, must also be considered within the context of a larger system, described at a much higher level of generality. Because

---

[29] Etzioni's concept of mixed scanning as a planning strategy is described in George Chadwick, *A Systems View of Planning,* New York, Pergamon, 1971.

more general descriptions can be synthesized from the specifics of a problem, one can reasonably deal with that problem in terms that are comparable to the general description of the remainder of the system.

The concept of mixed scanning is particularly important when developing a large and complex health system plan. It is surely beyond the capacity of most organization's to develop equally all elements of a health system plan in a short period of time, such as one year. Consequently, a feasible strategy for the organization is to describe the entire health services system in broad, general terms, to seek further definition of priority concerns in the community, and to provide sufficiently detailed descriptions that will enable decision makers to act in the priority areas. Gradually, the decision maker's attention can focus on other parts of the system, either by shifting priorities or acting on proposals that require reviews and recommendations. Such parts will then be described as fully as those that were first addressed in the plan development process. Eventually, this evolutionary process will lead to the construction of a uniform health system plan for all elements of the system.

Generic Planning Steps

Use of the rational model for planning would proceed in the following steps:

1. Identify the desired state (i.e., set goals and objectives).
2. Determine the discrepancy between the desired state and conditions that might occur if no action is taken (this involves forecasting).
3. Identify the resources that will probably be available to effect changes toward the desired state.
4. Develop feasible alternative methods for using these resources to make the necessary changes.
5. Evaluate the alternatives and select the ones that seem most likely to achieve the desired result within the limits imposed by resource availability.
6. Implement the chosen alternatives.
7. Appraise the performance of the alternatives, then make the

necessary adjustments to bring them closer to achieving the desired objectives.

Clearly, these steps constitute a highly simplified model of the planning process. Planning is not and cannot be a straightforward, sequential process. Instead, it must be regarded as a cybernetic system with many iterative loops; that is, at each step along the way, the planners must be prepared to review what has occurred in all the preceding steps and to reevaluate those activities in the light of current developments. For example, it is entirely possible that in the process of identifying available resources, the planners might discover that their initial objectives are either too high or too low. Should this occur, they must then go back and make the necessary adjustments to step one and proceed again through steps two and three. This iterative process will not be restated in this text but should be borne in mind in all considerations of planning.

Use of Information

Planning and related management activities can also be conceptualized as a series of data sets and decisions, as shown in Figure 5. The decisions in this figure portray the components of a complete plan. The initial part of such a document is a statement of the system's mission, which is determined through an analysis of the data representing the organization's values. The mission statement and facts about the environment become the basis for determining the organization's goals, which, coupled with its strengths and weaknesses (identified through an internal analysis), become the basis for deciding its strategy. The strategy, together with all previous data, allow the organization to determine what action options should be incorporated into its implementation plan. The priority actions from that plan become the basis for setting short-run objectives. When the objectives have been set, it is then possible to determine how they might be achieved. These decisions form the set of actions to be implemented and, together with information concerning the organization and its environment, are interpreted as time and resource requirements, which are translated into a budget. The budget then is combined with data about resource availability to determine the schedule of activities.

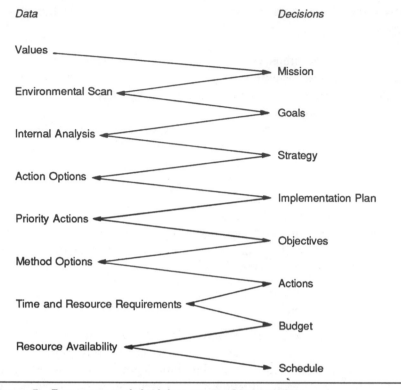

Figure 5   Data sets and decision stages for planning.

In short, throughout this series of activities, each decision be comes part of the data used in making the subsequent decision. As mentioned earlier, this does not imply that there is a simple one-way progression from data to decisions to the next stage of data to the next stage of decisions, and so on, until a final decision is reached. Ultimately, there is such a flow, but it develops as a result of an iterative process, during which prior stages are frequently reconsidered and modified in the light of knowledge gained as later stages are being developed.

Data Sets

Data sets are developed in a three-stage process. *Data gathering* is the first, and it must meet the following expectations.

1. All appropriate data sources must be used.
2. Data gathered must be valid (accurately measured and correctly defined).
3. Data reported must be relevant to the decision to be made.
4. Data must be reported at the appropriate level of detail.
5. Data must cover the appropriate time frame(s) (historical, current, future).
6. Explicit assumptions must be provided when relevant data are not available.

Information development is the second stage. In this phase, the data gathered are converted into information by analytic processes that yield answers to relevant questions. For example, cost and price data can be used to develop an answer to: How much service must be provided for the organization to break even? Standards for this stage include the following:

1. Appropriate analytic methods must be used.
2. Computations must be correct.
3. Presentation of results must be clear and effective.

Interpretation is the third stage. At this point, information from the second stage is transformed into "intelligence,"[30] which is the basis for decisions. In other words, information is necessary, but not sufficient for decision making. The decision maker explicitly or implicitly determines the significance of the information in the light of assumptions, expectations, and similar supplemental considerations. This is the point at which management changes from a science to an art. Successful development of intelligence requires the following:

---

[30] Intelligence is used here in the sense of military intelligence, but without the usual connotations of secrecy and covert data collection. For example, data on a potential enemy nation's oil production and the fuel consumption of planes, ships, and tanks can be converted into information concerning the length of time an all-out offensive could be sustained. This information can then be interpreted in the light of information, assumptions, and expectations concerning political, geographic, cultural, and economic conditions into an intelligence estimate of that nation's probable military strategy.

1. Interpretations must be consistent with prior decisions. For example, information from an environmental scan can be interpreted as threats and opportunities only in the light of prior decisions that determined the scope of the organization's mission.

2. Interpretations must be logical.

3. Interpretations must be focused on the decisions that are to be supported by the data. Interpretations lead to decisions, which become data for later decisions; consequently, the interpreters must focus on this ultimate purpose. For example, the interpretation of environmental scan information leads to decisions concerning threats and opportunities. These decisions then become part of the data set on which the organization's goals will be based.

Decisions

The purpose of an organization's planning activities is decision making. The value of information is determined by how much it contributes to improving the quality of decisions. As necessary, if not sufficient, conditions for the effective use of information, decisions must be:

1. Explicitly derived from the data sets
2. Consistent with decisions made at earlier stages
3. Expressed in terms that will permit evaluation
4. Focused on the data sets and decisions of later stages

Of course, the sufficient condition for making high-quality choices is the skill of the decision makers. Therefore, two critical roles of the planner are: helping decision makers improve their interpretive skills and ensuring that the information provided is of the highest possible quality.

SUMMARY

Planning to create the future must be normative, integrative, and cybernetic. It is also a three-tiered process. The first tier is policy planning, which establishes the values that will guide actions in the other two tiers. Managerial planning, the second tier, creates the instrumentalities to perform the functions required by the policy decisions. Finally, technical planning encompasses the specific tasks that are needed to carry out the system's functions.

The three tiers of planning are required by all systems, but the responsibility for each aspect may be allocated to different elements within various systems, particularly if they have dissimilar organizations. The assignment of responsibilities is often a very controversial decision.

This book emphasizes planning as a process that will allow leaders to maximize the performance of their organizations within a turbulent environment. The approach described involves a simplified, rational model with some discussion of the values on which required choices are based.

A decision was made to avoid the issues of plan implementation and the more or less administrative aspects of the planning process (e.g., plan format, activity scheduling), which nevertheless are key ingredients in planning. These topics are absent because their omission does not detract from a discussion of the plan development process, but their inclusion would have expanded this book into a multivolume work.

This simplified approach to planning should be useful in that it offers a basis for understanding the fundamentals of the planning process. Individuals can then adapt the process to meet the requirements of the various situations they will encounter during their professional careers.

APPENDIX TO AN OVERVIEW OF PLANNING

UNDERSTANDING SYSTEMS

To understand the idea of a health system plan, one must first have a good grasp of the concept of a system, which is well illustrated by a Zen proverb: "For the man who is ignorant, trees are trees, waters are waters, and mountains are mountains. When that man gains understanding, then trees are not trees, waters are not waters, and mountains are not mountains. And when at last the man attains wisdom, then once again trees are trees, waters are waters, and mountains are mountains."

Sometimes, a person cannot see the forest for the trees. In other words, one must examine the big picture in order to make valid decisions. True understanding or wisdom occurs when those who grasp the picture also understand the symbiotic interaction of all its components. This is the essence of the systems approach.

It is useful to consider a system in terms of its purposes and methods, as shown in Figure 6. This simplified diagram illustrates the basic idea of a system, which can be defined as a set of elements linked together in a purposeful way to convert *input* into *output*. The part of the diagram labeled *Process* represents the actions and interactions of the elements of the system that transform inputs into outputs.

When using Figure 6 as a simplified representation of the health system, one must realize that the *Final Output* is different from what

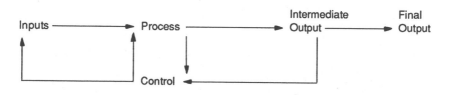

Figure 6   Simple schematic representation of a system.

one might expect to find in, say, a manufacturing process. One could say that *Inputs,* mainly health resources, are processed through the delivery system to create health services. These services, however, are not the end that is truly sought but simply a means to the ultimate end of health status, designated here as *Final Output.* A system, moreover, does not act in an uncontrolled fashion. Instead, it follows a cybernetic pattern in which those involved use information about what has occurred to adjust future actions so that they will be more likely to achieve the system's purposes. Specifically, information about the resources used, how they were processed, and the results is gathered into a *Control* element. Through this element, it is decided whether the system should function differently in the future to better achieve the desired outcome.

DEFINITIONS

Progression beyond this point will be difficult unless certain important terms are defined. The following definitions will be assumed throughout the remainder of this book:

1. *Environment.* Environment in this context does not relate to the physical or social milieu commonly associated with health planning. In other words, it does not mean clean air or pure water. In a systems context, environment refers to everything outside the system. The environment of the health system comprises the public education system, the public safety system, and the social welfare system, among others.

2. *Boundary.* The boundary of the system defines the system's scope in order to separate the system from its environment. To illustrate, the boundary of a health services system depends on what definition of health is adopted. A health planning body could, for example, adopt the very expansive definition of health proposed by the World Health Organization. Alternatively, it might decide to use a much more restricted definition, one that considers only medical care and services. The external boundary of an organization as a system is determined by its mission.

3. *Boundary Conditions.* This term can be used to describe how a system interacts with its environment. Usually, a system must make

exchanges with outside elements. For instance, health planners may need to seek assistance from those in public education to ensure that a health promotional strategy is successfully implemented. On the other hand, those in the educational system might find it necessary to ask health system planners to modify their activities in order to enhance the educational process (e.g., educators might ask health care providers to offer primary care services at various hours to minimize the number of school days lost when students obtain medical care). Longest[1] has developed an insightful analysis of how hospitals, as systems, must adapt their strategies to the demands and opportunities presented by their environments.

4. *Subsystems*. A system can be so complex that it often cannot be dealt with as a single entity. In such cases, the ability to manage the system effectively is much improved when one understands its components or subsystems.[2] In fact, one can imagine a hierarchy of systems. Each system is a component of a larger system and is itself composed of other smaller systems. For instance, one can envision a hierarchy extending from incredibly small subatomic particles to the expansiveness of the universe, with many intermediate levels. Within this range, each human being represents a system having a number of subsystems, such as the circulatory and respiratory systems. These, in turn, are composed of parts such as the heart and lungs. Moving in the opposite direction, we, as individuals, are part of larger systems: family, neighborhood, community, political jurisdiction, state, and nation. The question then becomes: How far should the planner explore in each direction when examining the expanses of the system? This is determined by the established boundary and by another concept, the *black box*.

5. *Element (Black Box)*. This is the lowest level of subsystem that concerns decision makers. They are interested only in the performance, inputs, and outputs of a black box and have no concern with its internal workings. The hierarchy of subsystems ending in

---

[1]Beaufort B. Longest, Jr. "An External Dependence Perspective of Organizational Structures: The Community Hospital Case." *Hospital and Health Services Administration*, 26:50–69, Spring 1981.

[2]LaPorte refers to this approach to dealing with complexity as the development of decomposable systems.

the black box can be illustrated by a familiar example. Each of us lives in a house or apartment, which is a shelter system. Within that system are various subsystems (e.g., for eating and recreation). The recreational subsystem has additional components, one of which could be a television set. For most of us, the television set is literally and figuratively a black box. In other words, we simply are not capable of or interested in critically examining the internal action of that device. Consequently, we concern ourselves only with the inputs (how much electricity does it consume?), the performance (does it begin to function as soon as we push the "on" switch?), and the outputs (does it provide clear pictures in realistic colors and a sound of reasonable fidelity?). Within health services organizations, the black box can be the program management unit (PMU). The PMU is a revenue center that provides closely related services (e.g., an oncology PMU or a cardiology PMU). In larger organizations, PMUs can be clustered into subsystems called strategic business units (SBUs).

6. *Attributes.* The characteristics of system performance that can be expressed operationally. Returning to our earlier example of the sound of a television set, we could ask for specifications of the audio output in terms of a frequency range, such as 20 hertz to 20 megahertz.

7. *Inputs.* Resources used by the system.

8. *Outputs.* Products or services the system creates by using its resources.

9. *Feedback.* Information on the system's performance that can be used to adjust its future operation. It is important to note that all the data in the feedback loop consist of historical information.

10. *Feedforward.* Information on expectations about future conditions in which the system will be operating. Feedback provides only historical information. The real concern is making changes in the system that will enable it to adapt to the circumstances in which it will be operating. This process is somewhat like leading the target in skeet shooting. Planners must anticipate where the system will be so that they can make appropriate adjustments and achieve the desired performance.

11. *Closed System.* For all practical purposes, this system is independent of its environment. Analysis of such a system focuses only on what occurs within the system itself and ignores interactions be-

tween the system and its environment. This clearly is not a realistic representation of the usual social organization, but it has great merit as an analytic device because it allows planners to make a less-complex analysis of the system's operation as a preliminary step to considering the greater complexity of an open system.

12. *Open System.* The open system involves exchanges of resources, information, and outputs with the environment. Usually, the number of interactions is very large, and, thus, the complexities introduced are great.

13. *Control.* The control element makes decisions that will affect the system's operation. These decisions typically affect the quantity and nature of the inputs used, the structure or functioning of the system's components (process), or both inputs and process. They are based on an analysis of feedback and feedforward in relation to values expressed as criteria and standards or as goal levels.

A CLOSE LOOK AT SYSTEMS

With these definitions in mind, one can take a somewhat more sophisticated look at a system diagram, as represented by Figure 7, which expands the simple system shown in Figure 6. The values, criteria, and standards that relate to the system's attributes are shown as important inputs to the control process. These inputs frequently derive from the environment rather than from the system itself. Similarly, it is evident that the final output—health status—is greatly affected by external forces, which reside primarily in the environment.

In the larger system, control is dependent on feedback from all components: external forces, final and intermediate outputs, process, and input. Without this array of information, an adequate assessment of the changes required is impossible. For instance, if the feedback indicates that the final output (health status) is unsatisfactory, one must know whether this represents a failure of the intermediate output (health services) or is the consequence of external forces over which we have no control. Similarly, one must be concerned with making the corrections that are most appropriate to the circumstances in which the system will be operating. Thus, one needs feedforward, which tells what to expect in the future in terms of external forces,

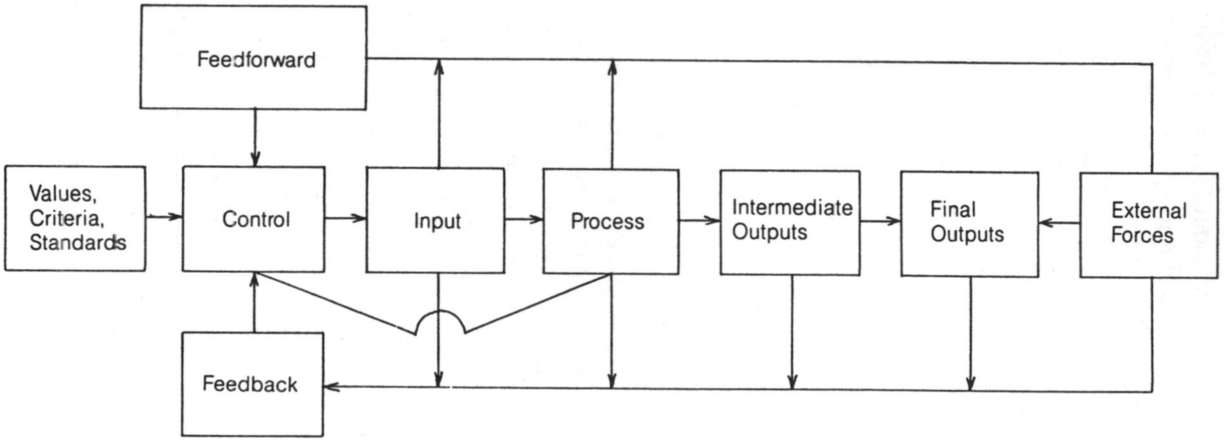

Figure 7   Schematic representation of a system.

processes (i.e., will there be a shift from solo to group practice in the provision of primary care?), and input (i.e., will medical education be changed to such an extent that future physicians will have different skills from today's doctors?).

A system has multiple purposes that can be described in terms of four specific functions. The first is goal attainment or achievement of the system's primary purpose.

The second is self-maintenance. If the system cannot survive as an entity, its goals cannot be achieved. In other words, the system must devote a certain amount of its energy and resources to acquiring additional resources for future operation. Frequently, the latter function is regarded as bureaucratic overhead and spoken of in pejorative terms. Managers of clinical personnel frequently will be told, "I don't have time to prepare next year's budget; I'm too busy taking care of sick people." This attitude shows no comprehension of the reality that an approved budget is needed to provide the required resources if sick people are to be cared for next year.

The third function is environmental adaptation. The system must maintain a satisfactory relationship with its environment or its efforts will be futile. This necessity implies a certain number of internal changes to accommodate the market for the system's output. In marketing, this is referred to as the exchange relationship. It also implies that when some environmental factor is detrimental to system performance, those in the system will try—through persuasion or other means—to effect a change that will accommodate the needs of the system.

The fourth function is the integration of subsystem efforts. Each system must balance the activities of its parts so that one part does not maximize its performance at the expense of other parts. This is a particularly pressing problem when dealing with professionals who are providing services. Because each professional is well aware of the importance of his work, he is strongly motivated to provide a maximum amount of that service to the beneficiaries. This attitude does not recognize that there is a point of diminishing returns, regardless of how excellent or important a service may be. For example, it is becoming clear that additional investments in high-technology medical care have far less impact on the health status of the population than do changes in environmental conditions or in individual behavior.

CHAPTER *2*

CONCEPTS OF PLANNING

THE ORGANIZATION AS A SYSTEM

The system concepts discussed in Chapter 1 are as relevant to individual organizations as they are to communities. Indeed, as organizations become more complex through diversification and integration, the need to manage them as systems becomes increasingly critical. Moreover, it is clear that now and in the foreseeable future, the success and even the survival of health services organizations are definitely dependent on effective interaction with the environment.

In short, it is important to remember that the discussion that follows is predicated on the presumption that the reader is aware of the multiple, varied internal and external effects of each individual decision.

Because of the complexity of health services delivery systems, a single plan will no longer suffice. Even though some organizations still appear to be freestanding single units, they must still plan, explicitly or implicitly, at several levels. Indeed, even small organizations must perform all the functions about to be described, but this is often done without explicit recognition. For example, a physician working as a solo fee-for-service practitioner has an implicit marketing plan, even though he or she may not recognize it as such. Consequently, this chapter will discuss planning as it relates to strategic management, business management, and the administration

37

of line functions, as well as the relationship between planning and the structure of the organization. We will begin, however, with a description of three generic types of plans.

TYPES OF PLANS

The types of plans described here will encompass the dominant managerial planning activities. Such things as disaster plans and contingency plans will not be considered.

Strategic Plans

Strategic plans are essential for all stages of management. Even the lowest echelon will have some kind of strategy for carrying out its mission. It is important to note, however, that the content of the plans will vary substantially between the different levels of responsibility within the organization. (This is shown in Table 2.) As a consequence, formal strategic planning usually will take place at only the corporate and business unit levels.

TABLE 2   Strategy Levels

Level	Content	Example of Focus
Corporate	Management of SBU portfolio Acquisition of resources Allocation of resources	Health services system
SBU	Range of service categories Distribution of services Promotion of services Allocation of resources	Acute medical services
Service Category	Scope and volume of services	Diagnostic imaging
Service	Specific service characteristics	CAT scans

Business Plans

Business plans are prepared at the business unit level, which, in single-purpose organizations, may also be the corporate level. They are prepared for each product line, whether new or existing. Unlike the strategic plan, the business plan will have a specific time horizon, usually two to five years.

Functional Plans

Functional plans are designed to meet the needs of each major line-management function within the organization. At minimum, these are marketing, operations, and finance. Staff functions, such as human resources management, and other line functions, such as research and development, also may develop similar plans. The purpose of these plans is to ensure that the activities of the unit are effectively directed toward the support of the organization's business and strategic plans and that they are compatible with the plans of other functional units.

In a large multiorganizational structure, it is possible that functional plans will be required at several levels, namely, when the functions are performed at both corporate and SBU levels. In such cases, it is important that the functional plans of one level are compatible and consistent with comparable plans of other echelons of the organization.

PLANNING AND STRATEGIC MANAGEMENT

Purpose of Strategic Management

The sole purpose of strategic management is to enhance the value of the organization from the perspective of the stakeholders.[1] Each

---

[1] R. Edward Freeman, *Strategic Management: A Stakeholder Approach,* Boston, Pitman Publishing, 1984, provides a thorough discussion of the concept of stakeholders and its application in strategic management. As a point of information, this current edition was written from the perspective of a broad definition of the term *stakeholders.* Some writers define stakeholders as only those who are affected by *and* who can affect the organization. This implies that managers should recognize as stakeholders only those people who control or otherwise have some power over the organization. A broader definition is used here, for two reasons. First, we believe that health services organizations have a social responsibility that is far more encompassing than that of commercial organizations. Second, even if this argument is rejected, a pragmatic manager must recognize that in most cases, even those with minimal personal power are usually represented by elected officials and/or other advocates who command the resources necessary to affect the organization.

decision must be made with one concern in mind. Will the "business" be better off? Can it create greater value for its stakeholders?

In purely commercial enterprises, these questions focus on the welfare of the stockholders—the ultimate owners of the corporate assets. There are many points of view concerning the level of social responsibility these organizations should accept, in addition to fulfilling their basic function of maximizing productivity.

The public expectation in the health services field, however, is that the values generated must be shared equitably among stakeholders. Thus, the organization must concern itself not only with the welfare of the owners of its assets, but also with the welfare of all who are affected by its activities. The list of stakeholders is impressively long. It includes patients, employees, medical staff, suppliers, purchasers of health insurance, governmental agencies, and the community at large.

To a large extent, public policy determines the appropriate trade-offs between economic efficiency and other social values (e.g., productivity versus employment of the handicapped).[2] The strategically oriented health services organization, however, must be proactive in attempting to influence the development of social policies that go beyond economic efficiency and in ensuring the well-being of its stakeholders.

Dimensions of Strategic Management

There are two elements in strategic management. The first is responding to changes in the environment. Managers deal with this element by developing responses to five sequential questions.

1. How do we perceive the environment?
2. How will it affect our organization?
3. What should we do about it?
4. What can we do about it?
5. What do we intend to do about it?

---

[2] J. David Seay and Bruce C. Vladeck, editors, *In Sickness and In Health*, New York: McGraw Hill Book Co., 1988, provide a collection of essays that highlight the dilemmas faced by health care providers who attempt to maintain the traditional role of a social service organization in an era of intense competition based largely on price considerations.

The second element is to creatively deploy internal resources to improve the organization's position, as part of the response to the final question. As suggested, this may entail the use of resources for political action, a perfectly legitimate part of strategy and usually essential in today's environment.

Most people are really referring to internal activities when they talk about strategy, but this is a very narrow and unrealistic view of the world. The need for management to continuously interact with a turbulent and often hostile environment has led to differentiating between the roles of the chief executive officer (CEO), and the chief operating officer (COO).

The CEO is the organization's chief strategist and planner. It is his or her responsibility to ensure the long-term survival and prosperity of the organization. The CEO also is the primary formal contact for all the elements in the organization's environment. The COO, on the other hand, is the individual whose principal concern is maintaining the efficient and effective day-to-day accomplishment of the organization's responsibilities.

Corporate Strategy

The three basic issues of corporate strategy are:

1. The number and kinds of businesses in which the organization will participate
2. The required degree of coordination among SBUs
3. The basis for allocating resources among SBUs

All decisions concerning these issues must be made for the express purpose of enhancing the value of the corporation; there is no other reason for the corporation to exist. Therefore, a corporations's strategy should include each of the following components:

1. Corporate goals to guide strategic decision making
2. Product markets in which the organization will compete
3. Level of investment the corporation will undertake
4. Means for developing synergistic effects among businesses
5. Basis for allocating resources among businesses

There are several significant assumptions that are fundamental to the development of sound corporate strategy. As is often the case with assumptions, they frequently are not recognized. The successful strategist may not always state these assumptions explicitly, but will not overlook them as essential ingredients of the final product. These assumptions are that

1. Strategy is derived from and guided by policy that is an operational statement of the organization's basic values.

2. Competition occurs at the business level. Diversified corporations do not compete with each other since they seldom have identical interests; businesses do compete because they have similar goals and objectives. Corporate strategy must increase the competitive strength of the organization's businesses.

3. Amalgamation of businesses into a corporation makes it more difficult to increase competitive strength, because integration into the corporate structure adds costs to the operations of business units. For example, supporting corporate overhead costs money. Also, business operations are hampered to some degree by the constraints of corporate policies, rules, and the like, and the transfer of information between levels within the corporation slows decision making. Consequently, decisions concerning acquisitions must be tested against particularly stringent criteria to ensure that they will truly create added value for the stakeholders.[3]

Decisions on strategic issues are implemented through four approaches to or concepts of corporate strategy.[4]

1. *Portfolio management* identifies attractive candidates for acquisition, provides capital resources to complete acquisitions, and provides objective guidance on decisions regarding management of the SBUs that comprise the corporation.

---

[3] These considerations may also lead to decisions to divest when it becomes apparent that the business to be spun off could operate more effectively without the costs of "corporate membership."

[4] Michael E. Porter. "From Competitive Advantage to Corporate Strategy." *Harvard Business Review,* 65(3):43–59, May–June 1987.

2. *Restructuring* includes taking over floundering companies, rejuvenating their businesses, and then selling them off.

3. *Transferring skills* requires establishing a synergistic relationship between parent corporation and an acquisition or start-up business. Both units must have similar activities that are related to competitive advantage, so that the transfer of skills has a significant impact.

4. *Sharing activities* is also based on synergy. It is similar to the transferring of skills, but it also requires that structure, incentive system, shared values, and style overcome barriers to collaboration between the organizational components involved.

Business Strategy

As previously noted, the business is the competitive unit. Consequently, business strategies are designed to create and sustain a competitive advantage. The choice of an appropriate strategy depends on the current structure of the industry; that is, what are the relevant threats and opportunities within the industry environment? This will lead to the choice of a competitive position that, in turn, will influence many resource allocation decisions.

Michael Porter[5] has identified three generic competitive strategies: cost leadership, differentiation, and focus.

The first depends on being a low-cost producer of the service. It is important to note that this says nothing about price. Pricing is a very significant element in marketing strategy, and a low-cost position can give the business an important competitive edge should a price-related marketing strategy be adopted, because the real issue is the difference between cost and price. So long as there is a positive difference, the organization is profitable. Consequently, the organization with the widest difference has the greatest latitude in maneuvering to meet the challenges of its competitors. In other words, it has the option of lowering its price, raising expenditures (e.g., by increased promotion), or both, until other organizations with narrower margins can no longer respond effectively to it's actions.

---

[5] Michael E. Porter. *Competitive Strategy.* New York, Free Press, 1980, Chapter 2.

A differentiation strategy is predicated on offering a service that is regarded by the target market as superior to the similar service offerings of other organizations. This approach is ordinarily applied to a large market segment that has distinguishable preferences, which can be accommodated by such things as a special design of the basic service or augmentation of the service.

A focus strategy is directed toward a limited market segment to which the result will appeal (e.g., low price or superior service). The strategy may be based on a cost focus or a differentiation focus. Because of the added expense for providing differentiated services, cost and differentiation are usually antithetical, but they may be combined if:

1. Cost is strongly affected by the size of the market share (scale)
2. Cost is greatly affected by intracorporate relationships
3. Cost is reduced by innovation
4. Competitors attempt to blend both without achieving conditions 1, 2, or 3

The first component of a business strategy is the choice of a competitive position that is based on an assessment of the threats and opportunities identified through an environmental scan. The options are, to become a

1. *Leader:* The goal of an organization positioned as a leader is to maintain market dominance. Such an organization will usually be a defender, but it will also need an offensive strategy to deal with a challenger. As a matter of fact, a growth-oriented strategy will often serve both purposes. It will preserve the organization's current position and can either prevent the growth of other organizations by absorbing unserved markets or reduce the strength of challengers by acquiring the market share that they are currently serving. The most frequently used techniques include an aggressive sales force, heavy advertising, an emphasis on quality and service, and production effectiveness and efficiency.

2. *Challenger:* The goal of a challenger is to overtake the leader by substantially increasing market share. A challenger may seek to achieve this end by attacking the market leader, attacking other

organizations that are not doing well and are underfinanced, or attacking smaller organizations. In other words, a challenger is most likely to engage in offensive strategy, but it could do this through flanking or guerrilla warfare in some circumstances. These attacks may be carried out through price competition, improved services, or innovative distribution.

3. *Follower:* Organizations in this group strive to maintain market share and avoid attack by either the leader or challengers. They may follow closely, follow at a distance, or follow selectively. A follower is pretty much a noncombatant, as are nichers, but both might use guerrilla warfare. Nichers, in effect, use a flanking approach, except that they have no aspirations for a big win. The most frequently used techniques of followers are imitative. They maintain high-quality service at a reasonable price by taking advantage of the service development and promotion activities of the leader and challengers. They select markets based on profitability rather than on size.

4. *Nicher:* Organizations that choose this position develop a specialized market which is not vulnerable to attack. The choice is often based on finding a target market that is unattractive to leaders and challengers. Niching is not unprofitable, however; it simply does not offer the large-scale opportunities that attract most organizations. Nichers may focus on a single aspect of the market or, if there is a potential for synergistic interaction or sharing of costs, multiple market facets. The techniques of the nicher include product specialization, geographic specialization, segment specialization, and quality/price specialization.

Once the desired competitive position has been identified, the strategy is developed, based on the following considerations.

1. What are the critical success factors for this business? (These will be the functional area strengths that are needed to compete in the service market.)

2. Among these, where does the organization have a distinctive competence that can be used to create a competitive advantage?

3. How can the organization ensure that this will be a sustainable competitive advantage that will provide the business focus?

TABLE 3   Cost Considerations for Various Strategic Thrusts

LEADING:	A leader has the biggest market share and should, therefore, seek competitive options that require fixed costs so that these can be spread over a large number of units.
CHALLENGING:	A challenger that holds a substantially smaller market share than the leader should emphasize competitive options that affect variable costs, since these will have an equal effect on each unit of both large and small producers.
HOLDING SHARE:	In a weak market, the organization should avoid investment, so as to become a low-cost producer, and then consider price competition to hold market share. In a growing market, the organization can use the prices of growth leaders as an umbrella to cover the added costs of increased capacity.
HARVESTING:	An organization using this strategy should get under the price umbrella of those that are spending, so as to stay in the market. Since it will have lower costs, this should provide a high profit margin.

4. Since a major test of any strategy will be the ability to maintain an acceptable margin between price and total cost, the organization must analyze the cost aspects of each strategy choice. This examination will include capital and operating costs related to inputs, operations, distribution, and overhead (general administration and all other elements of the business operation). When making these analyses, market growth[6] is assumed to have two significant impacts on costs. Capital costs (fixed costs) per unit will be reduced as volume increases. Operating costs should decline on the basis of economies of scale and movement up the experience curve. Table 3 presents descriptions of the cost aspects of several possible strategic thrusts.

As discussed, it is assumed that competitive advantage is based on distinctive competence in some aspect of the value chain. In other words, functional-area strengths are needed to compete effectively. Unfortunately, the critical success factors shift over the life cycle of the service. (For example, marketing, which is the dominant con-

---

[6] Market growth may be realized either through expanding the volume of business in a growing market or by increasing market share in a stable or contracting market.

sideration in the introductory phase of the product life cycle, becomes less important as the service reaches maturity. When this stage is reached, there is a need for greater efficiency in operations in order to sustain a cost advantage. Cost advantage is the dominant generic strategy in this phase of the life cycle, since most of the possibilities for differentiation and niching have been exhausted.) Consequently, no one aspect of the business can be pursued to the detriment of other aspects. Strategic balancing within the organization will be discussed in the functional planning section of this chapter.

PLANNING AND BUSINESS MANAGEMENT

Each organization must have some form of business plan. The possibilities range from the start-up plan of an independent new venture to the multiple periodic business plans of diversified corporations. Essentially, the business plan represents an "operationalization" of the organization's strategy.

Business planning has three purposes: resource acquisition, administration, and control. In the first case, a business plan is designed to persuade others to allocate resources to the product line. This may entail investment in a new venture or expansion of an existing service. It also is the basis for an annual budget of operating funds.

Second, a business plan provides the guidance necessary to manage the operation of the product line. This includes activity schedules and resource consumption patterns.

Finally, the business plan can be used, retrospectively, to determine whether activities and resource consumption are meeting expectations and, ultimately, to determine whether the stated objectives have been achieved. The periodic assessment of performance is essential for providing the opportunity for adjusting the plan to accommodate unforeseen circumstances or for modifying incorrect planning decisions that would otherwise prevent the organization from reaching its goals.

PLANNING AND LINE FUNCTIONS

The recognized purpose of functional plans is to devise schemes that will allow the function to maximize its contribution toward the achievement of the organization's goal. In this regard, a primary concern is that the functional plan must be consistent with the overall strategy as well as technically sound.

Another major concern that is often overlooked is that functional strategies must be mutually consistent and supportive in order to achieve business goals. This requirement is supported by the concepts of synergy, general systems theory, and the M-form organization.

Each functional plan is focused on a strategy that is appropriate for the particular activities for which that functional area has responsibility. Some aspects of the strategies for each of the major line functions are discussed in the sections that follow.

Marketing Planning

Marketing planning should focus on the following issues:

1. What market segments will we enter and with what products?
2. How will the products be priced, distributed, and promoted?
3. How will marketing resources such as sales force time, promotional funds, and managerial personnel be allocated across and within product groups?

Components of Marketing Strategy

The first element in the marketing strategy will be identification of the market segments. A health services market can be segmented using the same dimensions as any other service (e.g., demographic, behavioral, and psychographic characteristics), but the nature of the services and their uses makes it imperative to identify explicitly the functional needs of various age and sex cohorts.[7] For instance, an organization's disease prevention offerings for a young male population would be significantly different from the services offered for elderly females.

---

[7] A cohort is a group of people with similar characteristics who are born in the same time period. For example, all white women between 15 and 20 years of age form a race-sex cohort.

This observation leads to the second element in the strategy—selection of target market segments. Unless the organization plans to use a strategy of undifferentiated services, its offerings will not be suitable for everyone. Consequently, it must choose those segments that it wishes to serve. This choice will be based on organizational values (e.g., profitability, community service, research potential, etc.).

Since the organization cannot be all things to all people, it must develop a separate marketing mix for each segment. Once again, if the organization chooses a totally undifferentiated strategy or if it chooses a concentrated strategy only, a single product mix will be required. In all other cases, there must be a separate marketing mix for each segment. The organization can avoid excessive fragmentation of its marketing mix by trying to design offerings so that many, if not all, will meet the most important needs of several market segments. This requires careful analysis of the key characteristics of each segment with regard to all elements of the marketing mix. This process must be based on the results of fairly sophisticated market research. Intuition is a poor guide for determining the needs and wishes of others, especially if they are from a socioeconomic or ethnic group with which the analyst is not well acquainted.

The characteristics of the marketing mix will be influenced by such things as the economic climate, the life-cycle stage of the service, and the competitive position of the organization. It is particularly important to consider the likely responses of the competitors. There is little likelihood of developing a sustainable competitive advantage if this consideration is not taken into account during the design of the product mix.

Another element in the marketing strategy revolves around the *make versus buy*[8] decision with regard to marketing services, which can also be described as determining the degree of vertical integration of marketing functions. The purposes of make versus buy decisions for marketing activities are to reduce costs and to affect the degree of

---

[8] The discussion of make versus buy for marketing functions can be used as a model when considering vertical integration of other functions: for example, whether to contract out part of the operations or logistics activities.

control over the marketing process. Both these goals can involve significant problems if marketing services are available only from noncompetitive organizations. Factors affecting the decision on vertical integration are:

1. The degree to which functions are specific to the organization. (How long does it take a person knowledgeable in the health services industry to learn enough about your services and organization? Can you afford to rely on generalists to present your differentiated product?)

2. How closely must marketing be coordinated with other functions?

3. Are customer loyalties directed primarily toward the organization or the salesperson? (If the latter is true, keep sales in-house.)

4. Economies of scale. Are large providers of marketing services more efficient because they are:

   a. More intense in the use of their staff and facilities?
   b. Better able to attract and hold quality staff?
   c. Able to obtain quantity discounts (e.g., advertising rates)?

5. Environmental uncertainty. The organization needs direct control to respond quickly if the environment is uncertain. Environmental uncertainty depends on such things as:

   a. How accurate are sales forecasts?
   b. How frequently are new competitive products introduced into the market?

6. Inability to monitor performance. If the organization cannot adequately evaluate marketing performance using output measures, then it cannot effectively monitor what is being done for it by an outside agency, so it must bring the activity in-house in order to monitor the process.

7. Potential size of transactions. If the size of the transaction is small, the organization should contract. The size of transactions can be assessed by factors such as:

   a. The size of the advertising budget (advertising)
   b. The number of new advertising campaigns created in a year

    c. The average order size (distribution of products)

    d. Sales contacts per square mile in a typical territory (sales)

    8. Cost of administrative overhead for in-house activities. If this cost is high, the organization should contract the service.

Operations Planning

Operations planning should focus on the following issues:

    1. What will we make, and what will we purchase from other organizations?

    2. How will we configure the size, design, and location of our operations facilities?

    3. How will we recruit, train, and manage operations personnel?

It requires integration of:

1. Product design
2. Process design
3. Facility configuration
4. An information and control system
5. Human resources
6. Technology strategy
7. Suppliers' roles and relationships
8. Distributors' roles and relationships
9. Organizational structure and philosophy

Components of Operations Strategy

There are three basic components of operations strategy. An additional factor, the use of technology, must also be considered; therefore, we have included it in this section even though it applies throughout the organization.

    The first element in operations strategy is the establishment of one or more priorities. In other words, which of the following goals will be accorded the highest consideration in managing the operations function?

1. *Satisfying the most users.*

2. *Most important user.* This could mean satisfying the demands of a specialist on the medical staff or the "high admitters."

3. *Highest revenue.* This could be based on payer class or type of case (e.g., which will use the most chargeable ancillary services?).

4. *Least cost.* This might involve an attempt to avoid DRGs, where there is a high probability of high cost, and/or those cases in which there is uncertainty about the amount of resources that will be consumed. It also could be based on organizing services so that operations will be efficient; for example, by grouping similar cases on the schedule or by handling only cases requiring "standard" equipment.

5. *Focus.* The options are: undifferentiated, concentrated, and differentiated services. The choice is closely related to considerations of efficiency; the fewer the options, the lower the cost.

6. *Responsiveness to changes in demand.* How much capacity will be available to meet peaks in demand? An example of this issue is the trade-off between effectiveness and efficiency in determining the number of beds in an acute-care hospital. Similarly, what are the personnel policies that would affect the use of temporary employees to meet peaks in demand without creating "fat" staffing during periods of normal demand?

7. *Responsiveness to service design changes.* How much is spent to retrain staff, or are they expected to learn on their own time? Are changes deferred while the organization waits for attrition to allow it to hire people with the required new skills? Similarly, how quickly can the organization "unload" outmoded equipment (a factor in lease versus purchase decisions)?

The second element is the type of strategy that will be used. There are five types of operations strategy: capacity, innovation, efficiency, substitution, and deployment and readiness.

1. *Capacity-based strategies* are either anticipatory expansion or high utilization. Anticipatory expansion might be characterized as a preemptive move to discourage new entrants into a growing market. A high-utilization strategy seeks to create a cost advantage by maximizing the productivity of the organization's resources.

2. *Innovation-based strategies* concentrate on the development of unique processes yielding either reduced costs or improved quality, which will permit differentiation of the organization's service. It is important to note that the new processes are described as unique, which implies that they will provide a sustainable competitive advantage.

3. *Efficiency-based strategies* seek to minimize costs through application of tight controls.

4. *Substitution-based strategies* strive to maintain flexibility by purchasing inputs rather than producing them. Purchased inputs do not require commitment to any particular operations technology. New suppliers can be found as soon as a new input is desired. Changing internal production, on the other hand, implies at least the replacement of some equipment. Internal production is also predicated on large production runs to achieve economies of scale. Purchased inputs can be acquired in small batches, if necessary, to provide differentiation through customization of outputs.

5. *Deployment and readiness strategies* involve the dispersal of operations facilities to improve response time or to reduce transportation costs. These benefits must be weighed carefully against the advantages that can be achieved by consolidated operations, for example, economies of scale.

The third element in operations strategy should describe coordination with other functional efforts. In a service industry, it is especially important to strive for integration of service and marketing strategies, since the persons providing the service are often also key marketers. This idea is embodied in the concept of guest relations. If the operations strategy is incompatible with the marketing strategy, the service-delivery staff will be unable to fulfill their marketing responsibilities. For instance, an operations strategy predicated on maximizing throughput makes it impossible for the clinical staff to vary the length of encounters, which are based on the needs of individual patients, for product augmentation in the form of health education discussions.

Table 4 illustrates the relationship between operations strategy elements and marketing strategy.

TABLE 4   Marketing Strategy and Operations Strategy Elements

	Marketing Strategy	
Operations Strategy Elements	Customer Service	Price
Operations emphasis	Respond rapidly to customer requests	Produce at lowest cost
Organization structure	Tightly coupled	Loosely coupled
Priorities based on	Customer need dates	Steady flow
Reflexes	Fast	Slow
Focus	High, many options	Unfocused to achieve economies of scale

Technology Planning

The foregoing discussions make frequent reference to decisions that will influence and be influenced by the organization's use of technology.[9] This leads to the conclusion that an underlying strategy should be developed to achieve the optimum level of investment in technology. Such a strategy should be based on a technology situation assessment comprising continuous environmental scanning and periodic internal assessments. The internal assessments should produce a technology portfolio analysis that displays information in the familiar four cell matrix. The axes are technology importance and the organization's relative position. This portfolio analysis should be compared with the organization's business portfolio to ensure that technology investment decisions are compatible with the corporate strategy. For example, there should be a high level of expenditure in technology for a service that has great potential for growth and profitability and no investment for a service that generates little or no profit and has little potential for improvement.

---

[9] This includes both operations technology and managerial technology. Decision support systems are a good example of managerial technology.

A related issue of some consequence is the organizations's policy on research, development, and innovation. It should provide guidance in the form of answers to the following questions.

1. Will it attempt to be a technical leader in its field or will it depend on others for new developments?
2. If it intends to do research,

    a. How will the effort be divided between basic and applied investigations?
    b. What level of R&D spending will it seek to maintain, particularly in relation to other facets of the mission?
    c. How will R&D effort be allocated among the product lines?

Information technology provides a good example of the issues involved. It may have an impact at the following three levels, all of which are significant for the organization's strategies and plans.

1. *Industry-level effects*

    a. Change the nature of the service; for example, shift medical care from prescription to advice for do-it-yourself activities
    b. Alter distribution patterns; for example, specialists may be able to function on the basis of electronically transmitted images and clinical data without face-to-face contact

2. *Market-level effects*

    a. Alter the scope of markets; for example, service areas could expand as travel time is no longer relevant
    b. Change the economics of operations; for example, the elimination of paper records would have a significant effect on costs in terms of paper creation, transfer, and storage expenses

3. *Business-level effects*

    a. Change entry barriers; for example, investment will be required in the development or acquisition of software, hardware, and databases

    b. Facilitate integration; for example, networking will make it easier for various parts of the organization to communicate rapidly
    c. Change relationships with buyers; for example, remove some of the personal aspects of care
    d. Shift the balance among strategy options; for example, make it easier to become a low-cost producer by substituting information technology, such as expert systems, for human clinicians

Financial Planning

The two main issues in financial planning relate to profitability and maintaining a sound financial position.

Since the underlying purpose of corporate strategy is to increase the value of the organization, it follows that earnings must be satisfactory. The results of operations must provide at least as much increase in value as could be obtained from any alternative uses of the resources committed to the organization. Efficiency and growth are measures of contributing factors. Efficiency is a direct contribution to current profitability. Growth may be a step further removed, since profitability from growth may not be realized immediately. In other words, efficiency can be both a necessary and a sufficient condition for profitability; growth alone cannot be sufficient. The issues of efficiency are obviously closely tied to operations decisions, which, in turn, are affected by the marketing strategy. Efficiency is also related to capital outlays; that is, efficiency will depend on the availability of a suitable mix of plant, equipment, and staff. The availability of these resources will be influenced by the corporation's ability to provide the necessary financial assets.

Maintaining a "sound financial position" means that assets will be protected from an "undue" amount of risk while striving for profitability. For example, leverage is an attempt to increase stockholders' returns on their investments by supplementing their funds (equity) with borrowed funds (debt). As the debt increases, however, so does the risk, since debt increases the fixed demands (interest and principal payments) that could throw the organization into bankruptcy if they become too great in relation to the income/cash flow of the organization. Consequently, organizations adopt policies that affect the level of financial risk that will be taken. These policies, when considered in conjunction with policies on the amount of earnings that will be distributed to stakeholders, determine the amount of assets that will be available for growth or for replacement of existing plant and equipment.

Another aspect of risk avoidance relates to liquidity, which is reflected, in part, by cash flow. The cash position of the organization can be influenced by marketing decisions that relate to prices, discounts, and collection processes. It is also affected by operations decisions related to such things as inventory and staffing.

PLANNING AND ORGANIZATIONAL STRUCTURE

The organization is the vehicle for implementing the strategic plan; therefore, it must be suitable for the task. Some would argue that strategies are selected on the basis of compatibility with an organization as it exists. Since the organization is nothing more than a conception of how resources, processes, and authority should relate in a defined situation, however, such an approach places needless constraints on the number of available choices. It is far more productive to begin by assuming that any reasonable combination of structure, process, and behavior is acceptable regardless of historical antecedents. Stated somewhat differently, structure should follow strategy. Those who dissent from this point of view seem to feel that a better explanation is provided by the hypothesis focused on the fit between people and structure.[10] But there are also strong beliefs about the fit between people and strategy types. Consequently, the argument may be circular. In any case, several authors have prepared useful tables showing organizational characteristics in relation to types of strategy. Following are a few items from a table presented by Schendel and Hofer:[11]

---

[10] Dan E. Schendel and Charles W. Hofer (eds.). *Strategic Management.* Boston, Little, Brown, 1979, pp. 222–225.

[11] Ibid., p. 132.

Strategy Characteristics	Managerial Type	Organizational Characteristics
Growth	Entrepreneur	Must enable future growth
Earnings maximization	Solid businessman	Must provide flexibility at moderate cost
Harvesting	"Hard-nosed" operator	Must be low cost and no frills

Apparently, there is no controversy about the need to adapt processes to accommodate the strategies selected. For instance, it is clear that the evaluation-and-reward system for a strategy emphasizing current profit would be ill-suited for a strategy focused on research or long-range development. Bower[12] singles out two processes—specialization and integration—as particularly critical for successful implementation. Similarly, there seems to be agreement on the requirement that behavior support the chosen strategies. This implies that style and shared values must be compatible with organizational aims and the means chosen to attain them. The essence, then, of this step is the concept of achieving a strategic fit among the well-known *Seven S's*. The Seven S framework was developed by the McKinsey Corporation and has been widely used by successful firms.[13] In short, the decision makers must ensure a match between the strategy selected (the first S) and the organizational factors identified by the other six S's (see the following).

The S's

Factors Affecting Strategy	The Six S's Affecting Strategy
Structure	Structure, Staff
Process	Systems, Skills
Behavior	Style, Shared Values

---

[12] Joseph L. Bower. "Solving the Problems of Business Planning." *Journal of Business Strategy*, 2:38–41, Winter 1982.

[13] Robert H. Waterman, Jr. "The Seven Elements of Strategic Fit." *Journal of Business Strategy*, 2:69–73, Winter 1982.

The remainder of this section will focus on two aspects of these elements—the style and skills required of the organization's leaders and the structure of the organization.

Strategic management is usually distinguished from strategic planning by noting that it encompasses both strategic planning and implementation of the plan. It was pointed out earlier that strategic planning is a responsibility of the CEO. The successful CEO will want to ensure that the planning effort has not been a futile exercise; therefore, the organization's leadership must assume direct responsibility for the following activities:

1. Initiate the planning process and ensure implementation
2. Commit the resources required for the planning process
3. Manage conflicts induced by the planning process
4. Provide the group process skills that are required to formulate strategy and goals
5. Ensure that goals are doable
6. Gain the cooperation of neutrals or negatively disposed participants
7. Announce and promote the strategy
8. Be sure that the strategy is referred to as the basis for all major decisions
9. Avoid the production of excess paper
10. Review and renew the process at appropriate intervals

It has become commonplace for health services organizations to engage in restructuring as part of the strategic management process. This generally is rationalized by asserting that the goals of organizational restructuring are financial improvement, better management, expansion of a service, penetration of a market, tax advantages, regulatory advantages, or some combination of these. It is noteworthy that most of the intended results are tactical rather than strategic. Consequently, even when the restructuring is carefully designed, rather than merely a minor cosmetic change to be in vogue, there is a strong possibility that the revision may not be supportive of the fundamental strategy.

As architects and designers have often noted, form should follow function. This is as true for organizations as it is for buildings and equipment. For instance, Peter Drucker[14] predicts that organizations of the future will necessarily become much flatter, with widely dispersed authority, owing to the shift from an industrial society to one that is served predominantly by information-based service industries. This is consistent with the earlier assertions of Peters and Waterman[15] regarding loosely coupled organizations. It is also reinforced by the findings of Rosabeth Kanter,[16] that rigidly subdivided organizations tend to be less effective than those with more freedom of interaction among the organization's members.

The literature on organization behavior provides some useful insights with regard to this issue. It describes three generic organizational structures: U-form, H-form and M-form.[17]

A U-form organization is a unified, highly centralized structure. The subordinate units have no individual bottom line and they are unable to exist alone. The CEO is intimately aware of each subunit's functions and activities, which focus the CEO's attention on internal problems rather than external issues. In large organizations, this tends to become a layered bureaucracy. Many independent community hospitals of the 1960s and 1970s fit this pattern. Some of their most successful leaders have experienced great difficulty in altering their mindset; consequently, they often continue to function in a style that is inappropriate for the corporate structure adopted by their organization.

An H-form organization can be thought of as a holding company. It is extremely decentralized, and all business units operate independently. Each strives to maximize its own short-run profits, and there is no interaction among business units except on a purely commercial basis. The value created is the sum of the "bottom-lines" of all the business units within the corporation. The corporate office serves

---

[14] Peter F. Drucker. "The Coming of the New Organization." *Harvard Business Review,* 66:(1):45–53, January–February 1988.

[15] Thomas J. Peters and Robert H. Waterman, Jr. *In Search of Excellence.* New York, Harper & Row, 1982, pp. 112–113.

[16] Rosabeth M. Kanter. *The Changemasters.* New York, Touchstone Books, 1985.

[17] W. Richard Scott, *Organizations,* Englewood Cliffs, N.J., Prentice-Hall, 1981; William G. Ouchi, *The M-Form Society,* Reading, Mass., Addison-Wesley, 1984, Chapter 2.

primarily as the source of capital. It fills this role because it knows more about the businesses' operations than do outside investors. Presumably, this knowledge allows it to allocate capital more effectively than if the businesses were independently competing for capital in the stock market.

An M-form organization can be characterized as multidivisional; its management is partially centralized. The partially independent subunits share some common concerns (e.g., technology, marketing skills, etc.). On the other hand, each subunit produces a different service using different production processes. The subunits each have their own bottom line. (This is referred to as product-line management in current health services literature.) In this arrangement, the corporate office is still the primary source of capital, but it also seeks to optimize the performance of subunits and to facilitate collaboration when appropriate.

The M-form organization highlights the need for consistency between structure and the other six Ss. To illustrate, consider transfer pricing as an issue in system structuring and management. It is, in fact, a concern whenever diversification or vertical integration is part of the organization's strategy.

Vertical integration exists when a number of process stages are included within the organization. Diversification is a measure of the degree of separation between businesses that make up the organization. Vertical integration emphasizes interdependence of profit centers when each stage of operations is evaluated on the basis of profitability. Diversification emphasizes independence of businesses as profit centers.

If there was no vertical integration and no diversification, there would be no transfer pricing within a single stage-one business unit organization. This is the U-form organization. A variation of this arrangement is the situation where there is high integration and low diversification and the final unit is the only profit center. All other units are cost centers, and all units are rewarded on the basis of their contribution to corporate success.

If there was high diversification and no vertical integration or horizontal collaboration, each unit would seek to maximize its own profits without regard for the rest of the organization. This is the H-form organization.

The M-form organization, however, is composed of diversified units that are expected to collaborate to a great degree. The result is that the units compete but are regarded as part of an integrated corporation and are thus rewarded for both individual and corporate performance. In these circumstances, the corporate leadership faces a major problem in determining how to measure performance. If the bottom line of each unit is the major factor, then the units have conflicting interests. Each supplier unit is motivated to maximize its performance by charging as high a price as possible, while each user strives to improve its performance by minimizing costs.

When this kind of collaboration is mandated by the corporate *strategy* and the supporting organizational *structure,* top management must create a culture that regards corporate achievement more highly than the accomplishment of individual units. It must reinforce this *shared value* with a reward system that is capable of recognizing both collaborative and independent achievements of the individual business units. It must encourage a cooperative management *style* throughout the organization without stifling the motivation of business unit managers to maximize their unit's performance. It must recruit *staff* with the *skills* to develop policies that will optimize corporate performance by answering questions such as: What is the correct basis for transfer pricing? competitive market price? full cost? marginal cost? or full cost plus profit margin? Under what circumstances may a business unit manager try to get a better deal by purchasing supplies or services from an outside source?

SUMMARY

When the organization is viewed as a complex system, it is apparent that a single plan will not be sufficient for strategic management. Strategic management, which includes both plan development and implementation, requires strategic, business, and functional plans. These plans are essential for effective management of the relationships between the environment and the organization. This is particularly true when one considers developing and guiding organizational elements as subsystems.

Plans at the corporate, business, and functional levels include appropriate strategies. Corporate strategies focus on increasing the organization's value for its stakeholders by adjusting the scope of the corporation's enterprises, by acquiring resources, and by allocating them among the subsystems. Business strategies are competitive in nature. They seek to add value by gaining and maintaining a profitable position in the face of continuing threats from other organizations seeking to serve the same market(s). Functional strategies are designed to achieve corporate and business goals. Because of the great danger of suboptimization resulting from some function attempting to maximize its performance, particular attention must be focused on ensuring that the functional strategies are mutually supportive.

Finally, it was noted that the successful development and implementation of plans depends on compatibility between a variety of organizational characteristics. The compatibility of strategy and organizational structure was examined as one of the most significant of these relationships.

CHAPTER 3

COMMUNITY PLANNING

There is a general consensus (although certainly not unanimous agreement) that in a civilized, developed, and relatively affluent society such as that of the United States, every person should be assured of some minimum level of social services that will allow him or her to survive. Although there is less agreement about the level and scope of the services to which an individual is entitled, a majority of the population seems to accept the notion that some minimum level of health care is a right. There is also an abundance of evidence that the expectations for some acceptable level of social services cannot be achieved through sole reliance on the marketplace. In other words, there will always be some individuals in our society who will be unable to pay for even the minimum level of services at the time they are needed.[1]

Society has attempted to deal with this issue in several ways. First, there is the direct provision of services by a governmental agency such as a public health department. The second is based on the prevalent belief that governmental organizations are always less efficient than

---

[1] The persons in this situation will not necessarily be permanently dependent on others for their needs. Some will be long-term members of disadvantaged groups, but others will be without resources for only short periods of time (e.g., unemployed workers during the depth of a recession).

comparable units within the private sector, therefore, government funds may be used to reimburse or subsidize private organizations that provide care to certain categories of people.[2] Finally, tax exempt status is often used as a way to give an indirect subsidy to private organizations that are expected to provide needed services to those who cannot afford them.[3] Thus, government subsidies were augmented by philanthropic contributions, since the tax exempt status of the recipient organization created tax advantages for the donor. These subsidies and contributions have traditionally been supplemented by a process known as cost shifting; that is, charges that were assessed to paying patients have included a factor sufficient to cover the costs of care for nonpaying patients.[4] In any event, the net result was that members of the community have been investing large amounts of money, by one means or another, with the expectation that their investments would adequately support such social goals as care for the indigent, medical research, and medical education.

Observations about the results obtained, coupled with continuing pleas for greater infusions of money (either in the form of higher charges or larger donations), have led to public concerns about the efficiency of the health system. These concerns, in turn, have led to the establishment of various planning and regulatory programs.

Initially, these efforts were sponsored by local leaders in communities where a few dominant firms were faced with continuing pleas for support of hospital development efforts. The leaders attempted to rationalize the use of their contributions by establishing voluntary

---

[2] For instance, hospitals that received federal funds under the Hill-Burton Program are required to document the amount of uncompensated care that was provided up to the point where the amount of such care has "paid off" the hospital's obligation.

[3] The subsidy in this case takes the form of tax revenues forgone by the political jurisdictions that recognize the tax exempt status. Recently, there has been considerable debate about whether not-for-profit hospitals do provide a sufficiently large amount of uncompensated care to justify their tax exempt status.

[4] Nonpaying patients are not always unable to pay. In addition to the indigent, free care or discounted care has often been provided to special groups, such as members of the medical staff.

planning agencies. The term "voluntary" meant that no hospital was compelled to participate in the planning program or to abide by the recommendations of a community plan. On the other hand, those hospitals that participated expected philanthropic support as recognition of their cooperation.

The Hill-Burton Program, which was established in 1946, required each participating state to develop a statewide hospital development plan. In 1964, the Federal Government extended its support of planning by authorizing project grants for the development of local plans for health facilities.

In 1966, the Federal Government created the Comprehensive Health Planning Program through the enactment of P.L. 89-749. This legislation authorized federal support for health planning at both state and local levels. It is significant that the word "comprehensive" was used to convey the notion that all health services, not just hospitals, should be included in the planning process. Three other aspects of this law are noteworthy. First, it mandated participation by representatives of the consumers of health services. Second, it contained no sanctions that could be imposed on organizations that took actions which were incompatible with the plan; compliance was strictly voluntary. Third, it was a totally voluntary program with a relatively small amount of funds to disburse. At the same time, it required a substantial local effort to raise the required matching funds and to overcome political opposition. Consequently, only a small number of local agencies were established.

Several states, however, had already come to the conclusion that uncontrolled growth of the hospital segment of the industry would lead to expensive redundancies in service capacity. To avert this threat, these states enacted legislation requiring review and approval of projects before they could be implemented. Approval of a project led to the issuance of a certificate of need (CON). This document authorized the proposer to implement the project that had been determined to be in the best interest of the community.

At this point, the costs of Medicare, Medicaid, and other health services programs began to be viewed as a burden, because of the rapid and continuous escalation in the proportion of gross national product (GNP) that was spent on health. The Federal Government became increasingly concerned with finding some way to bring these expenditures under control. One such attempt was the adoption of the CON concept for reimbursing capital expenditures. This program was incorporated in the 1972 amendments to the Social Security Act and was popularly known as Section 1122—its location in that legislation. The program, however, had limited effect, since it applied only to that portion of the costs that were charged to Medicare and Medicaid.

The evident inadequacies of the Comprehensive Health Planning Program, the ineffectiveness of Section 1122 provisions, and the redundancy of other federally funded programs (notably Hill-Burton and the Regional Medical Program) led Congress to develop a consolidated planning program that required nationwide participation. The program also required that each state establish a mandatory CON process. This legislation, P.L. 93-641, established a national system of local and state agencies. The local agencies were called Health Systems Agencies (HSAs), since the law emphasized the need for a coordinated effort encompassing all aspects of health services. State agencies were known as State Health Planning and Development Agencies (SHPDAs). The law continued the requirement for consumer participation in the planning process at both state and local levels. Although it expressed concerns about the need to control the increase in health care costs, this consideration was balanced with issues of access and quality of care.

P.L. 93-641 was passed in the latter part of 1974. Activation of this complex legislation required a considerable amount of time. In fact, before it could be fully implemented, the Carter administration's effort to slow the increase in total health care expenditures by direct legislation was resoundingly defeated. At that point, the Federal Government began to make cost containment the overriding concern in all of its regulations and guidance to state and local planning agencies. CON was virtually the only tool that was available to local agencies attempting to comply with the demands of the Federal Government. Consequently, these agencies became even more stringent in granting approval of new projects. Each denial of a CON, however, increased the hostility toward the agencies.

The animosity of a majority of health providers complemented the antiregulatory philosophy of a new presidential administration, which began in 1981. This administration was firmly committed to the principles of the free market. It argued vehemently that competition was the only feasible mechanism for stabilizing the costs of health care. Although abolition of the planning program was a high priority on its agenda, the administration's efforts were thwarted for several years by Congress. It did succeed, however, in reducing available funds to a point where the agencies simply lacked the resources to carry out the responsibilities mandated by the law. The administration had enough support in Congress to prevent renewal of the legislation but, for several years, it was unable to prevent limited funding through continuing resolutions. Eventually, this war of attrition was won by the administration. Congressional support for the program waned, and efforts to secure funds for another year proved futile.

Since the national health planning framework created under P.L. 93-641 was abolished, the type and degree of planning activities at state and community levels has become very diverse. Despite the philosophical commitment to the effectiveness of the market, there is considerable evidence that some form of external oversight and guidance is essential. This evidence includes such things as business coalitions, committees appointed by state and local officials to give advice on health problems, the establishment of databases so that health provider performance can be scrutinized, and the creation of task forces to deal with pressing issues such as infant mortality, long-term care, health services for the uninsured, and AIDS.

Many of these programs appear to be achieving their objectives. It is important to note, however, that the objectives are limited and divergent. In some cases, they may even be conflicting. For example, a business coalition may be striving to limit the cost of health care purchases by its member organizations while a hospital association task force is seeking to increase revenues in order to meet the needs of the uninsured.

The diversity of these efforts makes it clear that a wide variety of stakeholders are seeking to influence the operation of the health services system. Some are dealing with the system at very broad policy levels, while others are considering very specific details (e.g., the differences among providers in terms of cost/value ratios for hospital services). Some community health planning programs are

TABLE 5   Comprehensive Plan Components

Mission
Megapolicies
Policies
Environmental Assessment
Goals
General Strategy
Functional Strategies
Objectives
Actions
Programs/Projects

very narrowly focused (e.g., infant mortality), while others cover an extremely broad spectrum (e.g., health care for senior citizens). In all cases, however, a framework is needed to guide data collection and analysis and to provide a foundation for recommendations.

The relevant question is how the interests of these stakeholders can be defined and reconciled as abstract values that, in turn, can be transformed into plans for specific actions that will lead to the achievement of their goals and, thus, to satisfaction of their interests. This can be achieved through the development of some form of a community health plan. A complete plan is depicted by the sequence of activities listed in Table 5. It is entirely possible, however, that some community health plans may only go to the point of establishing broad policy or of setting goals. In any event the process should proceed as follows:

First, the planning organization determines what the mission of the relevant health system will be.[5] Then the stakeholders' values

---

[5] This could be a comprehensive system, such as was envisioned by P.L. 93-641, or a very narrow subsystem, such as the Maternal and Child Health component of a city health department.

relevant to that mission are identified as megapolicies. The identified megapolicies *may* lead to a revision of the mission statement and *will* be used as a basis for specific policies that will guide all subsequent actions. The next action is an environmental assessment to identify the threats and opportunities on which the organization's goals are based. These goals, in turn, provide a focus for the development of a general strategy designed to accomplish the organization's mission within the bounds prescribed by policies. The general strategy is then expanded into more specific functional strategies for the achievement of objectives that will be steps toward goal attainment. Next, the organization will identify the actions that must be taken to achieve the objectives. Finally, the programs and projects that will comprise the actions are designed. In the final phase in particular, multiple options must be considered, and the selection of the preferred option will be based on criteria derived from the organization's policies.

POLICYMAKING

Metapolicy

Dror[6] identifies three levels of policy: metapolicy, megapolicy, and specific policy. The first can be defined as policy on policymaking. In other words, metapolicy sets the rules by which decision makers will establish all the policies within an organization. It includes such generic components as the policymaking system's mode of operation (e.g., its degree of stakeholder involvement), the system's organizational and personnel components (e.g., board/staff relationships), information inputs into policymaking (e.g., public hearings), policymaking methods (e.g., modes of policy analysis), and methods and criteria for evaluating policymaking. Metapolicy is important, but because it is complex and falls outside the scope

---

[6] Yehezkel Dror. *Design for Policy Sciences*. New York, Elsevier/North-Holland, 1971, pp. 63–79.

of this book, only two significant concepts, representation and accountability, are discussed further here.

Representation

Members of the community as actual and potential consumers are important stakeholders in the health services system. In the past, it often happened that consumers were not represented in the policymaking process, and their interests were considered only to the extent that they were known and accepted by professionals as valid criteria for establishing objectives.

The professionals' assessments of the consumers' knowledge of their own needs have ranged from complete knowledge to complete ignorance. At one extreme is the assumption that individuals are the best judges of their own welfare. Even though consumers cannot perform the services required, they do know when and how much service should be provided. At the other extreme is the implicit assumption that consumers simply do not know their own needs and therefore cannot evaluate the health services provided. Consider the issue of licensure of professionals. If one accepts the consumer-knowledge idea, one believes that licensure tends to create unnecessary monopolies. If, however, one accepts the consumer-ignorance idea, then one believes that licensure is necessary to protect the individual even though it might have certain undesirable side effects.

It is generally accepted that poor health persists in some areas because resources are applied in a manner that is inappropriate to a given situation. Usually, such misapplication is directly attributable to a lack of understanding between providers and recipients. It is natural—almost inevitable—that the optimal method of using available resources based on the assumptions and biases of providers is less than ideal from the standpoint of the consumer. When consumer input is not considered, the resulting consumer dissatisfaction is evident.

Sociologists have demonstrated that one group generally sees a situation quite differently from another group, even when members of the two groups are from the same socioeconomic stratum. Surely, if there are disagreements and feelings of disenchantment between if there are disagreements and feelings of disenchantment between two groups that have many similarities, such as consumers and providers from the same socioeconomic level, then the likelihood of dissatisfaction will be far greater between groups with many differences, such as recipients of public assistance and professional providers of medical services.

The disparity of views was confirmed by two large-scale national surveys conducted for the Equitable Life Assurance Society of the United States. These surveys reported that physicians are "out of step with the nation on many key issues." The surveys showed that physicians are more accepting of the status quo and less willing to accept innovative service delivery arrangements than consumers.[7, 8]

Dissatisfaction leads to avoidance. Thus, services predicated on inappropriate assumptions about the benefits and desirability of medical care become even less appropriate when those services are used only in crisis or last-resort situations. As a result, this use of resources tends to be ineffective even from the viewpoint of professional designers of the system.

An important factor relating to consumer participation in determining objectives for health services systems is the level of intellect, education, and experience of the consumers. Anyone who cavils at the determination of health needs by laypersons is confusing ends and means. The consumer knows well what the desired ends are and often has better insight into certain aspects of the means than does the professional. The insistence of the medical profession on maintaining the personalized doctor-patient relationship shows that medical services cover a broad spectrum of activities, ranging from technical to psychological. No one is suggesting that consumers have technical expertise, but they may be the only ones who truly know the proper choices for the social/psychological aspects of health care.

Two kinds of expertise, consumer and professional, must be recognized. They are not antithetical and, in most cases, are not even conflicting. There will be a few cases where these areas of expertise

---

[7] "MD, Public Attitudes Differ on Health Care Costs, Study Finds." *Hospital Week*, 20(24):2, June 15, 1984.

[8] *Today in Health Planning*, 6(12):1, June 11, 1984.

meet, but the vast majority of situations clearly will be on one side of this boundary or the other. The need, then, is to use the expertise available in both areas in a complementary fashion. This can be achieved if each group willingly accepts the contributions of the other. To rephrase this, there are six dimensions of medical care: quality, continuity, availability, accessibility, cost, and acceptability. In the traditional health care system in the United States, the first dimension has been dealt with by licensure and peer review. The others generally have been left to economic regulation by the mechanism of the free market, but this has not always worked. Therefore, other mechanisms, such as consumer councils in health institutions, have been designed to provide for more effective input by the recipients of health care, giving them meaningful control over these dimensions.

Consumer participation has led to many problems and misunderstandings. Often there is a definite difference in the degree of commitment as perceived by consumers and providers. For example, providers may feel that they are using an optimum amount of resources to deal with a particular problem; on the other hand, recipients may believe that the providers are slacking off or shirking their responsibilities because the problem is not totally solved.

Some, however, feel that consumer involvement conflicts with the professionalism of the providers. Professionals are those who are responsible for making decisions for people who are not qualified to decide for themselves. Thus, professionals have a fiduciary responsibility for providing health services; any delegation or sharing of this responsibility subjects them to criticism for actions over which they do not have complete control.

Despite these and other problems that may arise, sufficient reason exists to justify consumer participation in determining policies for health systems:

1. It reduces alienation between consumers and the institutions intended to serve them.

2. It provides consumers with an opportunity to influence the decisions that affect them.

3. It improves communication among all groups within the community.

4. It reinforces the underlying principles of our system of government. This factor is sometimes difficult to accept, but it may be that the strengthening of democratic institutions is more important than the efficient delivery of health services.

It is evident that participation will occur and will be maintained only if it is effective. Certain conditions for effective participation exist on both the consumer and provider sides of the interaction. These are outlined in the following series of questions on resources, motivations, and structure.

RESOURCES

Consumer

Does the consumer have the intellectual and knowledge resources required to deal with the situation?

Does the consumer have the material and economic resources required to participate effectively?

Does the consumer have the social resources, including leadership, that are necessary for effective participation?

Provider

Is the provider dependent on the consumer for resources such as money or information?

MOTIVATION

Consumer

Do consumers believe that participation will be effective?

Do consumers have relevant interests?

Do consumers feel that participation is personally satisfying?

Provider

Do providers believe that consumers have power?

Do providers believe that consumer participation is proper?

STRUCTURE

Consumer

Does the structure encourage participation rather than just permit it? For example, are there voting laws?

Provider

Is participation discretionary or mandatory?

On the whole, it appears that active consumer involvement in the policymaking process has had a positive effect; however, the potential for negative effects cannot be ignored. Cupps[9] identifies four categories of potential problems:

1. Decision makers may make shortsighted choices in an effort to be responsive to the demands of citizen groups (e.g., granting a certificate of need on the basis of accessibility considerations without regard to cost, quality, and availability).

2. Each advocacy group, however small, tends to assert that it represents the views of the entire community and that the public interest corresponds to the position it holds.

3. Some groups have resorted to tactics that have virtually paralyzed administrative systems (e.g., extending hearing and legal proceedings interminably in the hope that the frustrated majority will finally give up).

4. There is an absence of willingness to make, or even accept, balanced cost-benefit analyses. This leads to simplistic thinking that fails to consider that every benefit has a cost (e.g., total elimination of some form of water pollution may destroy the community's economic base).

The discussion of consumer input up to this point has focused on a relationship between professionals and laypersons, with the latter in a somewhat submissive role. Although this condition is still predominant, there has been a notable shift in consumer attitudes. Younger consumers, in particular, are taking individual and collective responsibility for more and more health-related decisions. This is reflected by the development of business coalitions representing large blocks of consumers and by some employers' demands for private utilization review programs to ensure that they are charged only for essential services. For many large corporations, the costs of health care have become a major drain on profitability and thus a critical issue in contract negotiations. In particular, businesses are seeking

---

[9] D. Stephen Cupps. "Emerging Problems of Citizen Participation." *Public Administration Review, 37*(5):478–487, September–October 1977.

arrangements that will overcome the bias toward uncritical use of health services.[10]

The greater independence of individual consumers is made evident by actions such as requesting second opinions, selecting nontraditional service delivery organizations (e.g., urgent care centers), and participating in wellness programs. Currently, many state legislatures (often at the behest of business coalitions) have enacted or are considering legislation that would give consumers access to information on the prices and quality of care offered by individual providers. This is intended as another step toward reducing consumer "ignorance," one of the major barriers to effective competition.[11]

The marketing orientation in organizational planning is another clear recognition of the size and significance of this phenomenon. Marketing is an effort to develop products and services that are responsive to the consumers' perceived needs. Thus, it follows that a process that includes consumer input in policymaking will facilitate market-oriented planning, since the resulting policies will guide the establishment of the system's goals, strategies, and actions.

Accountability

The concept of accountability encompasses representation, responsiveness, and reporting.

As a public policy principle, accountability[12] is intended to deal with a major problem of modern living: Few people can live in isolation from and independent of others. It is evident that the vast majority of stakeholders have neither the time nor the inclination to

---

[10] "Chrysler Exec Urges Automakers to Help Pare Health Care Spending." *Hospital Week*, 20(24):4, June 15, 1984.

[11] "Health Care Data Collection." *AHA Washington Memo #505*, June 15, 1984.

[12] The definition of accountability intended here is comparable to the conception developed by Etzioni. He discusses symbolic, political-process, checks-and-balances, and guidance approaches to accountability. The guidance approach, which is espoused here, is a combination of the first three approaches plus an additional component that requires the accountable agency to take an active role in educating and mobilizing the stakeholders affected by its actions. See Amitai Etzioni, "Alternative Conceptions of Accountability: The Examples of Health Administration," *Public Administration Review*, 35(3):279–286, May–June 1975.

monitor or participate in all of the collective decisions required in a modern community. On the other hand, each decision may have a significant effect on many stakeholders and, therefore, should be based on consideration of the interests and values of all affected. The solution to this dilemma is to delegate decision-making responsibility to a small group that presumably is responsive to the values of the community as a whole. Thus, in the health field, accountability could mean that the governing body of a health planning agency or the board of trustees of a community health services organization would inform the general community of each decision so that stakeholders could indicate approval or disapproval of all actions taken.

In this form, accountability has two weaknesses. It assumes that stakeholders often are considering many decisions individually and that any advice given to the governing body or board can only be a reaction to a fait accompli. On the other hand, if the planning agency or health services organization adopts a set of generic rules to guide all future decisions, stakeholders can focus on a manageable number of major issues and provide long-range guidance that will be used in making all future decisions. In other words, a governing body or board can become more accountable to the public by establishing clear, explicit megapolicies.

Megapolicy

Megapolicy consists of a set of master policies that provide general guidance for the more discrete specific policies. The contents of a megapolicy document are illustrated by the following sample (not exhaustive) list of components:

1. Organizational roles
2. Basic values and their priorities (e.g., quality compared to cost)
3. Theory of health on which decisions will be based
4. Health system boundaries or organizational mission
5. Range of topics to be considered within the system (e.g., public sector only, services only)
6. Type of change sought (e.g., incremental or comprehensive)
7. Time values applied to decisions (e.g., relative value of immediate results in contrast to long-range changes)

8. Level of acceptable risk and controversy
9. Assumptions about the availability of resources
10. Assumptions about the future
11. Acceptable instruments for implementing decisions
12. Threshold values (e.g., Will the goal levels set be the minimum acceptable or the ideal?)

This list indicates that the number of issues to be addressed through megapolicy is small and, furthermore, that the issues are couched in nontechnical terms which can be understood by any interested citizen. This simplicity and conciseness is essential, because the number and complexity of discrete policies tends to be very great, and presenting all of the specific policies to the stakeholders is not in keeping with the principle of accountability in a public decision-making body.

Policy

Just as megapolicies provide a means of achieving accountability, specific policies contribute to efficiency in the planning process. Without policies, decision makers will be engaged in repeated debates over the same crucial issues. This wastes time and adversely affects an organization's ability to execute its mission. Furthermore, policies provide guidance so that the staff can perform its assignments without waiting for decision makers to ratify each step along the way.

Kerr's[13] description of the conditions for establishing a policy implies a useful definition: A specific policy constitutes legitimate authorization for a designated agent to act in a particular way whenever a particular condition exists. It is, of course, expected that the specified condition will occur frequently. Successful policy also must meet other conditions:

1. The implementing agent must have both the capability and the resources to carry out the policy.
2. The required action must achieve the goals of the authorizing agent.

---

[13] Donna H. Kerr. "The Logic of Policy and Successful Policy." *Policy Sciences,* 7(3):351–363, September 1976.

3. The policy's purpose must be justified to the stakeholders, and the costs and side effects of taking the required action must be less than the benefits involved.

4. Finally, an effective policy must be adopted by a fair process. At the very least, it must be made known to affected stakeholders prior to implementation.

GOALS, OBJECTIVES, AND ACTIONS

Setting Goals and Objectives

The following is a useful definition of the term goals:

> Goals provide the basic framework for the plan by focusing directly on particular health issues or areas of concern. They are unconstrained by the present planning horizon and are not stated in terms of community or provider action. Goals are expressions of desired conditions of health status and health systems, expressed as quantifiable, timeless aspirations. Goals should be both technically and financially achievable and responsive to community ideals.[14]

The reference to community ideals makes it clear that goals are derived from policies that represent stakeholder value statements. Thus, goal setting becomes a major subsequent step in the plan development process. Goals, however, do not establish specific thresholds that tell decision makers the level or range of acceptable status or system performance. Consequently, another term—goal levels—must be introduced. *Goal levels* are "quantified targets set to indicate the achievement of specific goals." There should be a process for deriving the goal level from earlier policy statements. For instance, a megapolicy statement might assert that a community will strive to achieve system performance that is equivalent to the national average, and a policy statement might indicate that one measure of health status is infant mortality. In this case, the national average infant mortality rate, as reported by the National Center for Health

---

[14] U.S. Department of Health, Education, and Welfare, Bureau of Health Planning and Resources Development. "Guidelines Concerning the Development of Health System Plans and Annual Implementation Plans." Rockville, Md., 1976, p. 22. Mimeographed.

Statistics, would be used as the normative goal level against which the community's actual experience would be compared.

The normative statement is then contrasted with the current and projected status for the issue of concern, and that comparison becomes the basis for establishing an objective. An *objective* is defined as "a quantitative statement of what should be achieved within a specified time period." The level set for an objective may not be identical with the goal level; this depends on the decision maker's expectation of a system's ability to reach and/or maintain the goal level within the planning horizon.

Goal Indicators

A key issue in establishing goals and objectives is the selection of appropriate *indicators*.[15] These indicators must be established for each service, setting, and characteristic within the taxonomy adopted for a health planning process. This array of indicators can be envisioned as the content of a three-dimensional matrix, as shown in Figure 8.[16]

Indicators are essentially criteria for decision making; that is, they are measures of the factors to be considered by decision makers. Indicators are those elements of the issue deemed particularly important; they do not represent a total or complete description, as this would overload the information-handling capacity of decision makers.

Indicator levels serve a number of purposes. They describe the health system. They inform managers within the system of what is expected of them (although they do not attempt to state methods of accomplishment). They aid in the determination of objectives

---

[15] Adele Hebb. Presentation during Health Resources Planning Educational System, a course on health system planning sponsored by the Educational Testing Service; the U.S. Department of Health, Education, and Welfare, Bureau of Health Planning; and the Health Planning Development Center, Inc., Atlanta, Georgia, May 25, 1977.

[16] Some service-setting combinations will not exist (e.g., cardiac surgery in a home setting); therefore, all cells of the matrix will not be completed. Furthermore, many organizations will not wish to plan for a comprehensive system, but will, as noted earlier, focus on a smaller subsystem of particular interest.

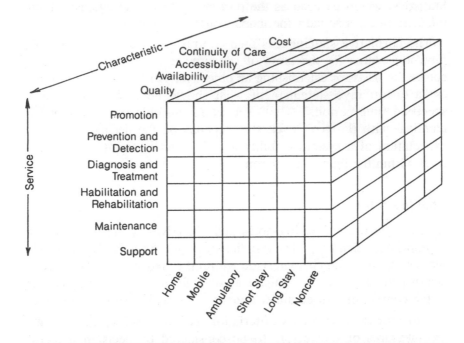

Figure 8   Indicators to be established for a health planning process.

and the setting of priorities. Finally, they are used to evaluate the performance of the system and of the planning organization itself. In other words, they are a basis for measuring whether the planning organization has affected the system.

An important consideration regarding these indicators is their level of specificity. Most organizations are inclined to develop standards that are far too specific in those areas that the planning staff knows well; such detail could stifle innovation and render the standards (which are based on current knowledge only) invalid in a few years, when the planning decisions will take effect. For example, in a field as dynamic as health services, technological obsolescence is always a possibility. Also, detailed, highly specific indicators may exceed a planning organization's capacity, because each indicator requires a substantial analysis before it can be accepted and must be reviewed frequently to ensure that it is current. Finally, a highly detailed health system plan would be counterproductive in the constraints that it would place on the managerial activities of the persons and organizations to whom it applies. This might be described as a jurisdictional aspect related to the boundary between stakeholder accountability and internal management responsibility. In simplest terms, at some level of specificity, stakeholder-established norms will begin to impair the health service provider's management capability to innovate, respond to opportunities, and deal with problems.

Indicators and levels of specificity can be selected in several ways. The "single best way" approach is based on a theory or on some analysis of empirical evidence. For example, evidence which has shown that faster treatment of trauma victims has positive results implies that the emergency medical system can best be improved by getting the patient to the hospital more quickly.

More often than not, there is no single accepted method of dealing with an issue. Consequently, it is frequently necessary to adopt what can be referred to as a "multiple perspectives approach," which attempts to determine all possible answers to problems and analyze how they overlap or complement one another. For example, physicians, parents, and teachers may have different views on mental retardation. Drawing on these varying perspectives, the modes of dealing with this problem are identified, and some attempt is made to reach a consensus.

There are a variety of techniques for achieving consensus in a group setting. One of the best known and most effective is the nominal group technique developed by Andre Delbecq et al.[17] Another method is to seek clarification and refinement of proposed measures by consciously establishing a conflict situation in which opponents will vigorously challenge one another's views. Through this process the "truth" may emerge. Although there are some obvious benefits to this sort of technique, its utility is quite limited because it requires an individual decision maker or an agency to exercise final judgment

---

[17] Andre L. Delbecq, Andrew H. Van de Ven, and David H. Gustafson. *Group Techniques for Program Planning: A Guide to Nominal Group and Delphi Processes.* Glenview, Ill., Scott, Foresman, 1975. The nominal group technique is a carefully designed procedure to maximize the productivity of a heterogeneous group seeking to develop a mutually acceptable set of ideas in relation to a specified issue.

between the contending parties. If the planning process has become at all controversial, the hostility that is generated may remain after a decision has been made and will probably be far more costly than the value of resulting benefits.

Regardless of the method used, there are five phases or steps in the process of developing indicator levels. Phase 1 is the establishment of general values, accomplished in the policy-development phase. Phase 2 is the conversion of these values into operational measures—the selection of indicators. Phase 3 is the determination of a feasible range of outcomes for each operational measure (in other words, What is the extent of the possibilities?). Phase 4 involves the selection of an acceptable outcome threshold for each measure. This is the point at which goal levels are initially set and balance is sought among the conflicting indicators (e.g., a relatively high goal level for accessibility may contradict a low goal level for cost). In Phase 5, measures and thresholds are validated in terms of values expressed in megapolicies.

Figure 9 displays in a three-dimensional matrix the possibilities for combining methods and participants in each of the five phases

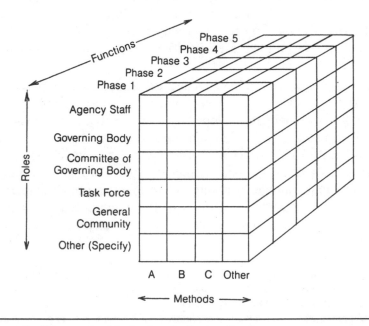

Figure 9 Phases in developing indicator levels.

of indicator-level development. For instance, the governing body of a health organization might undertake Phase 1 by using method B. Phase 2 might be carried out by a task force also using that method, whereas the staff might use method A for Phase 3. Alternatively, this phase could be accomplished by a technical task force also using method A. Phase 4 could be undertaken by the governing body, using a method other than A, B, or C (i.e., a voting process), and the general community might carry out Phase 5 in a series of public hearings.

Taking Actions

Actions can be defined as comprehensive collections of proposed programs aimed at achieving health status and health system goals and objectives. Actions describe the programs selected after consideration of alternative means of improving health and health system performance to desired levels. This definition makes it clear that actions are derived from objectives as another sequential step in the plan development process. An objective identifies a state or status to be achieved, whereas an action relates to the steps which are taken to achieve that state or status.

Some actions may affect numerous objectives; on the other hand, a single objective may generate multiple actions. For instance, the objective of achieving a reduced level of infant mortality might involve such actions as changing the availability and accessibility of obstetrical services or promoting disease-prevention subsystems, such as family planning services or prenatal care for mothers. Actions are important because they link status and services, services and resources, and resources and resource development plans. In other words, service actions are necessary to improve health status; resource actions are required to change services; and resource development actions are essential to alter the quantity and characteristics of resources.

Linkages

Linking Health Status and Health Services

Because the relationship between health services and health status is not well defined or well understood, the types of actions needed to achieve health status are not always apparent. Gradually, however, methods are emerging that will permit these linkages to be established. Some of the most important work in this area was done by the state of Georgia and by the Rand Corporation under contract to the U.S. Department of Health, Education, and Welfare.[18] There are distinct similarities between the approaches used in both cases; the following discussion draws heavily on each.

Both approaches involve a sequence of several steps. The first step is problem recognition, achieved by analyzing the data that might result from comparing goal indicator levels and the forecast status of a community population or from compiling information on publicly expressed discontent.

Once a problem has been identified, the next step is to analyze it for causes and risk factors. For instance, with infant mortality, one of the causal factors might be low birth weight, which can be attributed to a number of risk factors such as maternal age, number of previous pregnancies, poverty, educational level, availability and quality of prenatal care, cigarette smoking, and diet.

After the risk factors have been identified, the areas of potential intervention must be examined. In Georgia, these are categorized as biological, environmental, life-style, and health services factors.

Next, the preferred potential intervention must be determined, which might be done on the basis of a cost-benefit analysis. The large number of alternatives that emerge from such a view of the system, however, would make a full-blown cost-benefit analysis infeasible. Therefore, other heuristic methods must be chosen for selecting a few key contenders from the large list of possible actions. Table 6 illustrates the risk factors for immature infants and the categories of appropriate intervention, with the likelihood of success indicated for each category. An obvious first approach would be to eliminate all types of intervention not categorized as having a high potential for

---

[18] G. E. Alan Dever, *Guidelines for Health Status Measurement*, Atlanta, Georgia Department of Human Resources, Division of Physical Health, 1977; L. J. Harris et al., *Algorithms for Health Planners, Vol. 1, An Overview*, Santa Monica, Calif., Rand Corp., 1977. (See also other volumes in the set, which deal with specific health problems: *Vol. 2, Infant Mortality; Vol. 3, Breast Cancer Mortality; Vol. 4, Heart Attack Mortality; Vol. 5, Preventable Death and Disease;* and *Vol. 6, Hypertension.*)

TABLE 6   Analysis of Risk Factors of Immature Infants by Health Field Concept Components

	Potential for Programs Aimed at Risk Factors					*Potential for Reducing Problems by Eliminating Risk Factors*
Risk Factors	*Biological*	*Environmental*	*Life-Style*	*System of Health Care*		
Maternal Age	Moderate	Moderate	High	Low		High
Previous Pregnancy	Moderate	High	High	Moderate		High
Poverty	None	Moderate	High	High		Moderate
Educational Level	None	Low	Moderate	Moderate		Moderate
Availability of Care	None	Moderate	Low	Moderate		High
Quality of Care	None	Moderate	Moderate	High		High
Cigarette Smoking	Moderate	Moderate	High	Low		Moderate
Diet	Moderate	Moderate	High	Moderate		High
Family Mores	None	Low	High	Low		High

SOURCE: G. E. Alan Dever. *Guidelines for Health Status Measurement.* Atlanta, Georgia Department of Human Resources, Division of Physical Health, 1977, p. 72.

reducing the problem. Beyond this point, other criteria, such as length of time required for implementation or community acceptability, will further reduce the contenders to one or two. These could then be subjected to a rigorous cost-benefit analysis to make the final choice.

Linking Health Services and Resources

The next linkage to be established is between services and resources. The organizational planner is concerned primarily with resource productivity and cost. The community health planner, however, must consider both supply and demand. In this case, development of a full description of a system would enable an aggregation of the data on availability (i.e., quantity of specific resources available) and a determination of the overall level of demand for the various resources required to provide health services. Since achievement of this development presently seems unlikely, the planning organization may resort to a somewhat simpler strategy, based on the traditional ratio approach to estimating resource requirements.[19]

Thus, the policy portion of the plan can establish widely accepted ratios, perhaps national ones, as an ideal supply level to be used as the goal indicator level for resource requirements until the actual need—based on desired total service availability—can be computed. With this indicator level, the current and ideal supplies can be compared. If the former is greater than or equal to the ideal and a recommended action would increase the number of services in the community, then the total requirements of the community must increase by a sufficient amount to support the services to be added. If, on the other hand, the current supply is less than the ideal and recommended actions would once again add services to the community, then the increased services probably can be adequately supported, if the supply of resources is increased from the current level to the amount suggested by the resource goal indicator.

---

[19] U.S. Department of Health, Education, and Welfare, Public Health Service, Bureau of Health Manpower. *Review of Health Manpower Population Requirements Standards*. Washington, D.C., 1976. (HRA 77-22)

Linking Resources and Resource Development Plans

The recommended actions that are proposed to deal with resource shortages or surpluses provide an important link to plans oriented specifically toward resource development. This category includes a state medical facilities plan. It is also possible that a planning process for health manpower development eventually will emerge and that the recommended actions from community health system plans will provide important input to that undertaking.

THE RELATIONSHIP BETWEEN ORGANIZATIONAL AND COMMUNITY PLANNING

Although the concepts of systems planning are appropriate for organizations, there are some important differences between organizational and communitywide planning. The individual organization may be designated as the black box of a communitywide health system plan. The principles of systems hierarchy, however, show that the black box itself is a system with numerous subsystems.

Thus, community planning must recognize that each organization must be concerned with all of the four system functions: attaining its goals, acquiring resources, adapting to its environment, and balancing the activities of its own subsystems. Undoubtedly, the major focus of every organization is to attain its goals, and this function often obscures the importance of other functions. The function of acquiring resources usually depends on the availability of funds, without which the system or organization cannot maintain itself. This particular function, then, is frequently an overriding factor in decisions about changing the scope or methods of operation in an organization.

Tucker,[20] many years ago, highlighted the two major environmental adaptations made by organizational managers. For any hospital to survive, it must first maintain effective exchange relationships with both the patients and the medical staff. According to Tucker, patients demand certain amenities but also are influenced by the caliber or prestige of the medical staff. A good medical staff, in turn,

---

[20] Stephen L. Tucker. "Introducing Marketing as a Planning and Management Tool." *Hospital and Health services Administration*, 22(1):33–44, Winter 1977.

will demand the best of everything for its patients. Organizational management can refuse these demands, however, when the requested equipment or services will pose an economic threat to the organization's survival. Historically, most hospitals were reimbursed on a full-cost basis, so there was usually no reason for management to deny requests for more or better equipment and services. With the advent of reimbursement based on prospectively determined prices, management clearly has a major task in balancing the activity and use of resources among the various parts of an organization. Without that balance, inefficiency would soon result; those parts of the organization favored with resources would be producing large volumes of high-quality output that could not be fully used, and there would be inadequate output from those parts that were deprived of resources. Consequently, the hospital will lose the revenue that could have been generated by the less-favored units and will receive insufficient revenue from the favored services to cover their full costs.

The task of balancing activities and resources is significantly different in the two settings, however, because organizational decision makers have much greater influence over the activities they supervise. Thus, an organizational system is much likelier to respond quickly to its own planning initiatives than is the general community health system.

In fact, to some degree, the success of a community health planning process depends on the willingness of organizations (as components of the larger system) to cooperate and collaborate for the welfare of the general public.

The competitive environment fostered by policies of the Federal Government provides a particularly strong incentive to avoid voluntary cooperation for the benefit of the community as a whole. The organization that seeks to participate in collaborative efforts is likely to find itself outdistanced by its competitors, who have chosen to take advantage of any and all opportunities to increase the profitability of their individual organizations.

Nevertheless, when an agency is conducting community health planning, there will be opportunities for exchanging information and technical assistance to ensure that private endeavors will be compatible with community goals as well as the purposes of the sponsoring organization. When public and private sector organizations capitalize on such opportunities, public agency reviews of proposals by private organizations are likely to result in favorable recommendations.[21] If such results can be achieved, the organizational planning process will have made a worthwhile contribution to the organization it serves, and the organization itself will be better able to serve its community.

SUMMARY

The aims of planning are achieved by a sequence of processes that move from abstract values to very specific actions. This chapter discusses a number of processes that represent different ways of expressing the desired outcomes and then describes how activities focused at one level are the linkages that lead to the achievement of the stated aims of the next level.

Policies, especially megapolicies, identify the values sought by the system. Actually, the values sought are those that arise from interaction among the people who are stakeholders in the system. Consumers as stakeholders are becoming more influential in the health services system, so planners must pay greater heed to the consumer point of view. This is the essence of a marketing orientation. Consumer input at the policy level is especially appropriate since most consumers lack the expertise to express their wishes in the technical terms required to define goals and goal indicators or to specify the details of program operation.

A goal is a measurable accomplishment in terms of the health status of the population and the characteristics of the health services system that is congruent with the values expressed by policies; it is an ultimate ideal that may not be fully attainable within the planning horizon. An objective is a step toward the achievement of a goal that is to be accomplished by a specific time. An action is a set of programs and projects that will lead to the achievement of one or more objectives. Actions provide the linkages between health status,

---

[21] A majority of states have maintained some semblance of a certificate-of-need review process even though the federal program no longer exists. Also, most localities require review of major facility changes, often as part of the land-use and zoning processes.

health services systems, and health services resources. Although individual health services organizations are part of the community health services system, their participation in community planning has generally been quite limited. Since the advent of an overtly competitive environment, their motivation to participate has been even less than in the earlier period when their participation was sought and encouraged by planning legislation.

CHAPTER 4

ORGANIZATIONAL PLANNING

Organizations are involved in several types of planning, including contingency planning, project planning, functional planning, business planning, and strategic planning. Contingency planning involves the establishment of a course of action to be followed if certain unusual or unanticipated events should occur. Disaster planning falls within this category. Contingency planning should also include plans for holding the line when a strategic plan fails because it was based on incorrect assumptions or because of dramatic, unexpected shifts in the environment (e.g., the rapid introduction of a statewide, all-payer system of reimbursement). Since contingency plans are designed for short-term administrative responses to crises, they fall outside the scope of this book. Project plans are also excluded, since they focus on short-term administrative actions. Their purpose is simply to guide and control the activities necessary for implementing the organization's strategic, business, and functional plans.

STRATEGIC PLANNING[1]

Strategic planning is essential to the survival and growth of organizations. Until recently, it was generally assumed that health services

---

[1] Much of the material in this section was developed with the support of the American College of Healthcare Executives. It originally appeared in *Case Studies in Health Administration, Volume Three: Strategic Planning for Hospitals*, Chicago,

organizations (especially hospitals) were providers of essential and highly valued services and, thus, were virtually assured of survival so long as day-by-day management was competent and honest. The expansion of services fostered by this assumption has meant the allocation of ever-increasing portions of our national resources to the health industry, and now the value of health services relative to other uses of our nation's wealth is increasingly under question. More recently, shifts in federal policy away from widely accepted commitments to ensure access to needed health services with little regard for ability to pay have made it even clearer that there are definite limits to the amount of resources that are available for medical care and other health-related services. Thus, expectations about the future size and nature of the health services market have been altered significantly.[2]

The proportion of gross national product committed to health expenditures appears to be approaching an upper limit. In fact, it may be declining because of the priority assigned to competing uses (e.g., national defense). This limitation has become more severe with the slower growth of the national economy, which means that both the absolute and relative amounts of money available for health services are virtually certain to remain constant or to decrease. So, to survive, health services organizations must now compete vigorously for their share of fixed or shrinking resources.

This competition becomes more complex with the shift in payment policies. Most likely, there will be a shift in the demand for health services as certain economic groups become less able to avail themselves of needed services. This shift will be reinforced and perhaps amplified by the need for providers to maximize reimbursement to avoid bankruptcy. Strategic planning was originally developed to help commercial enterprises survive and prosper in such an environment. Leaders in the health services field anticipated a need for it years ago. Now this innovation is widely diffused throughout the

---

Foundation of the American College of Hospital Administrators, 1983. It is used here with their permission.

[2] Growth is not the expansion of physical facilities or market share only; it may mean maturation and transition into a new style or type of service that is more responsive to the demands of an evolving market.

industry, but it still is too new to be thoroughly familiar to most of those participating in it.

Definition of Strategic Planning

Every organization has a mission or purpose. *Strategy* is an integrated approach to move the organization toward accomplishing its mission. *Mission* is a high-level, abstract statement of what the organization should become. Strategy offers rules for making the trade-offs necessary to carry out the mission in a changing environment characterized by scarce resources. *Planning* is the process of making current decisions on the basis of their future effects. Ackoff[3] calls this "creating the future." In summary, *strategic planning* is making current decisions on the basis of rules designed to aid the development and maintenance of an ideal organization during a period in which that organization's environment is constantly changing and frequently hostile.

Clearly, strategic planning is different from operational planning, which is simply the development of schemes to accomplish specific, limited objectives (e.g., building a facility or setting up a new program). Furthermore, strategic planning is not necessarily long-range planning. Operational planning may have a very long time span; strategic planning may entail an immediate response to a sudden shift in the organization's circumstances (e.g., a change in the method for reimbursing hospitals).

Since strategic planning deals with a constantly changing environment, the process must be continuous. This is not to say that all steps of the process will be carried out concurrently and with equal intensity. It does mean that the organization must be continually scanning its internal and external circumstances and must be prepared to modify earlier decisions in the light of new intelligence. Strategic planning should be regarded as a continuous, cyclical process in which the plan completed during one phase of a cycle becomes the input for the first phase of the next cycle.

---

[3] Russell L. Ackoff. *Redesigning the Future.* New York, Wiley, 1974, pp. 3–4, 26–31.

Strategic planning is a continuous cycle of activities, referred to here as steps. Although it is possible and desirable to accomplish some of these steps concurrently, they are linked in a logical developmental sequence. Each of these activities is described in detail in the following section.

The Strategic Planning Process

Step 1: Establish the Planning Process

There are at least three general approaches to strategic planning: gap analysis, problem solution, and SWOT (strengths, weaknesses, opportunities, threats). In gap analysis, an ideal future situation is defined and contrasted to a reference projection[4] of current activities. The differences between this projection and the ideal are the gaps that strategic planning must address. The aim in problem solution is to focus the strategic plan on significant problems expected to exist at the planning horizon. These problems may be entirely new results of environmental shifts, exacerbations of current minor issues, or the persistence of currently serious deficiencies. The SWOT approach focuses on both the opportunities and threats likely to exist at the planning horizon. It also explicitly forecasts the strengths and weaknesses of the organization as factors that must be considered while developing strategies.

Regardless of the approach selected, the direction of the planning process within the organization—top-down or bottom-up—must be decided. Because of the widely accepted notion that a system is more than the sum of its parts, the bottom-up approach, which tends to be little more than an aggregation of plans prepared by lower echelons, is generally discredited as an initial approach to strategic planning. Instead, an organization's leadership must establish a mission that reflects both the contributions of individual organizational components and the effects of synergistic interactions between them.

The degree of involvement of others in the organization following

---

[4] A reference projection is simply an extrapolation of current activities to the planning horizon on the basis of historical trends. It must be remembered that strategic planning is not necessarily long-range planning.

this first step varies, but it is generally accepted that there should be some input from each organizational level. This could be done by organizing a planning team on which all levels are represented; or a sequential, cyclical process could be set up in which the output from one level's planning effort becomes the input for the next planning step by an adjacent level. For example, the mission developed by the top level in the first cycle becomes the basis for the intermediate level's goal development. These goals become the purposes for which the operating level designs functional programs. After validation by the intermediate level, these programs, in turn, become the basis of the top level's second-cycle activity—resource allocation. Ackoff[5] combines these two ideas by recommending that the higher level should have a representative involved in the planning process of the lower level.

The earlier discussion does not reflect this cyclical approach, but it does assume that many levels in the organization will help to create the final product for each stage in the process. This is related to Breindel's[6] recommendation that, rather than seeking to develop a total master plan, the organization should prepare a series of related documents. He believes that this will enhance the process by making it more flexible. To some extent, this proposal addresses Quinn's[7] assertion that a formal planning process may become an impediment to true strategic planning. More important is Quinn's message that the process is incremental and iterative—incremental in that major, far-reaching decisions are avoided for as long as possible so that leaders can have the best possible information before making a commitment, and iterative in that prior decisions frequently must be modified as a result of new knowledge gained through current activities; such modification usually leads to the repetition of all intervening steps to ensure agreement with the modified decision. Even more important are Quinn's concepts that the formal planning

---

[5] Russell L. Ackoff. *Redesigning the Future*, pp. 49–53.

[6] Charles L. Breindel. "Health Planning Processes and Process Documentation." *Hospital and Health Services Administration*, 26(Special II):10–17, 1981.

[7] James B. Quinn. "Formulating Strategy One Step at a Time." *Journal of Business Strategy*, 1:42–63, Winter 1981. (Those familiar with the writings of Charles E. Lindblom will recognize that he too does not equate incrementalism with "muddling," as that word is usually understood.)

process, if properly developed and used, is an essential complement to the related power-behavioral processes that affect implementation, and that incrementalism is a clearly conceived, carefully managed strategy of effective executives.

The planning process and its support structure must accommodate the characteristics of the organization, including size, management style, environmental complexity, and the nature of the production process (e.g., medical staff arrangements for hospitals clearly require a structure different from that of a hierarchical commercial enterprise). Despite these varying features, there are three roles (planner, chief executive officer, and chief operating officer) about which important generalizations can be made:

1. The planner should not do the planning. That is a responsibility management cannot delegate. The roles of the planner or planning office are to design the planning process, serve as a catalyst to carry it out, and provide continuing staff support. These responsibilities could be located elsewhere within the organization, but the required skills and knowledge have become so specialized, it is quite unlikely that a generalist manager could function as effectively as someone with special preparation for these tasks.

2. A related issue is the priority assigned to planning. Typically, if a person has both planning and operating responsibilities, the pressures of current situations will crowd out the seemingly postponable planning activities. This presents a dilemma for the chief executive officer (CEO), especially in a smaller organization. If the CEO's chief responsibility is the future survival and growth of the organization, then that person should delegate internal operating responsibilities to a chief operating officer (COO) and concentrate on strategic and external concerns. In a small organization, however, there may be no COO-type position, in which case the CEO would have to remain the focal point for operations and, to ensure that strategic concerns were not ignored, would assign some other member of the top management team as the organization's strategist[8]. Needless to say, there must be a concomitant reduction in the strategist's other duties.

---

[8] William W. Womack. "The Board's Most Important Function." *Harvard Business Review*, 57:48–54, September–October 1979.

Step 2: Define the Organization

The organizational definition describes the organization's philosophy, mission, and structure.

The organization's philosophy is a statement of its values. Many units aspire to accomplish many things, but at some point there will be a need to make difficult choices between attractive options. The decision will reveal what the organization values most highly. Likely contenders are quality service, technological leadership, community service, productivity, and competitive position. This dominant value is sometimes called the driving force. It is the factor on which the organization's quest for excellence is focused.

The organizational philosophy also addresses the issue of the unit's approach to growth. This is called the strategic thrust. Some feel that expansion is the only true measure of success. Alternatively, there are organizations that seek success by achieving stability—by assuring an existing market that it will be provided continuously with high-quality services.

The mission statement of the organization should state explicitly what products and services the organization will offer, the geographic scope of its programs, and the markets within that geographic area that it will seek to serve.

STRUCTURAL DESIGN

As noted earlier, the organization's structure can have a significant effect on its level of achievement. Unless the structure conforms to and supports the strategy selected, true success is unlikely.

There seems to be a general consensus that organizations should be viewed as systems. Theorists in organizational behavior have described rational systems, natural systems, and open systems. Within these broad frameworks, others have prescribed differing approaches to analysis. For instance, Lawrence and Lorch[9] have offered a contingency theory of organizational behavior, and Thompson[10] rec-

---

[9] Paul R. Lawrence and Jay W. Lorch. *Organization and Management.* Homewood, Ill., Irwin, 1969, pp. 185–210.

[10] James D. Thompson. *Organization in Action: Social Science Bases of Administrative Theory.* New York, McGraw Hill Book Co., 1967, pp. 10–13.

ommends that organizations be viewed as having three levels of activity. All of these are, in fact, elaborations of the organization as a complex system that must relate effectively to its environment.

If the organization is viewed in this light, the structural elements can be seen as a hierarchy that collectively accomplishes all of the generic functions of a system. The focus of such an analysis, of course, is the creation of desired outcomes, or the production of desired services, as a consequence of effective interaction between the system's components.

Corporate Organizations as a Hierarchy of Systems

System	Corporation
Subsystem	SBU
Black Box	Service Unit

Effective use of this analytic model requires explicit delineation of the system's external, intermediate, and internal boundaries. In other words, the scope of the system, the internal division into subsystems, and the identification of the specific productive units must be established.

External Boundaries

The external boundary separates the system from the environment, which contains independent factors that affect the structure and performance of the system. The system's boundary defines the point at which the system's discretion over the activities of its elements ends (e.g., behavior of staff members). An especially significant element in the environment is the set of stakeholders.

The system's boundary must be permeable, to permit desirable exchanges and prevent undesirable exchanges. In particular, the boundary must insulate the technical core—the productive units—so that they can behave as a rational, efficient system. The following are illustrations of the buffering functions of the boundary elements.

Coding: Identifying and excluding those clients who are ineligible to receive a service

Stockpiling: Assuring a supply of needed resources

Leveling: Smoothing fluctuations in input and output

Bridging: Making the organization effective in dealing with the external agencies with which it must interact

Contracting: Assuring the organization of an ongoing existence of the desired relationship and, thus, reducing uncertainty

Co-opting: Trading sovereignty for support by including persons from important segments of the environment in the system's processes (e.g., a banker on the hospital's board)

Joint Venturing: Limited pooling of resources to achieve a common goal

Merging: Totally absorbing units from the environment: horizontal mergers increase the scale of operations; vertical mergers ensure a supply of resources or a channel of distribution and thus reduce transaction costs

Factors that serve as external boundary determinants are:

Concept of Health: What is the technical scope of the health "industry"? For example, is a life-care community part of the health system?

Organizational Mandates: Many health services organizations are mandated to perform certain functions or to serve certain groups. These may be legislated mandates or societal expectations.

Perceived Needs: In addition to the external mandates, the organization's external boundaries are influenced by the perceptions of its own members with regard to the needs/demands of the community or the market that it proposes to serve.

Resources: A realistic determination of an organization's boundaries requires recognition of the constraints imposed by the type, quantity, and quality of available resources.

Intermediate Boundaries

The intermediate boundaries serve to identify the strategic business units, which are clusters of related services that are strategically and economically significant. This determination is affected by the factors related to technology—the process used to produce services. The following are some of the significant technology factors to be considered.

Complexity: This can relate to process complexity or to the skills of performers (e.g., professions). As complexity increases, it leads to more narrowly defined subunits.

Uncertainty: This refers to the lack of standardization in the process by which the service is rendered. It leads to decentralization of decisions and less formalization.

Interdependence: This is the extent to which the functioning of the system depends on interaction between the subsystems. As it increases, it requires higher levels of coordination.

As complexity, uncertainty, and interdependence increase, the need for information increases. When this occurs, there are two possible responses: (1) reduce the need for information exchange by reducing performance standards, or (2) increase the information handling capacity. The information processing capacity can be increased by adding managerial levels to cope with the increased volume of data or by increasing the efficiency of the information processing system.

Intermediate boundaries are structured on the basis of several organizing principles. They must be

Exhaustive: All elements of the system must be included
Mutually Exclusive: No boundaries should overlap
Understandable: By the staff and the relevant publics
Relevant to Strategy: In order to achieve the organization's purposes
Compatible with Input Categories: So that resources can be allocated appropriately
Compatible with Authority Structure: in order to provide clear lines of responsibility

The intermediate boundaries are most likely to meet these requirements if they are designed on a classification scheme based on one or all of the following factors: functions, products or services, clients, specialized resources, and/or processing sequence.

Product-Line Definition

The practical application of these concepts leads to the establishment of product-line management. The following steps will lead to a satisfactory definition of a product line.

1. Define the initial product
2. Identify other products with similar attributes
3. Establish the product line as a cluster of similar products
4. Identify additional products for the product line

This process is illustrated in the following example.

	Service A	*Service B*
Product:	Tonsillectomy	Cleft Palate Repair
Market Segment:	Pediatric Population	Pediatric Population
Stage of Production:	Surgery Outpatient	Surgery Inpatient
Clinical Specialty:	ENT	ENT

Product line = PEDIATRIC ENT

Product definition is the initial step in this process. It takes the following factors into consideration.

WHO? Customer groups served
WHAT? Customer functions served
HOW? Technologies used
SCOPE OF THE MARKET. A product's scope may be:

Concentrated	–	Narrow specific scope
Unfocused	–	Broad general scope
Differentiated	–	Broad scope but subdivided[11]

The possible combinations include concentration, differentiation, or focus with regard to each of the three other dimensions. This yields a total of 81 possibilities.

A product line is synthesized by combining individual products on the basis of shared functions, such as delivery site, housing, ancillary services, hotel services, management, promotion, and distribution channels.

Since each stage of these processes (e.g., ancillary services) can benefit from economies of scale and/or movement on the experience curve, abandonment of a weak product may cost more than it saves. This is especially true if such a product is evaluated on the basis of its contribution to fixed costs rather than on recovery of total costs.

---

[11] The subdivision may be based on internal differentiation among the organization's own products or external differentiation from competitors' products.

Internal Boundaries

The internal boundaries delineate the lowest organizational level from the perspective of corporate managers. In many organizations, this could be the SBU managing a single product line, in which case the intermediate and internal boundaries would be identical. On the other hand, it is quite possible for an SBU to be responsible for a number of product lines, in which case the product or product line would define the internal boundaries.

The point is to *not* provide unequivocal advice as to how an organization should be structured. Rather, the intent is to emphasize the need for the structure to be consistent with management style and strategy. Too many organizations are managed poorly because they have been restructured to resemble corporations, while management continues to function as it did when only a single organizational entity was involved. This is typified by the hospital administrator who has become the CEO of a diversified health services corporation but who continues to operate as though he or she was still responsible for only a single acute-care hospital.

Step 3: Scan the Environment

An environmental scan is the third component of a strategic plan. Although many organizations assert that this is the first step in the planning process, such an assertion is clearly incorrect, since it implies that the environmental scan is boundless. In other words, even though it is not explicitly stated, some concept of the mission has been developed to limit the scope of the environmental scan. The danger with such an approach is the probability that the participants may have differing concepts of the mission and, thus, will view the assignment to conduct an environmental scan in different ways. It is important to remember the earlier remark about the iterative nature of the planning process; that is, it is possible, indeed probable, that the initial organizational definition will be altered as a result of intelligence gained from the environmental scan. Thus, it is clear that the initial effort in organizational definition should aim to develop a working document rather than a final, definitive statement.

Similarly, a realistic assessment of organizational capabilities and the value of information should lead the persons preparing an environmental assessment to adopt a strategy of mixed scanning. For instance, even though the organization may have determined that its geographic scope is quite limited, the interconnectedness of the health system and governmental and national organizations dictates that the assessment includes information from national, regional, and local levels. On another, but equally important dimension, the scan should move from broad statements about the general environment to more refined estimates about the industry and, finally, to rather precise information about the organization's market.

Since the aim of the scan is to provide intelligence about the future environment in which the organization will be operating, it is necessary to include data about the past and present as ingredients in the forecasting process, described in Chapter 10. This requirement, coupled with the array of topics, is once again a clear signal for the use of mixed scanning. Determining the level of data on each of the following topics is a true challenge for the analyst's skills. The substantive areas covered by an environmental scan should include the following:

Economic Environment
    Macro trends
    Income
    Spending patterns
    Resource availability

Political and Legal Environment
    Property rights vs. welfare rights
    Competition vs. regulation
    Interest groups and political parties
    Enforcement agencies
    Attitudes of courts

Technological Environment
    Level of research and development
    New technologies
    Rate of innovation

Cultural Environment
    People's relation to:
        Themselves
        Other people
        Institutions
        Society

Demographic Environment
  Age
  Race
  Sex
  Education
  Population growth
  Population location

Epidemiologic Environment
  Death
  Disease
  Disability

Furthermore, the analysis should take into account the probable interactions between these areas rather than treating each one as a discrete entity. For instance, an economic forecast of a significant change in national income will clearly influence the political environment, which, in turn, will affect the technological (health services) environment in a variety of ways.

INTERPRETING ENVIRONMENTAL INFORMATION

Lenz & Engledow[12] have proposed several models that can be used to evaluate the data collected. It is important to note that these models are not mutually exclusive; rather, they offer a variety of perspectives that can aid in the interpretation of the information. A description of each of these models follows.

COGNITIVE (Personal Experiences)

STRUCTURAL PROPERTIES: What the decision makers hold as a world view. The corporation's collective understanding of its environment. As a context for change, it includes both internal and external factors.

SOURCES OF CHANGE: Based on a retrospective analysis. When strategy based on an existing model fails to produce the desired results, the corporation looks for "reasons why not" and then modifies its cognitive model.

DATA SOURCES: Ad hoc, depending on circumstances. Always include internal feedback on performance of the organization.

---

[12] R. T. Lenz and Jack L. Engledow. "Environmental Analysis: The Application of Current Theory." *Strategic Management Journal*, 7(4):329–346, 1986.

INDUSTRY STRUCTURE

STRUCTURAL PROPERTIES: Consider competitive forces that create opportunities and threats, but their scope is limited to the specific industry.

SOURCES OF CHANGE: Actions of competing firms and other external events (e.g., governmental policies).

DATA SOURCES: Primarily the corporations's competitor analysis system.

ORGANIZATIONAL FIELD

STRUCTURE:

Hierarchical approach: Focuses primarily on the task environment, which comprises organizations that directly affect the goal setting and performance of focal organizations. Porter's[13] model of competition is a good example of this approach.

Nonhierarchical approach: A stakeholder framework, as described by Freeman,[14] may be used to analyze the political[15] dimensions of the organization's environment.

Alternatively, this analysis may be based on an interaction network that focuses on linkages among organizations; particularly on the efficiency and effectiveness of exchanges.[16] Linkages that may serve as mechanisms for interaction are joint ventures, federations, and mergers. The linkages may also be considered in terms of the following dimensions of interaction: formality, standardization, intensity, and reciprocity.

Finally, this approach may view the organization as part of a social system. In this case, it attempts to determine how the organization contributes to all four system functions. This includes both the role of the organization as a component of the larger system, and the exchange relationships and linkages between system components.

SOURCES OF CHANGE: Broad trends in the general environment that create specific changes within networks or within task environments are the principal sources of change for these analyses.

DATA SOURCES: Except for "opportunistic" surveillance, no data sources are suggested.

---

[13] Michael E. Porter. *Competitive Strategy*. New York, Free Press, 1980, Chapter 1.

[14] R. Edward Freeman. *Strategic Management: A Stakeholder Approach*. Boston, Pitman Publishing, 1984, Chapter 3.

[15] Politics may be defined as "Who gets what and who pays for it?"

[16] N.B. Organizational performance within any organizational field depends on intraorganizational characteristics, such as centralization, routinization, professionalization, and integration.

ECOLOGICAL AND RESOURCE DEPENDENCE

STRUCTURE: This is based on the general systems concept that the environment is everything outside of the system. The environment is described as placid or turbulent, and particular attention is paid to what resources are available and who controls them.

SOURCES OF CHANGE: The natural selection of organizations that are competing for scarce resources—survival of the fittest—is the change mechanism considered. Consequently, organizations seek an environmental niche (a role that assures them of a supply of resources) or seek to gain control of the flow of resources (vertical integration).

DATA SOURCES: Once again the organization's competitor intelligence system comes into play. It is used to identify groups that control critical resources, determine how they evaluate your organization, and evaluate the impact of alternative actions on the resource controlling group's perceptions of your organization.

ERA

STRUCTURE: This model examines the environment in three stages: the prevailing situation, a period of turbulent transition, and the emergence of a new order.

SOURCES OF CHANGE: Changes occur as a result of shifts in the prevailing culture,[17] which provide a basis for determining the acceptance of institutions, social norms, and economic and political relationships.

DATA SOURCES: Data for this model is derived largely from intuitive forecasts and the work of various futurists (e.g., megatrends).

Each of these models is limited in some way, and each is more appropriate for certain situations. Analysts must recognize the limitations and select the most appropriate model(s).

Cognitive Model – useful for evaluating the results of strategies and learning from them

Industry Structure Model – illuminates economic and technological forces within an industry

Organizational Field Model – focuses on relative power and the conflicting objectives of interdependent organizations and groups (stakeholders)

---

[17] Culture is defined as the meaning of social values, such as self-fulfillment.

Ecological and Resource Dependence Model – describes system/environment exchange relationships

ERA Model – analyzes societies over long time horizons

In summary, the environmental scanning process gathers data about a wide range of topics that are defined by the organizational description. Since the aim is to arrive at a forecast of the future, both historical and current data are collected. The level of detail is determined by a strategy of mixed scanning, using the value of information as a basis for decision making. The value of information should also be applied in determining what data to collect. In some instances, strong assumptions may be substituted for actual data in view of the limited significance of a given topic.

The data are analyzed using an appropriate blend of models and then are interpreted to produce the desired intelligence: opportunities and threats.

Step 4: Establish Goals

Data for determining goals are the opportunities and threats that are developed through the environmental scanning process. The organizational definition is the basis for analyzing the data. Specifically, the decision makers must determine how to respond to the opportunities and threats in the light of the mission statement. To make this transition from mission to goals, three relevant questions must be answered: What do we *want* to do? What *should* we do? and What *can* we do?

At this point it is possible to frame tentative responses to the first two questions. The final question can be considered only after the internal assessment has been completed. In other words, the goal statements take the broad generalities of the mission and translate them into specific aspirations. These aspirations will seek either to capitalize on identified opportunities or to avert or diminish serious threats. Goal statements serve three purposes. They set the directions in which the organization will move; they focus the attention of the organization's members on the activities that are most important to the organization, rather than leaving this to the discretion or insight of individuals; and they provide a basis for evaluating the organization's achievements. Goals are expressed as indicators that must satisfy the following criteria.

MEASURABILITY   The indicator must be objectively observable so that it will be possible to conduct a meaningful evaluation. An indicator does not have to be quantitative. An example of a qualitative yet measurable goal would be the achievement of accreditation by JCAHO.

COMPARABILITY   The indicator must permit comparisons over time so that the organization can assess its own progress. Ideally, the indicator will also allow the organization to compare its performance with that of other organizations, both locally and in other areas.

RELEVANCE   The indicator should focus on a topic that the decision makers regard as significant.

CLARITY   The indicator must be understandable to decision makers, managers, staff, and the community at large.

UNIDIRECTIONAL   The indicator must be unambiguous with regard to the desired direction of change, for example, Is more medical care always good?

PRECISELY DEFINED   There should be no ambiguity in terms and statistical constructs; for example, neonatal mortality is clearly distinguished from infant mortality in most statistical systems.

BASED ON AVAILABLE DATA   The required data can be obtained with reasonable effort and cost.

SUSCEPTIBLE TO ACTION   The organization or some agency that it can influence can take actions that will lead to improvements in the indicator.

Step 5: Conduct an Internal Assessment (Organizational Analysis)

The content of the organizational analysis is focused largely by a review of past and projected performance and contrasted to expectations and aspirations. This gap analysis of actual and anticipated achievements provides a basis for assessing the effects of past and present strategy. The assessment should identify any strategic problems that the organization has encountered. Strategy evaluations based on outcomes, however, can be meaningful only if they take into account factors that might have affected performance. Relevant factors include the organization's structure, resources, processes, and systems. In other words, the internal assessment must be conducted from the perspective of the organization as a system. An alternative framework for analysis would be the value chain described by Michael Porter,[18] which provides a particularly useful identification of the process components in a productive system. In either case, the analyst must be especially attentive to the interactions between components of the organization.

An interaction analysis of this sort must focus on both competing values (intrasystem, intersystem, and among markets) and the primary and secondary effects of decisions, as described in Chapter 1. The analysis of competing values will identify issues of equity and equality, which are inevitable in complex modern organizations. Consider the problems that arise when the manager of an SBU is obliged to "purchase" a service from another element of the organization (e.g., tests from the pathology laboratory) in order to allow the corporation to achieve economies of scale, although the SBU could obtain these services at a lower cost from an outside agency. How should the SBU's contribution to corporate well-being be valued in relation to the resulting reduction in the SBU's profitability? If the laboratory is also treated as a profit center, how should its performance be evaluated under these circumstances?

Quantitative and qualitative assessments should be used to estimate the primary, secondary, and tertiary effects of management decisions. Quantitative estimates may be more precise, but they are often more difficult to complete and interpret (e.g., goal programming). It is possible, however, to create simpler analytic models that will provide substantial amounts of information. For instance, it is no great feat to prepare a spreadsheet model that shows the interactions between policy decisions on leverage, earnings retention, and rate of growth.

---

[18] Michael E. Porter. *Competitive Advantage.* New York, Free Press, 1985, pp. 33–50.

On the other hand, when variables cannot be estimated precisely and interactions are very complex, the value of information may dictate the use of a qualitative interaction analysis, such as the illustration of the systems matrix (Figure 4) in Chapter 1. Qualitative analysis may be hazardous, however, since it allows managers to take an unduly rosy view of the organization's strengths and weaknesses and, thus, to defeat the purpose of the analysis.

If this assessment of strengths and weaknesses is unrealistic, it will not be possible to make valid reassessments of goals. As one of the iterative steps, goals should be revised after the organization has determined the answer to the last of the three questions, What *can* we do? Similarly, an inaccurate assessment will lead to managerial errors in the next phase of the process, designing the organization's strategy; that is, determining how the goals should be reached.

The data gathered should be analyzed to produce the following internal assessment products: product characteristic profiles, life-cycle position analysis, portfolio review, process audits, resource reviews, and an organizational profile.

The information derived should then be interpreted to determine critical success factors, distinctive competences, and competitive advantages. Each of the critical success factors should be identified as a strength or a weakness. The weaknesses will indicate either unalterable constraints on strategy design or areas where strategy must incorporate remedial action. The strengths will indicate the organization's distinctive competences, which can become the bases for gaining competitive advantage.

The product characteristic profiles should examine closely the variety of services offered, the diversity within each service, and the complexity of services. Furthermore, each service should be evaluated with regard to acceptability, accessibility, quality, and continuity. Finally, the capacity of each service-producing unit should be assessed in relation to anticipated demand.

The estimation of demand requires a life-cycle position analysis, since this will clearly influence the future demand for the service. Moreover, life-cycle position data will assist in the formulation of strategy, since a different strategy is appropriate for each phase of the life cycle, to increase total revenue and reduce overall costs.

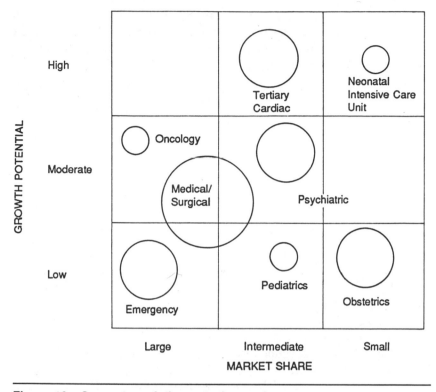

Figure 10   General portfolio analysis matrix.

The portfolio review will assess the performance of individual services or SBUs in several dimensions.[19] It serves to evaluate the balance of SBUs within the organization. Usually these dimensions relate to market share and growth potential. Figure 10 illustrates a widely used method of portfolio analysis. A three-dimensional matrix may be needed for health services, since growth and relative market share may not ensure profitability.[20] For example, a large and growing share of the Medicaid market could be disastrous if Medicaid

---

[19] Usually the organizational components assessed will be defined by the internal boundaries discussed on pages 29–31.

[20] Gary C. McCain. "Black Holes, Cash Pigs and Other Hospital Portfolio Problems." *Journal of Health Care Marketing*, 7(2):56–64, June 1987.

reimbursement is too low, but it may not be possible to discontinue Medicaid services. In such circumstances, the organization would have to develop other profitable markets or services to offset the losses incurred in the Medicaid market.

The process audits must review the performance of each of the organization's major subsystems. The following is a list of typical subsystems and the suggested content for each audit.

MARKETING AUDIT

> Marketing Mix
> Marketing Plans
> Marketing Research
> Marketing Organization
> Organization's Orientation to Marketing

OPERATIONS/PRODUCTION AUDIT

> Technology in Use
> Capacity
> Utilization
> Flexibility
> Efficiency
> Dispersion of Production Sites
> Vertical Integration
> Production Planning, Scheduling, and Control
> Compatibility with Marketing Strategy

FINANCIAL MANAGEMENT AUDIT

> Budgeting
> Management of Current Finances
> Acquisition of Capital
> Cost Analysis Capability
> Support of Marketing and Production Strategies

GENERAL MANAGEMENT AUDIT

> Organizational Structure
> Management Style
> Management Skills
> Management Systems
>> Information Systems
>> Planning, Programming, and Control Systems
>> Human Resources Management Systems
>> Logistics Management Systems

The final component of the internal assessment is resource reviews encompassing personnel, facilities, equipment, and finance. Each of these should be evaluated with regard to its cost and its ability to sustain and enhance the projected performance of the organization. Particular attention to the organization's access to the supply of these resources is necessary. If a reliable and responsive supply of suitable, reasonably priced resources cannot be assured, the organization may adopt a strategy of vertical integration to reduce this threat to its success.

The major competence assessment product will be an organizational profile. This should depict each facet of the organization as a strength or weakness, in light of the organization's mission and goals. Without this context, any attempt to identify the organization's strengths and weaknesses will be meaningless. To ensure objectivity and consistency in making this determination, the organization must establish criteria and standards on which to base its judgments. The criteria are those aspects of the factor that are important (e.g., the percentage of the medical staff who are board certified, as a proxy measure for quality of service). For each criterion there must be a standard—the value that will determine whether the situation is satisfactory or unsatisfactory (e.g., at least 75 percent of the medical staff must be board certified). The profile may be in narrative form, but a graphic presentation will reinforce the intelligence contained in the verbal description. This is illustrated in Figure 11.

A document of this scope could easily overwhelm the decision makers. Consequently, it is again necessary to resort to the strategy of mixed scanning, with detailed analysis limited to those elements that are critical success factors for this organization. Identification of these factors will not only contribute to the design of strategy, it also will provide management with a basis for loose/tight control decisions. In other words, it will show those elements of the organization that top management must monitor closely and continuously and those elements for which decision-making authority and responsibility can be delegated.

Distinctive competences are determined by interpreting the organization's profile in light of competitive intelligence gathered as part of the environmental scan; that is, a distinctive competence arises when the organization's strength on a critical success factor is high,

ORGANIZATIONAL COMPETENCE ANALYSIS

Factors	Very Strong	Strong	Average	Weak	Very Weak
Resources					
Facilities					
Equipment					
Funds					
Staff					
Management					
Clinical					
Administrative					
Logistic					
Skills					
Management					
Clinical					
Administrative					
Logistic					
Systems					
Management					
Clinical					
Administrative					
Logistic					
Programs					
(Life Cycle)					
Inpatient					
Outpatient					
Ancillary					
Organization's					
Structure					

Figure 11   Organizational competence analysis.

relative to the strength of competitors. It is a necessary, but not sufficient, condition for success in a competitive environment. A distinctive competence is important even if an organization is in a noncompetitive or monopolistic situation, but again, it only offers a potential advantage. The successful organization will actively use its distinctive competences to enhance its performance in any case and to gain a competitive advantage when such an action is appropriate. As Ian MacMillan[21] points out, however, a competitive advantage is

---

[21] Ian C. MacMillan. "Controlling Competitive Dynamics by Taking Strategic Initiative." *The Academy of Management Executive, II*(2):111–118, May 1988.

usually short-lived. Once competitors recognize it, they will take steps to copy and often improve on it. Consequently, the successful organization will be seeking new competitive advantages as soon as present ones are effectively implemented.

Step 6: Select Strategies

Owing to the significant differences between corporate strategies and business strategies, the two will be discussed separately, in turn. A single entity that is both a corporation and the sole business unit may find it necessary to combine elements of both strategies. It should, however, emphasize the elements of a business strategy since it is, for most practical purposes, a business that has assumed a corporate structure for reasons that probably have little to do with its primary functions.

CORPORATE STRATEGIES

Corporate strategy encompasses three activities: management of the portfolio of SBUs, acquisition of resources, and allocation of resources among the SBUs. Thus, the basic issues of corporate strategy are the number and kinds of businesses in which the corporation will participate, the degree of coordination among SBUs, and the bases for allocating resources among SBUs.

All decisions on these issues must be made with an eye toward enhancing the value of the corporation; there is no other reason for the corporation to exist. In other words, the purpose of corporate strategy is to enhance the value of the corporation from the perspective of the stakeholders. Note the use of the term stakeholders as opposed to stockholders, which is used in business literature. Stakeholders are a much broader and diverse group of persons than stockholders. They include stockholders (if there are any), employees, patients, medical staff, governments, and the community at large.[22] In a sense, it is the focus on stakeholders that distinguishes the traditional not-for-profit health services organization from commercial enterprises. Many

---

[22] R. Edward Freeman. *Strategic Management: A Stakeholder Approach,* Chapter 1.

have questioned the desirability of commercializing health services.[23] It is important to understand that strategic planning and business strategies are simply tools. They can be used for the aggrandizement of a small group of beneficiaries (e.g., hospital management, medical staff, or stockholders) or they can be applied to achieve the altruistic goal of serving the full range of stakeholders.

Approaches to Corporate Strategy Development

There are three approaches to corporate strategy development.[24] Each involves all of the various levels of the corporation, but the degree and type of involvement is significantly different and yields quite different results.

The strategic planning approach gives corporate decision makers virtually total control. This approach would be most appropriate for the U-form organization. SBUs may develop recommendations, but the corporate headquarters ultimately modifies and/or approves the detailed plans of individual SBUs. This style of management balances SBU strategies and encourages integration. It also favors long-term goals, because managers are free to develop creative SBU strategies to achieve corporate goals. The corporation handles financial balance so maximizing short-run profitability in all units is not necessary. On the other hand, it reduces lower level commitment to the plan in that the lower levels feel no responsibility; it may diminish flexibility since the corporate office will not receive information signalling the need for change as quickly as will the SBUs.

The approach that emphasizes financial control is compatible with the H-form organization. In this situation, the SBUs independently develop their individual plans, which are approved by corporate headquarters so long as they project a suitable level of financial success. This method emphasizes short-run profitability and tends

---

[23] J. David Seay and Bruce C. Vladeck (eds.). *In Sickness and In Health,* New york, McGraw Hill Book Co., 1988. Contains a set of papers that discuss thoroughly the issues surrounding the role of voluntary health services organizations in the United States in the competitive environment fostered by national policy as a solution to problems of high levels of expenditure for health services.

[24] Michael Goold and Andrew Campbell. "Many Best Ways to Make Strategy." *Harvard Business Review,* 87(6):70–76, November–December 1987.

to increase risk aversiveness. On the other hand, it encourages managers to change quickly if their strategy is not working well and, thus, it develops strong executives in the individual SBUs. It works particularly well in highly diversified corporations, since there are few opportunities to achieve synergy among disparate enterprises.

The strategic control approach combines the two approaches in an effort to get the best of both, but it creates conflicting signals that lead to ambiguity and, thus, to problems in motivating and controlling SBUs. Under this scheme, the SBUs are responsible for developing independent plans while corporate executives guide this planning toward the creation and maintenance of a balanced, integrated organization. Financial targets are set in a budget that is separate from the strategic plan so as to emphasize long-run perspectives of strategy. Obviously, there will be occasions when the short-run considerations of the budget and the long-term orientation of the strategic plan will conflict. Such situations create ambiguity for the SBU, which is being measured on performance in relation to both the budget and the strategic plan.

Principles of Strategy

Strategy development, regardless of the managerial approach, should recognize certain principles. One set of these are derived from the adaptation of military strategy to competitive management.[25] The most important of these can be summarized as follows.

Concentration: Do not spread the organization's resources over too many undertakings. It is important to have enough resources to achieve each goal of the enterprise with a bit left over to cope with unforeseen circumstances. In an attack strategy, in order to overwhelm the targeted competitor, pick one or two points of vulnerability and focus the aggressive effort on them rather than engaging in an across-the-board challenge. This is particularly important in view of the power of defense.

Power of Defense: An established organization is always stronger than an attacker. The existing organization, unless it is hopelessly

---

[25] Al Ries and Jack Trout. *Marketing Warfare.* New York, McGraw Hill Book Co., 1983.

inept, has many advantages such as client familiarity (brand loyalty), established channels of distribution and supplier relationships, and an operations staff that has gained efficiency as a result of experience.

Surprise: The advantage of the defender can be reduced if a major challenge is initiated before a coordinated response can be implemented. If the organization is moving into an area that has not been addressed by any of the existing organizations, surprise will allow it to gain a foothold and the advantages of defense before competitors can develop their own plans to offer a similar service.

Retain Initiative: As noted earlier in the discussion on competitive advantage, an organization cannot assume that its competitors will passively accept its success. It is far more likely that they will seek to gain rewards for themselves by "counter attacking," thus, the organization must actively seek to retain and capitalize on the position it has achieved.

General systems theory provides equally valuable additional principles to guide strategists.

The Whole Is Greater than the Sum of Its Parts: An organization must seek opportunities to create synergistic combinations of enterprises. An organization that is simply an aggregation of unrelated enterprises is probably less productive than the individual units would be if they operated independently.

Optimize Performance of Parts: A major task of corporate management is to ensure that resources are allocated in such a way that the overall productivity of the corporation is maximized. In some instances, this will require some units to perform at less than their maximum capacity so as to maintain a balance among the SBUs or product lines that are using the same type of resources. For instance, an established rehabilitation program might have to operate at less than full capacity so that an innovative sports medicine program (designed to position the corporation as a leader in innovation) will have sufficient physical therapists to reach a break-even level of activity.

Adapt to Environmental Changes: This is the essence of strategic planning. The organization must engage in effective exchange relationships with its environment in order to survive over the long run. As marketers point out, an exchange relationship will endure only if it is mutually satisfactory. In the past, many health services organizations, especially hospitals, operated on the premise that their services were inherently good and that the community naturally would accept the organization's judgment about what specific services were desirable and necessary. One of the most beneficial effects of the attempt to use competition to stimulate responsible and responsive behavior by health services providers was the belated recognition of the validity of the exchange relationship concept in an environment of informed consumers.

Information for Developing Corporate Strategies

Portfolio analysis is a significant input to corporate strategy development. It is exemplified by the well-known Boston Consulting Group's four-cell matrix and the General Electric Corporation's nine-cell matrix. The analysis usually focuses on two dimensions—industry attractiveness and competitive strength. Industry attractiveness is a weighted measure (index) of market size, market growth rate, profit potential, intensity of competition, emerging opportunities, capital requirements, and technology requirements. Competitive strength is a weighted index of relative market share, relative profitability, and the organization's strengths and weaknesses vis-à-vis the product.

A thorough analysis should also include a product evolution matrix that will reflect the life-cycle positions of the corporation's services. The businesses in the portfolio should be distributed over the different stages of the life cycle so that there will be a steady stream of new products available to replace those that are stagnant or being phased out because of maturity and decline.

The intelligence derived from interpretation of these analyses will lead to decisions concerning poor performance, obsolescence, or both. Possible actions include the following:

1. Alter strategic plans for some or all SBUs
2. Add new SBUs to the portfolio
3. Delete weak SBUs from the portfolio
4. Use political action to alter environmental factors that are contributing less than the desired performance
5. Reduce corporate goals

Strategy Options

Generic corporate strategies focus on all of the above except 4; that is, they address expansion or reduction in the number or scope of the SBUs within the corporation or the improved performance of specific SBUs. These strategies are described in the following paragraphs.

Concentration in Single Business: This strategy is the same as a competitive business strategy. It is usually the starting point of an organization. A decision to expand into other businesses must consider four criteria to ensure that the value of the organization will be increased.[26] They are:

SCALE – The additions to the organization will lead to increased benefits, such as economies of scale in operations or the added "political" power associated with large size.

RETURNS – The earnings of the new businesses must be greater than the cost of the capital required to add them.

DURATION – The increased earnings stream must be sustainable.

GROWTH – The additions must have the potential for expansion so that there is a likelihood that the organization will realize more than simply the immediate gains of the addition.

Unrelated acquisitions must be self-justifying on all four criteria. Related acquisitions must be based on the benefits realized from synergistic interaction with the current business. Acquisitions may be desirable if:

1. The market is not consolidated or the proposed new entrant has a means to destabilize a consolidated market (e.g., new technology).
2. Underlying industry trends are positive.
3. There is an opportunity for synergy.
4. There is good strategic logic (e.g., averting a threat by vertical integration).[27]

---

[26] Michael E. Porter. "From Competitive Advantage to Corporate Strategy." *Harvard Business Review*, 65(3):43–59, May–June 1987.

[27] Ibid.

Vertical Integration: This strategy will expand the organization's scope within the same industry either by moving backward into the supply segment or by moving forward into distribution activities. It reduces risks and transaction costs by incorporating the supply or distribution functions within the organization, but it also creates problems of capacity balancing and reduces the organization's flexibility, since the organization now owns the supply or distribution facilities and their capital equipment, staff, and the like. If such a strategy is to succeed, management must understand the "added" processes (e.g., distribution).

Horizontal Integration: This strategy simply adds more of the same type of business by acquiring other organizations.

Related Diversification: This strategy extends the scope of the organization's activities into new businesses. Like vertical integration, it demands that corporate management be able to direct effectively the efforts of a business that is to some degree unrelated to the existing line of endeavor. The risks of diversification are reduced to the extent that there is a strategic fit between the organization and its newest member. Examples of strategic fit are:

Marketing fit (e.g., advertising with similar themes)
Operating fit (use of the same technology)
Management fit (shared skills)

Related diversification builds upon existing expertise and fosters synergy. It may enhance capacity utilization; for example, it may fill empty hospital beds and it may increase the organization's strength in dealing with suppliers. Also the "added" services may benefit from the image of the acquiring organization.

Unrelated Diversification: With this strategy there are no synergies. Consequently, the decision must be supported by some other rationale. Some possible reasons for unrelated diversification are to balance cyclical demand for services of the basic business; balance the risks of the basic business by having the safety of income from a very different business; gain either the cash or capital, or both, that the added business will bring with it; continue corporate growth after the demand of the basic business is saturated; or make the most profitable use of the surplus funds that are under the control of the corporation.

Turnaround: When some part of a corporation is doing poorly, the corporate-level options are to harvest or divest the money-losing units and use the proceeds to replace them with new profitable units; launch corporate-wide cost-cutting (profit improving) programs; or restore the profitability of money losing units. The third option is a turnaround strategy. It requires the corporate decision makers to allocate a substantial set of resources (managerial talent, in particular) for the rejuvenation of a faltering enterprise. It requires conviction that the enterprise can be restored to its former strength. This belief must be based on an objective analysis rather than a sentimental attachment to a unit that historically has been an effective member of the corporation.

Retrenchment: When turnaround is infeasible, the next alternative is retrenchment, a cut-back in the face of adverse conditions. It may be across the board or applied selectively to part of the SBU's activities. It can be designed as either a temporary or a permanent change in the status of the SBU.

Divestiture or Harvesting: If it is apparent that the problem SBU is unlikely to return to profitability through either turnaround or retrenchment but that it still has the potential for some degree of success, divestiture or harvesting are reasonable options. If the SBU might fare well in different circumstances, divestiture would be a suitable choice, which entails selling the business to another organization or spinning off a separate entity in which the corporation retains a partial interest. If a change of circumstances is not likely to result in substantial improvement, but there is still a reasonable level of demand for the services provided by the SBU, harvesting is in order. Harvesting entails milking the business, with only sufficient additional investment to maintain the level of operation. Since there is no expectation that the business will improve in the future, the corporation should seek to maximize profitability without concern for the long-term consequences.

Liquidation: When a business cannot be divested or harvested, the corporation should seek to sell the enterprise's assets at the best possible price; in other words, it should get rid of the business with a minimum loss. Although it is most apparent in this case, the strategist must be aware, regardless of the strategy used, of the human resources implications involved in altering circumstances or reducing levels of

TABLE 7   Strategy Selection Guidelines

Competitive Position	Market Growth	Preferred Strategies
1. Strong	Rapid	Concentration Vertical integration Related diversification
2. Strong	Slow	Diversification Joint ventures into new areas
3. Weak	Rapid	Merger with firm in same business Vertical integration Diversification
4. Weak	Slow	Diversification Harvest or divest Liquidate

1. Strengthen current market position; expand market share
2. Use strength to move into more profitable areas of business
3. Gain strength to capitalize on the opportunity presented by rapid growth
4. Diversify into more favorable business or get out with maximum possible gain

operations. Similarly, the needs of the communities served by the corporation must be considered. These are but two illustrations of stakeholders' concerns, as opposed to stockholders' concerns.

Restructuring: This is actually a combination of several of the foregoing strategies. It entails radical surgery on the corporate portfolio to change the composition and/or proportional mix of the corporation's businesses. It may drastically change the nature/mission of the corporation; for example, a community hospital becomes a specialty hospital or vice versa.

Table 7 presents some rules of thumb that can guide corporate decision makers in the choice of strategies.

Frequently it is necessary to identify an existing corporate strategy that has not been stated explicitly. Such situations may arise within an organization that lacks a well developed planning process. More often the need will occur when developing a profile of a competitor. The components that will allow the analyst to infer the corporate strategy are:

External Elements

Overall direction of the corporation
Composition of portfolio
Number and types of units added
Number and types of units removed

Similar or dissimilar
Strategic fit

Methods used to add units

In-house development, joint venture, or acquisition

Internal Elements

Criteria for allocation of resources
Corporate functional strategies
Efforts to integrate SBUs
Strategic goals and performance measures

An analysis of these elements should indicate whether there is a coherent strategy and, if so, what it is.

BUSINESS UNIT STRATEGY

The purpose of business unit strategy is to contribute to the achievement of corporate goals by developing a sustainable competitive advantage. As noted earlier, if it is not possible to gain a permanent competitive advantage, an organization can seek to achieve a protected position by early market entry, pricing structures, franchising, concentration on a particular market segment, differentiation of services/products, or using alternative distribution channels. Although these opportunities exist, they are not used equally by all businesses. Research has shown that there are four types of business strategists.[28]

Defenders engage in little or no product or market development. Their organizations usually are in a niche that they can control by strategies related to stability and efficiency.

---

[28] Raymond E. Miles and Charles C. Snow. *Organizational Strategy, Structure, and Process.* New York, McGraw Hill Book Co., 1978.

Prospectors continually seek new market opportunities. Because they are pioneers/entrepreneurs, they may not be able to sustain a stable operation that demands efficiency based on routinization.

Analyzers are an intermediate type. They make slower and less frequent changes than prospectors. This characteristic is partly attributable to a need for more "data" to convince them that a new undertaking is feasible. On the other hand, they are less committed to stability than defenders.

Reactors have no consistent strategy. They make ad hoc opportunistic moves that may lead to Porter's "stuck in the middle" type of strategies.[29] Organizations with this type of leadership tend to be "low performers".

A basic decision is the size and scope of the business. This is usually defined in terms of product-mix length, product-line width, and individual product depth. It also includes the market domain. Consequently, there are three domain expansion options: to serve a new market with existing products, to serve an existing market with new products, or to serve a new market with new products. Recently, it has been proposed that many health services businesses will find it necessary to reduce their domain.[30] Often a reduction of scope is assumed to mean getting rid of the most recent additions to product lines and markets; this may be a poor choice, since the newest products are not necessarily the least profitable.

Another significant input into business strategy selection is an environmental description. Every organization is to some degree dependent on its environment. These dependencies can pose a threat to organizational survival; consequently, organizations seek to manage dependencies in two ways. They attempt to minimize the cost of complying with external demands through organizational design (e.g., vertical integration). Alternatively, they reduce dependence by:

1. Choice of domain (e.g., they do not deal with certain distribution channels)

---

[29] Michael E. Porter. *Competitive Advantage*, pp. 16–17.
[30] Charles L. Breindel. "Nongrowth Strategies and Options in Healthcare." *Hospitals and Health Services Administration*, *33*(1):37–45, Spring 1988.

2. Control of who operates, and how they operate within the environment (e.g., franchise, CON, licensure, practice acts)

3. Establishment of advantageous relationships through cooperation or by dominance through competitive advantage

The environment is composed of supporters (customers, suppliers, etc.) and competitors who are trying to attract the same set of supporters. The goal of the organization's attempts to adapt to the environment is to retain the loyalty of supporters. It does this by meeting their expectations in mutually satisfactory exchange relationships. Therefore, the environment can be described in terms of the relative densities of supporters and competitors.

Competitors	Supporters	Environment
Few	Few	Bilateral Oligopoly
Few	Many	Monopolistic Competition
Many	Few	Oligopsony
Many	Many	Competition

Approaches to Business Strategy Development

Although culture and governmental policy mediate the effects of concentration within an industry (e.g., the level of exploitation of monopoly power), the concentration of competition and the level of production standardization significantly influence the relationship between businesses. Production standardization is the degree to which there is a generally accepted "best way" of providing the service. This set of influences leads to the identification of four approaches to acquiring power over the environment.

Cooperation: Appropriate when the organization cannot directly control critical dependencies because of concentrated competition. The objective is to ensure a supply of supporters and to keep new competitors out. A cooperative strategy gets commitments through exchanges between both competitors and supporters that reduce uncertainties for both parties.

Innovation: This is based on monopolistic competition. The organization attempts to create a quasi-monopoly by differentiation of its services. An alternative is to innovate through diversification, to minimize dependence on any particular set of actors.

Consolidation: A defender strategy that is intended to maintain a monopoly or quasi-monopoly position. Institution building legitimizes the monopoly position through such devices as licensure requirements and practice acts. Formulation of standards also creates problems for competitors, since the existing organizations have the experience/technology required by the prescribed standard. Furthermore, differentiation is difficult within the constraints of the standard.

Competition: This approach is most similar to the idealized perfect competition among producers of a homogeneous product. It uses low prices, which are made possible by internal operating efficiency, to undermine the ability of competitors to get resources from supporters.

Concentration	*Standardization*	*Relationship and Strategy Example*
High	Low	Cooperation (Joint venture)
High	High	Consolidation (Capturing regulators)
Low	Low	Innovation (Differentiation)
Low	High	Competition (Cost advantage)

Factors in Developing Business Strategies

Three generic business strategies have been defined by Michael Porter.[31] They are cost leadership, differentiation, and focus.

A low-cost strategy is based on a superior production process. It should be used when there is little opportunity for differentiation, purchasers are price sensitive, or there are few switching costs. The risks associated with this strategy are that it tends to lock the organization into current technology, and rivals may copy the production methods.

A differentiation strategy is based on technological superiority, quality of service, or product augmentation. It should be used when buyers have diverse needs and the value of features exceeds the cost differential. The risks inherent in this strategy are that it leads to a much higher cost for specialized production, and rivals may imitate the special characteristics of the service.

A focus strategy is based on price advantage or service differentiation in a limited market. It should be used when market seg-

---

[31] Michael E. Porter. *Competitive Strategy*, Chapter 2.

ments have enduring needs for different products or the organization has insufficient resources to compete in the total market. The risks of this strategy are that the needs of the target segment may change, that broad-based rivals may find a way to meet the needs of the target segment, or that broad-based rivals may subsegment the target segment.

In any event, the organization must choose one of the three. An organization seeking to apply both cost leadership and differentiation will be "stuck in the middle" and will succeed at neither, because competitors who emphasize any of the alternatives can perform better on the dimension they have selected. Strategists should be keenly aware of the control implications of these two approaches. Differentiation deals with environmental variables, that is, consumers' expectations, over which the organization has limited influence. On the other hand, cost strategies deal with internal variables and are thus more certain, because these variables are under the organization's control.

Business Strategy Options

In this formulation of generic strategies, there are two major options: volume and low cost derived from economies of scale and extensive experience, or differentiation of product performance and service, which tend to increase the costs of production. In the future, the two options may not necessarily be mutually exclusive. There is a strong likelihood that it will be possible to decrease the cost of specialized production through the use of new technologies such as expert systems and robotics. If this is the case, combination 3 below will become an addition to the set of feasible options now composed of only combinations 1 and 2.

Combinations	Cost	Differentiation	Competitive Advantage
1	Low	Low	Pure Cost
2	High	High	Pure Differentiation
3	Low	High	Cost and Differentiation
4	High	Low	No Advantage

These generic strategies form the building blocks for specific strategies. The choice of specific strategies is strongly influenced by the life-cycle stage of the service. The following sections will illustrate the differences in the strategies, which are appropriate for various stages of a service's market development.

Strategies for a New Market

The first entrant has the advantage of a preemptive strike. Low cost also creates a barrier to entry. It can be achieved by selecting the correct technology and by rapid movement up the experience curve. The first entrant can choose among the following options. Early followers can gain a foothold in the market by basing competitive moves on either lower prices or differentiation, since the sole producer has no motive to incur the added costs of a differentiated service.

GROW AND BUILD is a middle-of-the-road strategy between the next two extremes. It is based on either low cost or sustainable differentiation.

MARKET SKIMMING seeks to maximize profit to provide a strong resource base for further growth.

MARKET PENETRATION attempts to maximize market share and, thus, to create a significant barrier to entry by competitors. It requires either low-cost production or a willingness to accept a minimal profit in the short run.

Strategies for a Growing Market

In a growing market, there are opportunities for many organizations to prosper without engaging in directly hostile competition. Each organization may seek to reach previously unserved clients. All will seek to consolidate and improve their position through such tactics as pricing based on sophisticated analysis of costs (e.g., when competing for managed-care contracts), process innovation to reduce costs, or improving services and increasing sales to present customers. It is also possible to undertake relatively riskless aggressive action by taking over or buying out smaller rivals.

The choice of strategy will be dictated to some extent by the market position of the organization. The leader or dominant organization will seek to keep the offensive in order to continue its growth. In some circumstances, a hold and maintain position may be adopted, but that opens opportunities for challengers to capture the leadership position by simply growing larger than the present leader. In general, the leader should defend its position vigorously, but, at the least, it should always harass its competitors to make them realize that they cannot challenge it without some cost.

A strong runner-up usually will resort to a variety of devices in its quest to grow. Some of the available options for growth are to serve unserved markets, become a specialist in the general market, offer a superior product, create a distinctive image, or grow by absorbing smaller rivals. Another way to survive and prosper is to adopt the role of a nonaggressive follower.

A weak runner-up may seek to become stronger by using a turn-around strategy, or it may settle for survival. The latter choice implies a willingness to accept the present low level of profitability. If this is not the case, the organization must resort to harvesting or abandonment.

Strategies for a Mature Market

A mature market is one in which virtually all demand is being satisfied by existing providers. This does not mean that growth is impossible, but it does indicate that any significant growth will be achieved only at the expense of some other provider of the service. Theoretically, it is possible to maintain the status quo as a sort of equilibrium situation, but as a practical matter, there will be circumstances that motivate some organizations to expand their level of activity. Those organizations that wish to seek more than their current market share must use the strategies described earlier in a more aggressive fashion. Suitable approaches will be described as offensive strategies. It is axiomatic that no organization is so well entrenched that it can safely ignore an attack. Consequently, responses to challenges will be discussed as defensive strategies.

OFFENSIVE STRATEGIES

Direct Offensive: This attack on existing competitors will yield the largest gain in market share, but it will also require the greatest commitment of resources and carry the greatest risk. A focused attack on a competitor's strength is a head-on attack. Since the defender has the advantages noted earlier, the attacker must have superior strength. If this is not the case, the logical alternative is a focused attack on the competitor's weakness. The risk and resource commitment can be reduced by attacking the weaker competitors in the market, but the gain in market share will be correspondingly smaller. The attacks just described conform to the principle of concentration. An organization might consider simultaneous attacks, but this approach would still require the attacker to have considerable strength so as to sustain multiple efforts. Moreover, to succeed, an attacker also must have superior management ability to coordinate the several efforts.

Bypass Offensive: This type of attack entails a move into parts of the market that are not served by competitors; it may require development of a special version of the service to meet the needs of the target market segment. It avoids some of the problems of the direct offensive, but since the remainder of the market is saturated, the amount of growth that can be achieved is limited.

Guerrilla Offensive: This method of competition requires maintenance of a strong and secure base of operations to support attacks that are frequent and dispersed to keep the competitor off balance. These challenges focus on small targets that the competitor will not defend strongly.

DEFENSIVE STRATEGIES

Concentration: By focusing all of its resources on current products and markets, a defender can amplify the advantages inherent in a defensive posture. This will make the challenger's task of overwhelming the defense far more difficult.

Mobility: This is a less-passive defense that also serves to increase the difficulties faced by the attacker. If the defender makes frequent changes to keep abreast of changing market conditions, the attacker will be compelled to continually alter its activities to respond to the new situations created by the defender.

Preemption: This strategy allows the defender to minimize the strength of the attacker. The defender does so by gaining control of the major sources of supply or channels of distribution (e.g., through exclusive contracts).

Dissuasion: A low-cost strategy that averts major conflicts by convincing competitors that an attack will cost more than any possible benefits that might be realized. The defender must appear to be unbeatable. Such an image can be created by psychological warfare based on continuing efforts in publicity, public relations, and advertising. It can be reinforced by prompt punitive attacks on "upstarts" and new entrants. The evident cost of victory can also be raised if the defender appears to be irrationally committed to maintaining the status quo even though this would be suicidal. For example, if the defender makes it clear that it will maintain a weak service even if it is extremely unprofitable so as to fulfill its mission as a full-service provider, an attacker could be dissuaded from launching a guerilla attack.

Strategies for a Declining Market

Inevitably, every market will reach a state of decline either because virtually all effective demand has been satisfied or because the service has been made obsolete by the introduction of a new service. In these circumstances, the organization must still decide how to maximize the value created for the stakeholders. The following options are available.

REJUVENATE DEMAND: For most stakeholders, this would be the preferred solution; however, it requires unusual creativity to find new applications for an existing service.

RETRENCH: Reducing the scale of the operation while maintaining profitability can be achieved by focusing on the strongest segments in the market. A market leader may willingly relinquish control of these segments if it is no longer possible to maintain sufficient volume to achieve the economies of scale required to sustain the leader's strategy. An organization following a niching strategy may find this to be a very profitable arrangement.

DIVEST: The organization may be able to create considerable value by selling the business to another organization that believes there is an opportunity to operate profitably. For instance, the market leader may be able to sell its business to the nicher on the premise that purchase is less costly than the other methods of acquiring the target market's business. The proceeds of the sale can then be invested in other ventures with a higher rate of return than could be realized by any of the other options.

HARVEST: If divestiture is infeasible, an organization can seek to maximize the value obtained from a business through the process of harvesting. Harvesting entails maximizing the difference between costs and price; however, it should never lead to a degradation of quality. The organization should maintain quality for two reasons: first, to maintain the loyalty of the persons using the service when they finally switch to a replacement service; second, any reduction of quality could adversely affect the overall image of the organization and, thus, have a negative impact on the marketability of its other services.

Step 7: Evaluate Strategy Options

It is clear that an organization will face many situations that have a variety of plausible strategies. Selection of the preferred strategy must begin with an examination of the alternatives to maintain consistency with the organization's mission and goals. Special attention must be given to the degree of support for the driving force.

Options that survive this initial screening should then be evaluated on the basis of four general tests:

1. FOCUS TEST: Does the strategy focus on critical success factors?

2. COMPETENCE TEST: Does the strategy pose problems that can be solved by application of the organization's skills and competences?

3. WORKABILITY TEST: Does the strategy require only those resources that are available to the organization? Will it produce the results sought?

4. ASYMMETRY TEST: Does the strategy create or exploit an asymmetry, or difference, constituting an advantage over rival organizations?[32]

---

[32] Richard P. Rummelt. "Evaluation of Strategy: Theories and Models." In: *Strategic Management.* Edited by Dan E. Schendel and Charles W. Hofer. Boston, Little, Brown, 1979, pp. 199–203.

The options for passing these tests should be assessed on the basis of additional, more specific criteria. Various authors have proposed comparable sets of criteria; the following list was developed by Steiner:[33]

1. Is the strategy consistent with the environment?
2. Is the strategy consistent with internal policies, management styles, philosophy, and operating procedures?
3. Is the strategy appropriate in the light of resources? (This is analogous to the workability test previously described.)
4. Are the risks in pursuing the strategy acceptable?
5. Does the strategy fit the product life cycle and market strength/ market attractiveness situation?
6. Is the timing of the proposed implementation correct?

Steiner provides 34 questions that make these criteria operational. Two other factors also deserve consideration. The first is the degree to which the strategy will create or contribute to synergistic interactions. The second is the strength of the competitors' probable responses to the strategy when it is implemented.

The four tests previously described yield "yes" or "no" decisions. Thus, a proposal either survives or is rejected. The criteria, however, can be met to varying degrees, so the issue to be decided is which strategy is best. The answer is ultimately judgmental, but rating schemes such as those mentioned in Chapter 8 can be very helpful to the decision maker.

The Business Planning Process

Although business plans may have three seemingly different purposes, there are many similarities in their content, since the ultimate aim is to persuade some set of decision makers to allocate resources to the business, whether it is a new venture or an ongoing enterprise. Consequently, the following discussion will be organized to avoid redundancy by moving from a plan designed for creating a totally new undertaking (start-up plan) to one for acquiring an established

---

[33] George A. Steiner. *Strategic Planning*. New York, Free Press, 1979, pp. 144–145.

organization (acquisition plan) and, finally, to a plan for supporting the continued operation of an ongoing business.

Since both the start-up and acquisition plans involve new business ventures, they must be preceded by a feasibility study. Indeed, these plans are, to a large extent, reports of the results of a favorable feasibility study.

Start-up Plan

1. DEFINITION: The first component of this plan is a definition of the proposed business or service that will describe what benefits will be offered to which clients. An item that should receive particular emphasis is the new venture's relation to the organization's mission.

2. SITUATION ANALYSIS: This section provides general environmental information, especially the economic and demographic features of the proposed market. It also discusses product information, with particular reference to the state of technology, the life-cycle stage of the service, and the potential for competitive advantage through either low-cost production or service differentiation.

A demand estimate is included in this section to show the total potential market and the population data and utilization rates that were used to estimate the total demand. The discussion of demand should also address price sensitivity and the difference between need and effective demand. This information should be complemented with an indication of the market share available and a description of the status of the competitive factors, current participants, other potential entrants, the availability of substitute services, and any potential problems that may be related to acquisition of the resources required. Finally, any aspect of governmental activity that would affect demand or competition should be identified.

The information derived from analyzing these data should be interpreted and reported as a summary of threats and opportunities.

3. ORGANIZATIONAL ASSESSMENT: Those characteristics of the organization that represent strengths and weaknesses in relation to the venture under consideration should be reported. This information, coupled with the previous competitive analysis, should be interpreted so as to recognize any distinctive competences. The interpretation

should also discuss how these characteristics could be used to gain a competitive advantage.

4. COST ESTIMATE: A valid cost estimate will consider all elements of the business. Michael Porter's[34] value chain provides a good checklist to ensure that all facets of the business have been included. For each element, there should be an estimate of the capital required and the operating expenses, expressed as fixed, semivariable, and variable costs. These data can be used to develop supplements that show capital requirements and a cash flow analysis. This section should conclude with an estimate of the break-even cost for a range of the probable levels of activity.

5. PROFITABILITY ESTIMATE: This should begin with a price-range estimate based on break-even costs (as the floor) and the competitive situation (as the determinant of the maximum feasible price). The total profits at the most likely level of activity can be used to evaluate the proposal on the basis of the organization's financial criteria, such as return on investment. It is also important, however, to emphasize any nonfinancial gains that the organization is likely to experience if it enters this business.

6. RISKS: These should be discussed in a separate section to ensure that they are not overlooked by an unduly optimistic proponent of the new enterprise. In particular, this component of the plan should identify the likely results of a strong, aggressive response by competitors. Environmental changes that would have an adverse effect should also be reported.

7. CONCLUSION AND RECOMMENDATIONS: The conclusion should identify the action that will be most advantageous for the organization. The recommendations will describe how the organization should implement the preferred course of action, including the scope and timing of the program if it is feasible.

Acquisition Plan

1. DEFINITION: The first component of this plan is a definition of the proposed business or service that will describe what benefits will

---

[34] Michael E. Porter. *Competitive Advantage*, pp. 33–61.

be offered to which clients. An item that should receive particular emphasis is the new venture's relation to the organization's mission.

2. FINANCIAL PERFORMANCE: Since the goal is to increase the value of the existing organization, the proposed acquisition must be carefully scrutinized to ensure that its financial condition will not become an undue burden on the acquiring organization. This is not to say that only profitable organizations should be considered for acquisition; rather, the acquiring organization must have a clear understanding of the nature and size of the likely effects of the acquisition. At minimum, the financial analysis should include information on the break-even level of activity, projected cash flows, dollar volume of business, gross and net revenues, and ROI (return on investment).

3. FINANCIAL BENEFITS: In addition to the direct financial results, the analyst must also consider the indirect financial benefits that may result from the acquisition. This section should consider such things as contribution to overhead expenses and impact on payer mix.

4. MARKETING POSITION: What is the current and projected demand for the service(s) offered by the proposed acquisition? What market share does it now possess, and what are the opportunities for growth? Particular attention should be given to the stage of the life cycle that the service(s) have reached. What segments of the market does it serve, and will these customers offer opportunities for expanding the acquiring organization's other businesses? Is the pricing of the acquisition's service(s) proper, and is it compatible with the pricing strategy of the acquiring organization? Similarly, what effects will the acquisition have on the image of the acquiring organization? For example, will it change the acquiring organization's positioning in the overall market from a secondary acute-care hospital to that of a tertiary-level medical center? What effect will the acquisition have on the competitive situation? This last question must address both the responses of competitor organizations and the reactions of regulatory agencies such as the Federal Trade Commission.

5. REQUIRED INVESTMENTS: In addition to purchase costs, the acquiring organization must be prepared to provide the resources that are required by the acquisition. These may include expenses to

provide fixed capital resources (e.g., new equipment) and infusions of operating capital to sustain the growth of the acquisition until it can become a self-sufficient cash generator. The acquisition may also require the investment of human resources as, for example, the acquisition of a potentially profitable but poorly managed organization.

6. MEDICAL STAFF FACTORS: In many health services organizations, the medical staff represent an especially important variable that is not under the direct control of the organization's management. When this is the case, the analysis must consider the willingness of physicians to participate in the activities of the acquisition. For instance, will community physicians in the appropriate specialties agree to bring their patients to the acquired organization? Also important is the reaction of the existing medical staff; will they see the acquisition as fostering unwelcome competition to their private practices or as generating referrals that will enhance their situations?

7. ETHICAL AND LEGAL CONSIDERATIONS: Most health services organizations have been assigned unusual social responsibilities by their stakeholders; for example, provision of uncompensated care for the indigent. What effect will the proposed acquisition have on the perceptions of the relevant stakeholders?

Regardless of one's opinions concerning the desirability of such a situation, the fact remains that the health services industry is one of the most highly regulated industries in the United States. Regulation usually is managed by governmental agencies, but some nongovernmental agencies also are given credence as valid overseers; for example, the Joint Commission on Accreditation of Healthcare Organizations (JCAHO). Since conformity with the mandates of regulators is essential for the parent organization's survival, it must always be concerned with how the acquisition will affect its ability to remain in compliance.

8. STRATEGIC FIT: Many organizations, both in and out of the health services industry, have learned to their regret that growth alone is not a valid criterion for acquisition. These organizations discovered that the principles of span of control and specialization remain valid. In other words, their acquisitions increased the size of the organization but decreased its value to the stakeholders. The net result was that the acquisitions were subsequently divested, so the

organization experienced the expenses of acquisition and divestiture while suffering an overall loss in its value. Often the reason for the decrease in value was attributed to a lack of knowledge of the unrelated business. This is but one of many reasons for such an outcome. The entire set can be grouped under the rubric of lack of strategic fit.

Strategic fit encompasses such factors as the organization's mission, values and strategic market position, development opportunities, and the relationships between services, between the processes by which the services are provided, or both.

9. CONCLUSION AND RECOMMENDATIONS: The conclusion should indicate whether the acquisition will be advantageous for the organization. If acquisition is desirable, the recommendations will describe how the organization should acquire the other organization and the timing of the various phases of the acquisition program.

Continuation Business Plans

These documents are designed to make a persuasive case for the allocation of resources for the continued operation of a particular business enterprise within the organization. The total set of business plans will represent the corporation's overall commitments. The *business plan* also serves as a control document against which the performance of the business can be evaluated.

1. THE INDUSTRY AND PRODUCT ENVIRONMENT: This section describes the general state of the health services industry and the particular circumstances of the service offered by the business. For example, maternity services might be greatly affected by levels of support for Medicaid reimbursement.

2. THE CORPORATION AND ITS PRODUCT LINES: Here the plan should discuss the place of the SBU within the corporation and the relationship of the SBU's service(s) to the total product lines of the corporation. A corporate portfolio analysis, described earlier, provides important data for the development of this section of the plan.

3. THE MARKET: Past, current, and projected market information concerning the service. This analysis should be presented for the total

market, as well as for individual market segments. It should include demand, market share held by the organization, and a description of the competition.

4. FUNCTIONAL PLANS: Even though the SBU may not have totally independent functions, it should present a distinct and complete plan for the business in each of the following areas: marketing, operations, and finance. These were described in detail on pages 47–57. If, for example, marketing is a function performed only at the corporate level, then the corporate marketing plan would include an integrated presentation of the marketing plans presented in the plans for all of the corporation's businesses.

5. CRITICAL RISKS AND PROBLEMS: This section should identify threats to the successful execution of the business plan. It should include contingency plans that are appropriate for dealing with the most serious hazards.

6. SCHEDULE AND CONTROL PLAN: As noted earlier, the business plan should be the basis for evaluating the unit's performance. Therefore, the plan must make a commitment to achieve definite objectives by specific dates and should provide a mechanism for periodically informing management of the degree of its success in meeting these obligations.

The purpose of this comparison of planned results with actual events is to ensure progress, efficiency, and effectiveness. It requires that any deviations from the plan either are acceptable or become the basis for remedial action. Monitoring should focus on factors that are likely to have consequences of major significance. These may be input, process, output, or outcome factors.

Effective monitoring requires measurable objectives, effective means of measuring accomplishments, valid processes for analyzing the data gathered, and explicit decision rules. A decision rule should specify what factor is to be measured (a criterion), what level of performance is satisfactory or better (a standard), and who has the authority to act when performance is unsatisfactory.

There are a variety of techniques for monitoring continuing programs. These include activity summaries, budget analyses, and statistical control charts. Monitoring techniques for discrete projects, as opposed to continuing programs, include Gantt charts and network charts (PERT/CPM). To use these techniques one must make a list of tasks to be completed and, for each task, identify the preceding tasks, time required, resources required, and responsible individual. This information can be used to develop the sequence of tasks, which then yields the schedule for the total project.

Functional Plans

This section will discuss plans for the three primary line functions of marketing, operations, and finance. Although the specifics will differ among the three, they can be organized on the basis of the following standard components.

Generic Functional Plan Content

1. SITUATION ANALYSIS: This should be a description of the relevant circumstances affecting the performance of the function. For instance, in the marketing plan, it will describe the market characteristics, demand, supply, and competition. It provides the database for establishing the function's goals.

2. GOALS: The measurable achievements that the function manager proposes to accomplish in support of the organization's mission and strategy.

3. STRATEGY: A detailed description of the strategy that was developed to achieve the goals and the rationale supporting it.

4. RESOURCES: A time-phased statement of the resources that will be required to implement the strategy and an inventory of the current and projected relevant resources of the corporation.

5. ACTION PROGRAM: A statement of the short-range activities that will be undertaken to implement the strategy. It will contain the following sections.

   a. *Objectives*: Subgoals or specific steps that must be taken to achieve one or more goals and the dates by which each will be completed.

   b. *Actions*: The individual activities that must be accomplished to reach each objective and the person or unit that will be responsible for performing them. Each action must be linked explicitly to the objective(s) it supports.

   c. *Schedule*: A display of the time periods in which various actions must be completed so as to meet the dates established for accomplishment of the objectives.

   d. *Budget*: A time-phased allocation of resources for accomplishment of the actions. A budget of personnel resources is often a useful addition to the traditional financial budget.

   e. *Controls*: A description of the process by which progress will be monitored.

Specific Functional Plan Content

   1. MARKETING PLANS[35] should consider the following issues:

   a. *Market Research and Analysis*: Potential service users, market size and trends, competition, estimated market share and sales, and future of the market.

   b. *Marketing Plan*: Overall marketing strategy, product and service policies, pricing, distribution, sales tactics, advertising and promotion, and marketing budget.

   2. OPERATIONS PLANS[36] should address the following topics: service delivery methods, service delivery sites, facilities, equipment, and operations budget.

   3. FINANCIAL PLANS[37] should include the following items: profit and loss forecasts, break-even analysis, pro forma cash flow analysis, pro forma balance sheets, capital requirements, sources of capital, and costs of capital.

---

[35] Philip Kotler and Roberta N. Clarke. *Marketing for Health Services Organizations.* Englewood Cliffs, N.J., Prentice-Hall, 1987. Chapter 7 provides a thorough description of the contents of a marketing plan.

[36] D. J. Bennett, "Operations Planning and Control," in: *Operations Management in Practice,* edited by C. D. Lewis, New York, Wiley, 1981, pp. 194–223; and Joseph G. Monks, *Operations Management: Theory and Practice,* 2d ed., New York, McGraw Hill Book Co., 1982, Chapters 7, 10, 11, and 13.

[37] William O. Cleverley. *Essentials of Healthcare Finance.* 2d ed. Rockville, Md., Aspen Publishers, 1986, pp. 155–181.

4. ADMINISTRATIVE PLANS may be added. If they are, the following should be included: organization structure, management team, support services, control and evaluation process, and administrative budget.

5. RESEARCH AND DEVELOPMENT PLANS[38] will be relevant for only a few organizations. When such a plan is appropriate, it should address the following topics: life-cycle status of the service, development of service improvements, research on replacement services, and research and development budget.

SUMMARY

This chapter describes the strategic, business, and functional plans required by organizations. It includes discussions of the content of each type and also provides guidance on the development of strategies for both corporations and businesses. Throughout the chapter, the concept of the organization as a system is stressed as a framework for analyzing data to develop the information required for planning decisions. Although certain parts of the chapter mention the organization's relation to its environment, the organization's role in community health planning activities was not discussed. This issue will be covered in Chapter 5.

---

[38] William G. McLoughlin, *Fundamentals of Research Management*, New York, American Management Association, 1970, pp. 131–145; and Anthony J. Gambino and Morris Gartenberg, *Industrial R&D Management*, New York, National Association of Accountants, 1979, pp. 29–63.

COMMUNITY HEALTH SERVICES PLANS

There are many advantages to the systems approach to health planning. The concepts of the systems approach can be incorporated in community health services plans. The term *health system* includes the combinations of health services and settings that are within the boundaries established by the decision makers. The matrix in Figure 12 portrays health services and settings that constitute a comprehensive community health system.[1]

Policies and assumptions, community description, health status, health services, and health resources form the components of the health system plan. Figure 13, a flowchart of the process for developing such a system plan, shows the relationships between the plan's components.

POLICIES AND ASSUMPTIONS

The first, and perhaps most important, part of a community health system plan embodies statements of system policies and assumptions. This section of the plan contains statements of the system's general

---

[1] A community health plan may be a comprehensive plan covering a wide range of health concerns and services, such as the plans envisioned by P.L. 93-641, or it may be more narrowly focused, such as a plan to cope with a particular health problem, for example, AIDS.

goals, which provide the context and overall guidance for all other planning activities and make a major contribution toward the goal of an accountable planning process.

HEALTH SYSTEM SERVICES		HOME	PUBLIC	AMBULATORY		SHORT STAY INPATIENT		LONG STAY INPATIENT		FREE STANDING SUPPORT	COMMUNITY
				HOSP	OTHER	HOSP	OTHER	HOSP	OTHER		
COMMUNITY HEALTH PROMOTION AND PROTECTION	Health Education Services										
	Environmental Quality Management										
	Food Protection										
	Occupational Health and Safety										
	Radiation Safety										
	Biomedical and Consumer Product Safety										
PREVENTION AND DETECTION	Individual Health Protection Services										
	Detection Services										
DIAGNOSIS AND TREATMENT	Obstetric Services										
	Surgical Services										
	Diagnostic Radiology Services										
	Therapeutic Radiology Services										
	Clinical Laboratory Services										
	Emergency Medical Services										
	Dental Health Services										
	Mental Health Services										
	General Medical Services										
HABILITATION AND REHABILITATION	Medical Habilitation and Rehabilitation Services										
	Therapy Services										
MAINTENANCE											
PERSONAL HEALTH CARE SUPPORT	Direct Patient Care Support Services										
	Administrative Services										
HEALTH SYSTEM ENABLING	Health Planning										
	Resource Development										
	Financing										
	Regulation										
	Research										

HEALTH SYSTEM SETTING

Figure 12   Health services and settings matrix.

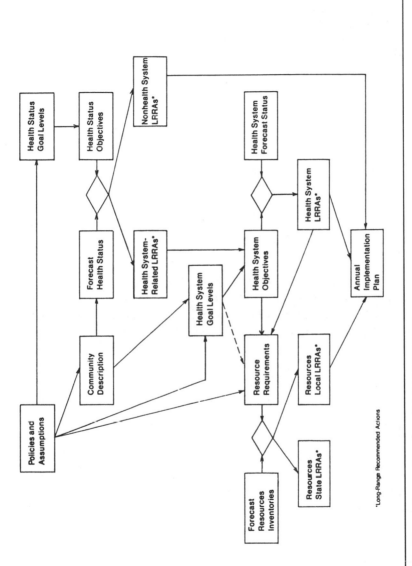

*Long-Range Recommended Actions

Figure 13 Health systems plan development process.

TABLE 8 Suggested Health Plan Policy Topics

1. Planning horizon
2. Emphasis on current or future program
3. Relationships with "peer" organizations
4. Board/committee/task force relationships
5. Board/staff relationships
6. Quality of information required by decision makers
7. Basic values and their relative priorities
8. Theory of health on which plan is based
9. Boundary of health system
10. Population groups to receive special attention
11. Subsystems to receive special attention
12. Goal levels uniform for entire health service area or variable
13. Assumptions about resource availability
14. Goal levels and objectives expressed at what level (minimum, national average, ideal)
15. Preference for investment or consumption activities

In addition to value statements, the system's governing body[2] must clarify its assumptions about the health care system and its future. Some of the requirements here include an explicit definition of the boundaries of that system and a determination of the planning horizon to be used in the decision-making process. (*Planning horizon* is simply the end of the time period for which planning has taken place. If a health system planning process establishes a five-year planning horizon, a plan developed in 1990 will have a planning horizon of 1995.)

The governing body must also state its expectations about the level of investment and operating costs that the community will approve for the health system during the planning period. Table 8 presents a list of topics that might be included in the policy section of a health system plan.

---

[2] The term *governing body* as it is used here means the decision makers who control the community health planning process. It may be an elected or appointed quasi-governmental body or a group that has formed a voluntary association, such as a business coalition.

COMMUNITY DESCRIPTION

The next major component of the health system plan is a community description. The concepts of marketing call for a population-based plan (i.e., a plan based on the needs of area residents as a whole rather than a process that deals with the proposals of individual organizations or providers as a basis for making planning decisions). In addition to describing the population to be served, the plan also should describe the conditions within which the plan will be implemented, including the social, economic, geographic, and political dimensions of the community. These factors are important from two perspectives. The social, economic, and political conditions will affect implementation of the plan. More important, they also will have great bearing on the health status of the population, if one assumes that an ecological model of health is to be used in the planning process.[3]

Because of these considerations, planners must incorporate the relevant data into this section of the plan. The word *relevant* is of particular significance, because many plans have described communities in exquisite detail but have failed to indicate to the users of the plan the relationship between the community characteristics described and the health status of those to be served.

HEALTH STATUS

Health status is the next component of the health system plan. Goal levels are established on the basis of the values expressed in the policy portion of the plan and are set for an indefinite time in the future. Consequently, the organization must move from the goal levels to a time-related set of objectives. In other words, planners must decide on reasonable health status levels at the planning horizon. These levels become the objectives that are compared with a forecast of

---

[3] An ecological model of health implies that health status is affected by many factors in addition to medical care. These often are grouped into three categories: biological (e.g., maturation and aging), environmental (e.g., housing conditions), and behavioral (e.g., leisure activities).

community health status for the same time period. The forecast is developed from information provided in the community description.

The comparison of the health status forecast with objectives for the planning horizon will indicate the areas in which there are discrepancies–where problems exist. It must then be determined whether these discrepancies can be attributed to the health system or whether they are caused entirely or in part by factors outside the system. In the latter case, the organization might initiate appropriate actions vis-à-vis those who have power to make the necessary changes. This move is represented in Figure 13 by the box entitled "Nonhealth System LRRAs" (long-range recommended actions).

When some or all of the health status problems can be attributed to the health *system,* the planning organization must seek to correct them by changing the system. It cannot plan long-range recommended actions related to health *status;* there is no action, for instance, that will directly reduce infant mortality. Instead, the organization must design long-range actions that will somehow change the health system, the environment, or both, in such a way that the causes of infant mortality will be reduced.

HEALTH SYSTEM

The health system goal levels in Figure 13 are derived from the values expressed in the policy section and from the community's characteristics.

The goal levels are translated into health system objectives that are appropriate for the planning horizon. These objectives can be compared with the LRRAs for health services that arose as a result of the examination of health status problems.

If the health system objectives are compatible with the LRRAs related to health, the planner can be confident that those objectives are appropriate. On the other hand, if they bear no relationship to each other, the planner can assume that the system's objectives should be modified to encompass those actions that are needed to deal with a clearly defined health status problem. The health system objectives are contrasted with a health system forecast. This forecast is an inventory of the health system projected to the planning horizon, so the planner can compare the two. This comparison is made along a number of dimensions represented by the attributes or characteristics that the governing body may have selected. Characteristics that are frequently cited include availability, accessibility, acceptability, quality, cost, and continuity.

In the event that the system's objectives differ from the forecast status of the system, the planner must then develop strategies and LRRAs that will bring the system's status into agreement with the objectives. At this point, it should be noted that a surplus may be as great a problem as a deficiency. As reimbursement shifts from a cost base to a prospectively set price, underused service capacity can become a serious drain on the financial resources of the system.

RESOURCE NEEDS

Whatever the case, the LRRAs for the health system generally will imply some adjustment in resource requirements, another important section of the health system plan. Ideally, one would hope that these requirements could be determined on the basis of the general values expressed in the policy portion of the plan, plus an aggregation of the more specific statements in the health system goal levels and objectives.

When such aggregate resource objectives are developed, they must be adjusted on the basis of the health system's LRRAs. In the interim, these LRRAs can be used to estimate changes in the projected supply of system resources. This supply is determined by taking an inventory of currently available resources and forecasting that inventory to the planning horizon. If the planners have succeeded in developing an aggregate system resource requirement, the forecast inventory and resource requirement can be compared to determine what action is necessary.

The adjustment that must be made in resources will become the basis for long-range recommended actions. In some cases, recommendations affecting the resource supply can be implemented at the local level, but many resource adjustments will require actions at the state or federal level. For instance, the state supposedly has control of facility development through the state medical facility plan. Similarly, a state might act to influence the output of the medical schools, but a community that is in complete control of the supply of physicians would be unusual. On the other hand, a community might influence the supply of inhalation therapy technicians through a community college that is the primary, if not the only, source of such technicians.

If the point of action is sufficiently remote, the system may have to set resource supply levels as budgetary constraints. If expenditures must be limited, the system can insist that no more than a certain amount of resources be allocated for the provision of specific health services. In such cases, LRRAs would be considered feasible only if their net resource requirements were less than the differences between the quantities of resources required to provide existing health services and the resource ceilings derived from statements in the policy section of the health system plan.

IMPLEMENTATION PLAN

The data from the health system plan become part of an implementation plan, which describes what actions the organization intends to take to attain the objectives established for the planning horizon. Figure 14 is a flowchart of the process for developing an implementation plan. The decisions concerning which of the long-range recommended actions are to be implemented during the coming year are dependent on knowledge of organization resources and other data that may be relevant to priority determination (e.g., availability of community resources) and on the policies and assumptions contained in the health system plan.

When all these factors have been taken into account, the organization can establish annual objectives related to changes in the health system, health resources, and those aspects of the environment that have an adverse effect on health status. For each of these objectives, planners will develop both short-range recommended actions (SRRAs) and project plans to implement them.

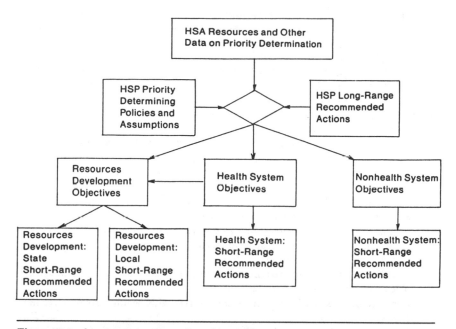

Figure 14 Implementation plan development process.

Table 9 presents a list summarizing plan development activities. This list should not be regarded as a sequential set of actions, since many of these activities can be accomplished concurrently. For example, once the indicators for health status and the health system have been determined, planners can begin to prepare the forecast of community health status, the status of the health system, and the inventory of health resources, because the indicators represent the decision variables, that is, the measurable characteristics of the system that are used in making decisions. Collection of other data would be unnecessary, since these additional factors would not be used in actions affecting the system.

The process of preparing a forecast is not affected by determining goal levels, and, consequently, the latter can occur concurrently with the preparation of the inventory. Obviously, however, both of these forecasts must be completed before they can be compared, as required in step 6 of Table 9.

TABLE 9   Plan Development Activities

1. Establish planning policies and assumptions
2. Prepare community description
3. Determine indicators and goal levels for health status and health systems; optimize goal levels
4. Set objectives on basis of goal levels
5. Prepare forecasts of community health status, status of health system, and inventories of health resources
6. Compare health status and health system forecasts with objectives
7. Arrange observed disparities in priority sequence
8. Design alternative means for eliminating disparities that have the highest priority
9. Choose preferred means for eliminating each priority disparity and designate it as a long-range recommended action (LRRA)
10. Examine health system objectives to ensure consistency with health-system-related LRRAs designed to achieve health status objectives; modify health system objectives as necessary
11. Establish health resource requirements on the basis of policies, health system objectives, and health system LRRAs
12. Compare forecast health resources inventories with health resources requirements
13. Design alternative means for eliminating disparities between forecast inventories and requirements
14. Choose preferred alternative means for eliminating each disparity and designate it as an LRRA
15. Inform state health planning and development agency of LRRA related to state resources development plans
16. Put all LRRAs into priority sequence
17. Establish one-year objectives for LRRAs that are feasible within existing resource constraints
18. Design alternative methods for achieving each objective
19. Choose preferred alternatives and designate each one as a short-range recommended action (SRRA)
20. Prepare project plans for each SRRA

Table 9 also shows items that are not fully addressed in the description of the health system planning flowchart (Figure 14). For example, step 3 calls for optimizing system goal levels. This step recognizes the need for trade-offs between certain attributes of the system—one would not expect the highest level of quality at the lowest possible cost. Experience has shown that in the initial process of setting goal levels, health care decision makers tend to establish a maximum as the desirable level. Unfortunately, maximization of all attributes is seldom possible, and it is particularly unlikely that the ultimate in other attributes (e.g., accessibility, quality) will be attained for a minimum cost. Therefore, after goal levels are initially stated, they must be reexamined to ensure that they are internally consistent. If they are not, then decision makers must seek to achieve a reasonable balance among the desired levels for each of the many attributes.

Several steps in Table 9 imply a choice among different options. For example, step 7 indicates that disparities or problems must be placed in priority sequence. This implies insufficient resources to deal with all the trouble spots or opportunities, so one must address the most important to the extent allowed by available resources. Similarly, step 9 requires decision makers to choose from a number of means for dealing with a problem to determine which is preferred in terms of cost and benefit. This is a constant challenge to planners and, in fact, can be seen as the real reason for planning. Because resources are insufficient to accomplish all possible aims, planners must help decision makers choose the most desirable achievements and determine how scarce resources can be used to attain them. The system plan and the process by which it is developed are the means by which planners can accomplish this task.

The system planning process is not dependent on the assignment of all planning functions to a single agency. The allocation of responsibilities is more of a political or administrative matter than a requirement of the process. It would be easy from a technical standpoint to separate the three levels of planning (policy, strategic, and operational) that are incorporated in the process. The shift of responsibility for policymaking from the planning organization to some other body would result in the establishment of two easily de-lineated sets of tasks. The line of demarcation between strategic and operational planning is less obvious, but it is significant because the strategic planning organization must understand clearly the implications of being involved in operational planning. Specifically, if the role of the planning organization were limited to strategic planning or to strategic and policy planning, its plan development responsibilities would end with the establishment of objectives for each attribute of each component of the health services system, in keeping with resource budget limits. The operational planning phase could then be carried out by the operating organizations.

The decision makers would hold the operators responsible for developing health services in accordance with the objectives and budgetary constraints. The organizations responsible for operational planning must have the high level of expertise needed to select the best means of achieving an objective (long-range recommended action) and the best combination of resources to carry out the chosen action. Furthermore, the effort involved in this kind of detailed analysis and planning is so great that the strategic planning group must either avoid the task or resort to mixed scanning. For this reason, planners must be concerned with two things: First, they must be especially meticulous in setting priorities, because they will be able to develop operational-level plans for only a few concerns. Second, they must not succumb to pressures to develop operational plans at the expense of completing the strategic plan. It is essential that performance standards (objectives) for the entire system be known when LRRAs are chosen, because the selection process must consider the likely effects of choices on the performance of other parts of the health services system.

SUMMARY

General systems theory provides a useful framework for planning the organization and delivery of health services. The integrative systems approach overcomes many of the deficiencies of earlier styles of planning, which focused on the acquisition of resources as the purpose of planning or on individual problems as discrete and isolated issues. A health system plan contains sets of elements, each of which evolves in a logical progression from the preceding elements. Policies and assumptions set the overall guidance for the plan. Within that guidance, a community description characterizes the environment and population that the health system is intended to serve. Health status data, as a subset of the environmental information, reflect the community's needs that are to be met by the system. The health system section describes the organizations and services needed to satisfy those needs in a fashion consistent with the community's policies. The next element of the plan identifies the resources that are required to maintain and operate the desired system. Finally, there is a specific action plan that describes what will be done to achieve the most immediate objectives of the health system plan.

CHAPTER 6

ENVIRONMENTAL ASSESSMENT

The health industry is undergoing tremendous change, driven by shifts in the macroeconomic environment. An understanding of these broad forces is the baseline for market assessment, outlined in Chapter 7.

An early and critical step in the strategic planning process is environmental analysis. This chapter focuses on those factors that are external to the organization or community undertaking the planning process; such factors are not directly or immediately impacted by the community or organization for which the planning is being undertaken. It also examines more closely those factors that directly affect the context of the planning process, the environment of the U.S. health industry, and the hospital or health organization.

Many of the approaches presented here for environmental analysis can be applied to either a community- or an organization-based planning effort. Because of the introductory nature of this book, the concepts that are considered basic to the health planning process are discussed in greater depth.

In some cases, the purposes and applications of community- and organization-based planning are the same. Often, however, the community planner and the organizational planner are forced to analyze the environment or organization differently because their purposes and goals are different. The community health planner is usually working toward the goal of improving public health. When community and state-level health planning are driven by regulatory programs, the purpose is a rationalized health delivery system within an extended series of political boundaries that encompass a number of individual service providers. The organizational planner, whether based in a hospital, multiorganizational health system, or other health organization, is usually seeking to compete and to gain financial viability in a much more narrowly defined market.

There are philosophical and ethical dimensions in the issue of how planning, from both the community and organizational perspective, relates to decision making. These factors include the role of consumers in health, the degree of altruism motivating the provision of health services, the profit and nonprofit motives, the impact of government reimbursement, and the use of technology. These conflicts among perspectives of key stakeholders strongly affect the desired outcome of the planning process (discussed in Chapter 1) and the manner in which both the environment and the organization are assessed. Planners and market analysts must be aware of the prevailing value systems so as to gather the proper data and develop the needed information for an environmental or internal assessment.

ENVIRONMENTAL ASSESSMENT

The term *environmental assessment* often is used to represent an analysis of all factors outside the organization's direct control that could affect its activities significantly during the time horizon covered by the plan. These "S.T.E.E.P." factors include:

Society and Consumers
Technology
Economy
Environment
Political and Legal

The health care market analyst may wish to include an additional factor—personal health status, which is more likely to be used in community-oriented processes than in organizational planning processes.

A description of the current status of each of these factors and a forecast for each are required for the planning process. Because of the broad nature of these factors, descriptions and forecasts tend

TABLE 10 Summary of Environmental Assessment*

Society	Economy	Political/Legal	Technology
Values and beliefs about	Income levels	Regulation of Health services	Medical New equipment
Health	Employment	Workers	New drugs
Life-styles	patterns	Reimbursement	New procedures
Cost controls		Certificate of	
Services	Inflation	need	Environment
		Zoning	
Expectations	Interest rates		Health services
Goods		Government	organizations
Services	Growth rates	reimbursement	
		policy	
Demographics	Local indus-		
Age trends	trial base	Changes in the	
Mobility		offing	
Birthrates	Investments		
Education	and savings	Taxation policy	
Religion			
	Wage levels		

*The elements included in Table 10 are examples of the information that might be included in an environmental assessment. This table would serve as a summary of the environmental trends and would be backed up by substantial narrative.

to be readily available from secondary sources, especially for the economic and sociocultural areas. The important task for the analyst is to determine and focus on those elements of each factor that are most likely to affect the organization for which the planning process is being undertaken. Table 10 presents a general model of an environmental assessment involving the factors identified. The elements included in the dimensions are only examples of what might be appropriate for an environmental assessment. The planner must analyze which elements are most appropriate to the organization, industry, and community that will provide the context for the more specific market strategies. Increasingly, health care organizations and trade associations are publishing environmental assessments for their constituents. Two good recent examples are *Forecast '89,* prepared by the Futures Research Program of UniHealth America, a Los Angeles-based health care company, and "The Trauma of

TABLE 11   Environmental Assessment of Factors Affecting Home Health Agencies

Society	Demography	Economy	Technology	Politics
Nationwide				
Increased awareness of sense of limits	Increase in aging of population	Decrease in percent of the GNP for health	Decrease in technological imperative	Increased conservatism in all levels of government
Increase in change of life-style to improve health	Decrease in birthrate	Growth likely over short run	Technological advances for the future	Decreased governmental regulation
Desire for alternatives to hospital care	Increase in chronic illness	Inflation will continue at a low rate	Ability to predict disease	Increased interest in home care
	Decline in the 15 to 44 age cohort	Reimbursement will stress lower cost care	Cure for cancer	Federal monies will be made available to home care field
			Improved nutrition of population	
Locally for Community X				
Better health education will make people aware of home health services	Population will continue to grow slowly	Growth will have lessened impact on local community	No short-run changes seen	County council will support home care
Home health will become accepted as an alternative type of care	Increase in incoming older population	Energy problems will cause increased costs		State will cut funding of all health programs
	Decline in the birthrate	Insurance will cover more home-care services		Local officials will promote home care but not with dollars

Transformation in the 1990s," prepared by Health One Corporation, a multihospital system in Minneapolis.[1] This environmental assessment is intended to give an information advantage to the health care executives and managers of this regional health system. Similiar reports are prepared and published annually by a number of national and state industry trade associations, as well as by consultants and suppliers.

Macroenvironmental factors need to be translated into strategic implications for the health organization and its long-range and market planning. Table 11 presents an approach to an environmental assessment that might be appropriate for a home health agency. In this example, the assessment of the environment for home care is undertaken at two levels. The first seeks to identify broad trends on a nationwide basis; the second attempts to identify the local or regional experience for those same trends.

Two-Tiered National/Regional Approach

Identification of national trends and local or regional trends is useful when good secondary data are available at the national but not the local level. Because regional experience can differ greatly from national experience in such areas as population demographics, employment patterns, and general income patterns, it is important to reflect the proper level of experience in the environmental analysis. The two-tiered national/regional approach allows the planner to clearly identify the degree to which macroenvironmental trends will, in fact, affect the local experience.

The purpose of environmental assessment is to develop information that will permit the identification of threats and opportunities. The assessment should establish the political decision-making processes, key actors in the health delivery system, target markets and segments, consumer behavior, and need and demand. It also should seek to explain the causal relationships between the environment and these factors.

---

[1] Lois Green, *Forecast '89*, Los Angeles, Calif., Lutheran Hospital Society of Southern California, 1988; see also "The Trauma of Transformation in the 1990s," Minneapolis, Minn., Health One Corporation, 1989.

Expectations of Outside Constituents

Constituents are those individuals and groups who have such an important interest in the affairs of an enterprise that their views should be taken into account in the planning process. For hospitals and health organizations, these constituents include patients and family members, employees, medical and nursing staff, suppliers, representatives of government, regulators, payers, consumer advocacy groups, and the general public. Larger companies are systematically examining these interests as a prelude to strategic planning and marketing.

George Steiner[2] cites the experience of General Electric (GE). In preparing its long-range plan, GE examined the demands of 14 groups of constituents and derived a list of 97, such as federal chartering of corporations, more stringent effluent/emission standards, provision of day care to working mothers, disclosure of more information about products, and an end to tax deferrals for offshore profits. These 97 demands were then ranked in terms of their convergence with major domestic trends perceived over the next decade. Future trends included increasing affluence, rising level of education, expanding technology, and greater emphases on the individual and quality of life.

The results of this anlaysis were summarized into six areas of challenge to companies like General Electric. These six areas, in descending order of importance to the company, are

1. Constraints on corporate growth—a spectrum of issues ranging from national growth policy through economic controls and environmental protection to questions of antitrust policy and industrial structure

2. Corporate governance—including matters of accountability, personal liability of managers and directors, board representation, and disclosure of information

---

[2] George A. Steiner. *Strategic Planning: What Every Manager Must Know.* New York, Free Press, 1979, pp. 126–127.

3. Managing the "new work force"—dealing with the growing demands for job enlargement, more flexible scheduling, equality of opportunity, greater participation, and individualization

4. External constraints on employee relations—the new pressures on government (employment opportunities, health and safety, "federalization" of benefits), unions (coalition bargaining), and other groups (class action suits, "whistle-blowing")

5. Business-government relations—including a redefinition of the role of the private sector in public problem solving

6. "Politicizing" of economic decision making—the growing governmental involvement in corporate decisions through consumerism, environmentalism, industrial reorganization, inflation control, and the like

Stakeholder Analysis

Business strategist James O'Toole[3] attests that organizations achieve the greatest success when they attempt to satisfy the legitimate claims of all the parties that have a stake in their companies: consumers, employees, suppliers, dealers, special interest groups, host communities, and government, as well as shareholders. The challenge for management of these competing interests is to anticipate the demands of each set of key stakeholder constituents.

Techniques for assessing the interests of stakeholders include opinion survey research, focus groups, interviews of key informants, Delphi surveys, literature reviews, and library research. Once the stakeholder groups have been surveyed for their primary concerns, statistical techniques such as weighted factor analysis and cluster analysis can be used to identify those concerns that appear with the greatest frequency and may have the greatest impact on the health organization.

---

[3] James O'Toole. *Vanguard Management: Redesigning the Corporate Future*. New York, Doubleday, 1985, pp. 42–49.

Content Analysis

John Naisbitt[4] has popularized the technique of content analysis, which provided the research base for *Megatrends: Ten New Directions Transforming Our Lives*. Content analysis is a technique adapted from military intelligence. It systematically tracks, sifts, and charts the content of news media. Researchers have found that only so many issues can hold the public's attention at one time. Societies are like human beings. A person can only concentrate on so many problems and concerns at one time. Likewise, a society sorts out its priorities as reflected in the "news hole" of stories the media chooses to cover at any point in time. In this forced-choice situation, society adds new preoccupations and forgets old ones. If new problems or concerns are introduced, some existing ones are given up. Over time, a variety of social issues emerge, gain, and then lose market share, as reflected in the inches of new stories in newspapers and magazines, or minutes of air time on television. Often the rise of one issue, for example, environmental pollution, directly displaces another, such as civil rights. Governmental action is frequently taken at the crest of interest in an issue; invariably, other issues are rising to take the place of that issue on the public scene.

Health organizations may use a media clipping service to track health-related trends in local and regional newspapers and magazines, or a media consultant to sample the content of local television news. Analyses of the amount and duration of particular issues can provide another perspective on the environment. Column inches of news coverage can be charted over time to assess the rise or decline of health-related concerns. Content analysis can be used both for health policy planning at the community level and organizational market planning. Trends from the media "news hole" indicate which issues will affect health policy decisions by local or state governments, as well as impinge on the market strategy of the health organization.

S.T.E.E.P. Analysis

The S.T.E.E.P. assessment process is a continuous scanning and monitoring of the environment that should identify changes as soon

---

[4] John Naisbitt. *Megatrends: Ten New Directions Transforming Our Lives*. New York, Warner Books, 1982, pp. 3–6.

as they occur and, in a competitive sense, before other organizations can react. Because organizations maintain their viability by being responsive to their environment, this process is one of the most critical ongoing parts of the planning activity.

The following discussions of each of the major factors in an environmental assessment suggest elements that are most important for the health planner. The purpose is to present a potentially useful range of elements rather than to identify specific elements related to various portions of the health services industry.

Society and Consumers

Social characteristics of interest to the health analyst include societal values and beliefs and basic population demographics. These descriptors help identify the direction in which society is moving. The beliefs and values of society and consumers directly affect the way in which we seek and deliver personal health services. The role of the planner is to understand the decision-making process and the important variables in that process so as to make the organization or community health system responsive to the population it serves.

Both society and consumers place demands on all of our social structures and systems. They specify the limits of acceptability, accessibility, and demand for health services. Hence, the planner needs to monitor the pulse of society and consumer needs to be able to include these factors in the planning process.

The methods used to identify societal changes generally are not highly sophisticated. The simple process of reading the newspaper and being aware of other news media will give major clues to societal change, as previously noted in the discussion of content analysis.

Polls and studies of societal expectations are especially useful. To gain direct access to the consumer perspective, the planner may engage in household surveys or interviews of major community agents (key informants), although the environmental assessment process usually does not require this level of activity.

Patients or consumers of health services are becoming increasingly sophisticated in their use of the health system. They are demanding more input in the decision to consume specific health services, are more knowledgeable about health and the delivery of health services, and are paying an increased percentage of the health care dollar. The U.S. health industry has become much more "market driven" in the past decade, as deregulation and consumerism trends have impelled health organizations to become more aware of consumer behavior.

Understanding consumer behavior is the technique of psychodemographics combined with the analysis of "use behavior" of consumers. Psychodemographics relates to the social class, life-style, and personality dimensions of the consumer. One of the best-developed psychodemographic systems is the VALS (values, attitudes, and life-styles) typology developed by SRI International. The VALS database is structured to profile nine key life-styles,[5] developed from 20 years of continuous consumer polling. VALS has been used by the Kaiser Foundation Health Plan, America's largest Health Maintenance Organization, as well as by other health care companies. The underlying assumption in psychodemographics is that consumer preferences and behavior patterns are predictable. Knowing the relevant demographic characteristics of a community or target market allows the planner to translate demographic data into forecasts of market behavior.

Use behavior focuses on consumer attitudes, knowledge, use, and/ or response to specific products and services. Consumer use behavior can be analyzed by using an array of market research approaches (see Chapter 7, Market Assessment), together with the standard demographic and geographic approaches to examining consumer behavior and traits, to serve as the basis of market segmentation—the division of markets into distinct groups of consumers who will need, want, prefer, or use different products or services.

In addition to changes in societal and consumer beliefs and values, basic demographic trends are important to the planner. Because the demand for health services will change according to the demographics of a population, these trends are vital to the environmental assessment

---

[5] Arnold Mitchell. *Nine American Lifestyles: Who We Are and Where We Are Going.* New York, Macmillan, 1983.

process. The market assessment process places much greater emphasis on detailed analysis of demographics than does the environmental assessment process. The basic trends are of prime importance here.

Specific population descriptors that are most useful in health planning will vary with the organization doing the planning. A long-term-care facility or continuing-care retirement center (CCRC) is naturally more interested in the aged. A children's hospital would focus on demographic trends affecting children, youth, mothers of childbearing age, and families. Some of the specific demographic characteristics of a population that might be of interest include:

1. *Population size* (i.e., the community's total population). This provides a basic indicator of the demand on which planning is based.

2. *Age distribution,* or the proportion of the population within each age group. This is usually studied in five-year cohorts. Mortality and morbidity vary considerably within different age groups, as do acute and chronic diseases.

3. *Sex ratio* (i.e., the proportion of males to females in the population). This ratio has a direct effect on marriage, birthrates, and family structure. It also is linked to occupational patterns and longevity.

4. *Racial, ethnic, and cultural characteristics,* measured as proportions of the total population. Mortality and morbidity vary with different groups, as does the use of health care services.

5. *Mobility,* measured in terms of immigration and emigration over a specific time frame. Mobility data are important in tracing population changes and also indicate community stability.

6. *Education data* for persons 25 years of age and older. The level of education affects both the use of health services and individual behavior in preventing accidents and illness.

7. *Housing characteristics* may be important to the health planner because of their link to the general health status of the population. Such factors as inadequate, overcrowded, or high-density shelters are closely related to the onset of certain diseases and mental health problems. Housing also is related to the economic base of the community; such data as median home value and average rent yield useful economic information.

Within any given geographic area there may be several subcultures or societal groups. Joel Garreau[6] has suggested that various regions of the United States have very different cultures and value bases. In *The Nine Nations of North America,* Garreau profiles the life-styles and attitudes that are unique to each subregion of the nation. These groups may hold various attitudes, beliefs, and values and, therefore, very different patterns of seeking care. Such situations require the planner to examine each segment of the community or market to understand the service needs of the community and the buyer behavior associated with these needs.

Technology

Two types of technology are most important to the health planner: medical technology and environmental management technology. There is currently an explosion in medical technology, and a wave of more than 30 new diagnostic and theraputic devices is expected in the 1990s, according to a recent technology forecast.[7] Medical technology can change a community's health services delivery system, as well as affect the quality of services rendered within the system. Medical technology, especially new technology and high technology, tends to be costly.

There are three major types of medical technology of interest to the planner: equipment, drugs, and procedures.[8] Most planners' interest in and needs for information will focus on equipment and, to some extent, drugs. It is important, however, to be aware of the potential impact a change in medical procedures could have on the system and the practice of medicine. The number of surgical procedures now considered appropriate for ambulatory rather than inpatient treatment has had a major impact on the delivery of health services, for example, cataract surgery. As technology and medical practice advance, additional procedures that were once done only

---

[6] Joel Garreau. *The Nine Nations of North America.* New York, Houghton Mifflin, 1982.

[7] "New Technologies for Your Hospital to Consider: A Strategic Planning and Capital Budgeting Checklist." *Health Technology,* 1(4):138–148, July–August 1987.

[8] Gary S. Whitted. "Integrating Technology and Strategic Planning in Hospitals." *Hospital and Health Services Administration,* 27(4):22–40, July–August 1982.

on an inpatient basis will be reclassified and reimbursed on an ambulatory basis, for example, cardiac catheterization studies.

In addition to being costly, implementation of new medical equipment technology could have secondary effects: The new technology itself may create health problems. For example, the introduction of computerized axial tomography (a computerized diagnostic X ray technique) in the health delivery system brought a valuable diagnostic tool to the physician. The first impact of this technology was high capital costs, since the early models cost close to $750,000. A second immediate impact was the need to train or hire a new set of technologists to use this equipment. After the technology was used for several years, a new problem surfaced—the effect on health of the levels of radiation associated with its use. A similiar cycle may now be evolving with the widespread dissemination of magnetic resonance imaging (MRI) devices.

Historically, most health planners have addressed this type of technology only from a cost and marketing perspective. But, clearly, the issues of the impact of technology on the productivity of the delivery system and on the health status of the community also are important. This can easily be seen in the computer revolution, which has drastically changed the cost of health services and the way in which they are delivered. Unfortunately, few sources of data or assessment techniques are available to help the planner deal with these considerations.[9]

Economic Factors

Economic factors may be the most influential forces in the future of health care organizations. The failure of more than 50 hospitals in Texas between 1983 and 1988 may be more directly related to the economic weakness of the "Oil Patch" than any factor related to health policy or finance.

---

[9] Sources of information and reports on technology assessment include the Congressional Office of Technology Assessment, located in the Library of Congress, Washington, D.C., and the National Center for Health Services Research, U.S. Department of Health and Human Services, Rockville, Md.

The economic characteristics of interest when conducting an environmental assessment include the general vitality of the economy on a national or regional level, as well as the economic condition of the population being served by the organization undertaking the planning process. Economic analyses that focus on interest rates, growth, inflation, and expenditure of income are readily available from many sources.[10] Government, universities, and industry make these forecasts and predictions frequently and with various levels of detail. The planner's job is to find the one or two most appropriate analyses for use. These broad economic characteristics are of less importance to the planner in a community that is financially insulated from the cost of health care as a result of employment or insurance coverage. To the extent that the cost of care is shifted more directly to the consumer, these measures will become more important.

Economic characteristics of the population can be further categorized into income and employment. Specific income characteristics that are important to the health planner include per capita income, median family income, and number of persons below the poverty level or receiving public assistance. All of these are closely related to a population's ability to buy and use health services and are directly linked to employment levels. Other key economic characteristics are major sources of employment;[11] the natural resources that are available (e.g., water and land); and transportation systems, which affect the success of health care services.

Data on the economic characteristics of a community, as related to individuals, are frequently used as a surrogate measure of community health status and often help predict the use of a community's health services. Traditionally, income and the volume of health services consumed have had a direct relationship. Recently, however,

---

[10] Sources for the reports include the U.S. Department of Commerce and most business/economics journals. Most major newspapers publish an economic forecast edition for local areas in early January of each year. A number of state universities prepare an annual economic forecast.

[11] Employment levels are also important in terms of the health insurance provided by local employers. For example, if employers in a given area are competing for workers in a low unemployment market, they may use benefits such as dental or vision care as an incentive. Such coverages will have a definite impact on the use of these services in the community.

financing of health services programs for the poor has complicated this relationship. Variations in the relationship between income and use also depend on the type of service and the extent to which it is covered by third-party reimbursement mechanisms such as Medicare or private insurance. For example, since general hospitalization is covered by most third-party payers, the relationship between income and hospitalization is weaker than that between income and dental services, which are not as frequently covered by third-party payers.

Factors related to the financial and investment markets and the cost of capital are of prime importance to the organizational planner. The fact that almost 70 percent of the funding for hospital construction now comes from debt or the sale of bonds indicates the need for substantial analysis of these factors. Many hospitals and health systems have available in-depth economic analyses, prepared when the organization or system was securing new debt. These analyses, prepared by accounting firms and financial specialists, are important contributors to an analysis of the environment.

Environmental Factors

If twentieth century medicine is dominated by heart disease, today's number one cause of death, the twenty-first century may be medically focused on cancer. Increasingly complex biochemical interactions with the environment—mostly man-made—are suspected to be creating a wide range of cancer-producing toxins that will have widespread social and health impacts in coming decades.

Calculating the adverse health effects of air pollution, water pollution, toxic chemicals, hazardous wastes, and carcinogenic compounds is still in its infancy. Public health is becoming increasingly focused on environmental health issues, as medical care becomes more widely accessible. Thus far, most of the medical attention to environmental health has concentrated on specific diseases such as "black lung" and "brown lung," many of which are workplace acquired. Occupational medicine is searching for more linkages between worksite health and safety factors with disease. It will be a long-term process, and medical knowledge is still quite limited.

Environmental management technology is another type of technology that the health planner is concerned with. The specific technology that is used to cope with problems of air pollution, solid-waste disposal, water purification, and other environmental factors certainly can affect a community and its health needs. In this area, the health planner is dealing with issues of prevention rather than of diagnosis and treatment. The costs and impacts of environmental management programs are often of a much longer duration than those of health services technology, and their results may be just as important.

Environmental health is primarily a public-sector issue for the public policy analyst and public health planning. Few hospitals, outside of a limited number of academic medical centers, have any significant involvement in environmental health.

Although public health planners often have little jurisdiction over environmental management technology, they must attempt to address the issues arising from its development and use. They may find themselves confronted with issues that are related to environmental impact statements. Consequently, they should develop relationships with the environmental protection agencies in the community to enable them to assess the health impacts of environmental projects.

Political/Legal Characteristics

America's political/legal systems mirror many societal beliefs. It is through the political/legal process that society implements many of the underlying values of its people. Health care is a basic value of society, which presently consumes more than 11 percent of the gross national product. Of this, the government (federal, state, and local) pays more than one-third. Government has made many direct inroads to the health delivery system as the American people have come to depend on it for health services to the elderly. Government is likewise deeply involved in the protection of the public's health against communicable diseases and incompetent practitioners. As the number of elderly rises, Medicare is becoming one of the most significant factors in planning for health care organizations. The government's role in the regulation and financing of health services is increasing at the federal level, despite efforts to increase competition in the health industry and some trends toward deregulation at the state level.[12] While health industry trade organizations are actively involved in governmental affairs, these political/governmental actions are beyond the direct reach of health providers.

Political jurisdictions are key environmental influences for health organizations, because they have lawmaking, law enforcement, and taxation powers. Governments at all levels frequently influence the delivery of health services through regulation, financing of health services for certain populations, or direct delivery of services to a broad population. Unfortunately, the patterns of health services delivery rarely coincide with the boundaries of political jurisdiction. Most health planners—whether community or organizational—must assess multiple jurisdictions and multiple levels of government.

The policy direction and climate of the political jurisdictions in which the health organization is planning can often be assessed through the analysis of newspaper articles, interviews with key political figures, examination of polls taken within the area, and the like. A problem arises when the political directions of several adjacent or overlapping jurisdictions conflict. For example, a state may be moving politically in directions that differ from a county or city, yet may affect the planning process. The problem is worsened when a medical market area overlaps multiple states. This situation requires careful analysis to predict a general direction of the future political climate.

The health planner is especially interested in several categories of governmental action: provision and regulation of health services, regulation of workers, taxation and regulation of organizational structure, and zoning. Because the government regulates, finances, and provides health services, its actions have a major impact on all sectors of the health delivery system. Small changes in any of these areas can have a major effect on an organization or a community. These changes occur most frequently at the federal and state levels and

---

[12] Victor R. Fuchs, "The 'Competition Revolution' in Health Care," *Health Affairs*, 7(3):5–24, Summer 1988; Robert H. Brook and Jacqueline B. Kosecoff, "Competition and Quality," *Health Affairs*, 7(3):150–161, Summer 1988; and Jeff C. Goldsmith, "Competition's Impact: A Report from the Front," *Health Affairs*, 7(3):162–173, Summer 1988.

are relatively easy to chart. There are numerous publications that perform "government watching" services in the health arena.[13]

Regulation of what for-profit and not-for-profit organizations may or may not do as corporate entities has become increasingly important to the planner. The corporate structures being used by health services delivery organizations have diversified and become more complex in recent years. The trend toward corporate restructuring of the health industry has opened many new avenues and opportunities to health care providers and has made the job of the planner more complex. As these trends continue, however, governments will become more concerned with the competitive practices of the restructured industry. Proposals to limit the tax-exempt status of hospitals or to restrict access to tax-exempt bonds reflect the concern of some lawmakers that the health industry is becoming more of a business than a social institution.

Governmental policy plays a key role in human resources management, with many strategic and operational consequences. Regulation of the worker is important from two perspectives: its impact on the health of the population being served and its impact on the way in which health services can be delivered. The governmental agencies that regulate workers have become increasingly concerned with the health of the American worker. Occupational health and safety requirements have placed demands on health services delivery organizations to meet the needs of employees in industry. Likewise, many health workers are highly regulated through licensure, certification, and other governmental and nongovernmental regulatory processes. Employee safety is a governmental concern. Federal regulations for "universal precautions" to protect health workers against the threat of AIDS have had a major impact on health services delivery.

A final political/legal factor that is important to planners within specific communities is zoning. The ability to locate health facilities in specific areas has major implications for the success of those facilities and the health of the community. Frequently, concerns

---

[13] Two examples are *Health Care Competition Week*, Alexandria, Va., Capital Publications; and *The Blue Sheet*, Chevy Chase, Md., Drug Research Reports, a Division of F-D-C Reports, Inc.

for the nature of a neighborhood conflict with the needs for health services. As hospitals evolve towards multiunit "campuses" and ambulatory-care centers proliferate, zoning becomes a key issue in the location of facilities and services. Trends in this area are an especially important issue for facilities planners.

Federal Government actions in providing health care services for portions of the population are of major importance. The recent trend of shifting more of the cost of health services to consumers, physicians, and organizations is causing a substantial change in the health services delivery system. The shift from fee-for-service approaches to prospective payment systems has dramatically lowered Medicare payments to providers, pushing many hospitals into financial deficits. Rising medical costs under Medicare may bring payment reform for physician services. Recent policies that require higher copayments by Medicare beneficiaries mean that they must now pay for "catastrophic" medical care and drug benefits. These governmental policy shifts may constitute the most important political/legal factors in the next few years. The reactions of state and local governments to these moves will likewise be important trends for planners to track.

Health Status

As with the other dimensions of the environmental assessment, the planner's interest in health status depends on the organization and the perspective from which the planning is being undertaken. From a public policy perspective, the health status of the community is exactly the outcome that the planner is attempting to affect. Inclusion of health status is essential in a comprehensive assessment of the environment that public health policy seeks to influence, through disease prevention, interventive medical care for the medically needy, and biomedical research and development.

Community health status is also an important concern of the market analyst in a hospital or health organization. Although individual health services delivery organizations may have limited impact on the overall health status of a community, they can tailor programs and services to respond to below-average health levels found in the community, for example, high rates of uncontrolled hypertension or diabetes. Organizational market planning should include some general indication and forecast of health status in the environmental assessment.

There also are important conceptual ramifications to the planning process, based on how the organization defines "health" within this process. Because these ramifications tend to help define the scope of the planning process and are not always within the direct control of the organization undertaking the planning, health status is included as a part of the environmental assessment portion of the process. In many cases, it will be included as part of the market assessment of particular services, for example, cardiac care.

Measuring health status is an elusive and difficult task because neither a generally accepted definition of health nor a generally accepted model of health status exists in the United States. For measurement purposes, health status historically has been defined as the absence of disease. This definition has been used even though it is generally considered inadequate.

The definition put forth by the World Health Organization in 1948 is more comprehensive: "Health is a state of complete physical, mental, and social well-being and not merely the absence of infirmity." Although this definition is more conceptually adequate, its breadth complicates the process of making operational measurements of health status.

Examples of four models that can be used to define health status are described in the following list, beginning with the model narrowest in scope:

1. The *medical model* focuses on individuals and emphasizes the absence of physiological malfunction or disease. This fairly narrow model of health status uses a physician to determine the status of individuals, with the total absence of disease being the highest obtainable level of health.

2. The *epidemiological model* focuses on groups of individuals and views disease as the result of disequilibrium among agent, host, and environment. In this model, the measurement of health status is accomplished by identifying incidence and prevalence rates, which reflect disease dynamics within a population. Again, this model establishes the lack of disease as the highest level of health.

3. The *ecological model* uses a methodology similar to the epidemiological model but examines a wider range of variables and interactions. This model focuses on preventing illness and shifts the responsibility for health more to the individual than to the professional. It is more readily adaptable to the study of mental health problems than to the epidemiological model.

4. The *Georgia model*,[14] an ecological model, views health status as a function of four major variables: human biology, environment, life-style, and the system of health care organization.[15] It is depicted in Figure 15 in more detail. The Georgia model provides one of the most comprehensive approaches to health status, but it is one of the most difficult models to use from a measurement point of view.

Regardless of the model the health planner uses in defining health and health status, measuring the absence of health is an important part of the process. The three major measurements are mortality, morbidity, and disability.

Mortality is described by crude or overall death rates or death rates adjusted for age and sex, as well as cause of death. Infant mortality generally is considered a useful indicator of a population's health level because it is responsive to many conditions within the community (e.g., nutrition, availability of prenatal care, and education).

Morbidity measures the incidence and prevalence of a disease and other conditions.

Incidence is the number of new cases occurring during a specific period, usually one year.

---

[14] The title, *Georgia model*, is used because it was in Georgia that the model's concepts were first applied within a formal health planning program. The general structure seems to have originated in the work of the Canadian Marc LaLonde (*A New Perspective on the Health of Canadians,* Ottawa, Government of Canada, 1974) and has been eloquently advocated by a number of authorities in the United States, most notably Henrik L. Blum. See Henrik L. Blum, *Planning for Health: Generics for the Eighties,* 2nd Edition, New York, Human Sciences, 1981; and _____, *Expanding Health Care Horizons,* 2nd Edition, Oakland, Calif., Third Party Press, 1983.

[15] G. E. Alan Dever. *Guidelines for Health Status Measurement.* Atlanta, Ga., Department of Human Resources, Division of Physical Health, 1977.

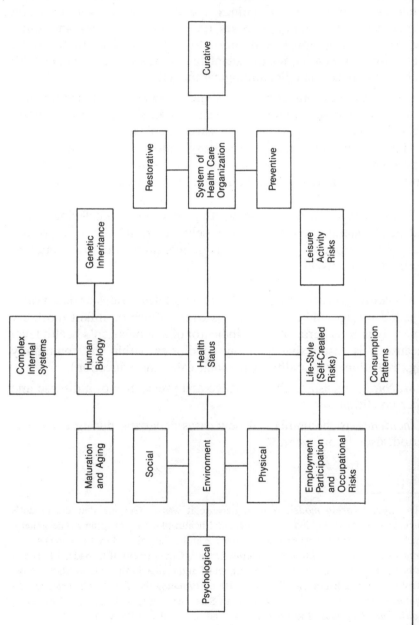

Figure 15   Georgia model to measure health status.

Prevalence is the number of cases in a given population at a single time (usually one day), such as the first day of the year.

Disability carries morbidity one step further by relating the effects of disease on the population. This usually is measured as either bed days or restricted-activity days. A *bed day* generally is a day in which an individual is bedridden because of a certain condition. A *restricted-activity day* is one in which an individual must limit some portion of normal daily activity because of a health condition.

Few attempts have been made to measure the positive rather than the negative aspects of health status because of the difficulties in defining "positive health." Attempts made to date usually have relied on subjective judgment or observation.

Health status characteristics are used both as direct indicators and as tools to create indexes of health status. When used as indicators, this information becomes a general descriptor; that is, the statistics are used as numerator data to build rates and ratios for morbidity, mortality, and disability. These data are then compared with similar statewide or national data. The following example illustrates the use of mortality rates as a health indicator in the creation of the Unnecessary Death Index (UDI) for the community,[16] which can be defined as:

$$UDI = DRA - DRE$$

where DRA is the actual death rate for the community and DRE is the expected death rate.

The DRE may be state or national data adjusted for the local population. The UDI can be calculated on the crude death rate, age-specific death rates, or cause-specific death rates; the index is simply a way to describe the local experience compared with state or national experience. The DRE also can be established as a normative definition of what is acceptable to the community. In this case, the UDI expresses the degree to which the death rate exceeds the standard desired by the community. It should be noted that when the index becomes a

---

[16] L. Guralnick and A. Jackson. "An Index of Unnecessary Deaths." *Public Health Reports*, 82(2):180–182, February 1967.

negative rather than a positive number, the community is doing better than expected.

Although health status characteristics have been used to develop indexes for aspects of health status, a generally accepted health status index, normally defined as a multicomponent composite indicator (i.e., a single number, such as the consumer price index, that attempts to express price increases), has not yet been developed. Several attempts have been made to develop a health status index, but none has gained wide acceptance in the United States.

Direct measurement is the ideal source of health status information. Health planners, however, may sometimes resort to proxy measures, of which hospitalization is the most frequently used. This proxy does not measure the actual health condition of the community in terms of a specific disease, but it does indicate the existence of conditions requiring care. Other proxy measures include patient days, number of physician visits, and number of medications or prescriptions issued during a given period of time.

Health status data often are available from the National Center for Health Statistics (NCHS) of the Department of Health and Human Services. NCHS publishes a *Monthly Vital Statistics Report* and an annual publication, *Vital Statistics of the United States,* which are the best sources of mortality and natality data (these data also are available from each state). The mortality data in these federal sources are very good in terms of total numbers of deaths, but their cause-of-death information is somewhat questionable. Morbidity statistics are available from several sources. Most state health departments gather some morbidity data in disease registries. The quality of these data varies widely from state to state and according to the type of disease being reported. For example, venereal diseases and tuberculosis are among the most commonly reported diseases, but information on them is not always reliable. Hospital discharge data usually include morbidity information coded to conform with the international system for classifying diseases. Morbidity data also are available on a survey basis in the National Health Interview Survey, conducted by NCHS on a sample of the nation's population. The data from these two sources are good at the national level, but the samples are too small to provide local-area estimates of morbidity. Disability data also are gathered as part of the NCHS health interview survey.

SUMMARY

Environmental assessment is the process of identifying the trends in society, technology, the economy, the environment, and the political/ legal arena that are external to, but impact on, the organization for which planning is undertaken. These S.T.E.E.P. factors will have an important role in shaping the assumptions on which policy decisions and market strategies will be developed. The planner's role in conducting an environmental assessment is to identify and forecast those factors that are most pertinent to the process. Although much of the information needed for an environmental assessment is available from secondary sources, it may be necessary for the planner to fill in some gaps.

The specific factors chosen for the environmental assessment depend on the focus of the planning process. Community health planning and organizational market-based planning will use similar processes but quite different foci. Health status may not be included in all environmental assessments, but it is a useful complement when linked to the policy or market objectives of the health organization.

CHAPTER 7

MARKET ASSESSMENT

Assessment of the market in which the health organization operates may be the most critical step in the planning process. Many important operational and financial decisions are influenced by assumptions about markets—demand, utilization, preferences, and market behavior. The development and mangement of health services, from the program or service level (micro) to regional or national systems (macro), are shaped by a baseline understanding of markets. Today's health organizations are shifting to product-line planning and portfolio management. It is essential to align product and operational strategies with highly tailored market analysis.

Market assessment is equally central to health policymaking. Decisions about the allocation of scarce resources, the solution of public health problems, or the provision of services to populations in need, are all influenced by analyzing market needs and patterns.

Beyond the local and regional market assessment, a broader understanding of the environment is essential for planning and health care management, as discussed in Chapter 6. The health industry is undergoing macroeconomic changes that will significantly affect the future of health services delivery. Approaches for assessment of these societal trends are presented in Chapter 6. Methods for forecasting both environmental and market trends are the focus of Chapter 10, Forecasting.

APPROACHES TO MARKET ASSESSMENT

Population-based Planning Versus Market Planning

Governmental agencies and public health organizations have traditionally conducted population-based planning, focusing on the health needs of a defined population. This approach is sometimes called community-based planning, at the heart of which is the public-private nature of health planning.

Population-based planning is typically used in the public sector for policymaking, program planning, and budget decision making. The intent of population-based planning is to provide an equitable approach to the allocation of scarce public resources so as to solve the identified health problems of a defined population. The outcomes of population-based planning are quantitive estimates of the prevalence of a disease and measures of unmet need for health services. The use of a population-based planning approach allows policymakers to construct funding formulas that are quantitatively derived and perceived as fair by the public. Population-based planning is used worldwide by public health authorities; it was systematically applied by Health Systems Agencies (HSAs) to develop regional health plans in the United States, as described in Chapter 3.

In recent years, the health industry has developed a strong interest in market planning. Many of the concepts, techniques, and tools are similiar to the approaches of population-based planning. For example, a planner may talk about the "population at risk" for a specific illness, whereas a marketer would discuss the "market segment" that is at risk for the illness. Although there are minor differences in the two approaches, the differences are more in style than method. This chapter uses terms and concepts from both marketing and population-based planning.

Market planning is essentially private sector oriented. It is the framework for competitive analysis. By definition, market planning recognizes and accounts for the impact of competitors on the market being served; it also recognizes the nature of the exchange relationship in health care. Populations at risk are also consumers with needs, some of which are being satisfied by competitors. It is essential to analyze the use of competitor services and to gain insights into the attractiveness of competing health organizations for well-targeted planning, marketing, and operational decisions.

The consumers or market for some health services can include both patients and providers (e.g., physicians, dentists). At yet another level, major purchasers of health services are also consumers of these services. Health care markets may be analyzed at three levels:

1. *Direct consumers* of service (e.g., patients)[1]
2. *Referral sources* (e.g., physicians, school health nurses, senior centers, diagnostic centers)
3. *Major purchasers* (e.g., employers, unions, government, insurance companies, HMO/PPO-managed health care plans)

MARKET DEFINITION

Market boundaries may be defined as broadly as the "community of solution"[2] and as narrowly as the ZIP Code or household. Marketers use the concepts of *publics* or *segments* in a similiar fashion. A public or segment is a subgroup of the population that has a real or potential need for a service or product and has the resources to exchange with the organization for benefits received.[3]

Setting market boundaries and defining markets are a combination of demographic analyses and market planning objectives. Although the community of solution concept is difficult to define, this does not render the concept useless.[4] Defining potential markets is a multidimensional task that integrates a number of planning criteria, including:

---

[1] For a discussion of derived demand, see Roice D. Luke and Jeffrey C. Bauer, *Issues in Health Economics,* Rockville, Md., Aspen Systems Corp., 1982, p. 337; see also Russell C. Coile, Jr., "Physician Channeling," *Hospital Entrepreneurs Newsletter,* Rockville, Md., Aspen Publishers, February 1988, pp. 1–5.

[2] National Commission on Community Health Services. *Health Is a Community Affair.* Cambridge, Mass., Harvard University Press, 1966, pp. 2–9.

[3] For a more complete discussion of the relationships between geography and health, see John Eyles and K. J. Woods, *The Social Geography of Medicine and Health,* New York, St. Martins, 1983.

[4] Philip Kotler. *Marketing for Nonprofit Organizations.* Englewood Cliffs, N.J., Prentice-Hall, 1975, p. 22.

1. Population at risk for the disease or condition
2. Population in need who actually have the disease or condition
3. Future consumers not now in need but who are forecasted to acquire the disease or condition within a specific time frame (e.g., five years)
4. Travel time and convenience, as defined by transportation studies and market research
5. Ability to pay, defined by payer source
6. Referral source (e.g., within 30 minutes of the office location of a member of the hospital's medical staff)
7. Pyschodemographic factors believed to influence demand and service-seeking behavior
8. Competitors' market, defined as the percent of the population in need who are currently served by another service or facility

SERVICE AREAS

Historically, market planning in the health industry has been based on the concept of service areas—those geographic areas having a population that can be expected to use the services offered by a specific facility. Many of the service area or market definition approaches have their roots in retail marketing theory.

The concepts of service areas and market segmentation are quite similiar. Both seek to identify homogeneous subgroupings of people who are logical markets for certain services. Health planning has, since World War II and the Hill-Burton Program, placed its focus on *beds* as the service unit for which geographic market planning was conducted. In today's complex market, as health organizations shift to product-line planning, analysis is shifting to the microlevel. Health organizations must be able to identify the service area and market for every product and service as the focal point of analysis.

Market Definition Methods

Two methods can be used to determine the market area for a given facility and its programs or services.

The first is the *boundary approach,* which seeks to establish a single continuous line around the service area of a given facility.

This approach identifies the equiprobability boundary between two facilities—that is, the line identifying the point at which a patient has equal probability of visiting either facility. Figure 16 illustrates the boundary, or equiprobability, approach. For example, contour 7 indicates a 70-percent probability that persons living along that line will use the services of facility A, and a 30-percent probability that they will use a different facility. The equiprobability boundaries are shown by the heavy lines in the illustration; they signify that people living along these lines would be equally likely to use facility A or facility B. Although equiprobability is a common boundary-setting approach, not all methods use it.

The second method is the *nonboundary approach,* in which the patient load for a given facility is defined and described in terms of geography but no specific boundary is established for market planning purposes. Figure 17 illustrates the relationship of two facilities using the nonboundary approach. The shaded part represents the geographic area from which facility A draws its patients, and the hatched area signifies the territory for facility B patients. Patients in the overlap area may use either facility.

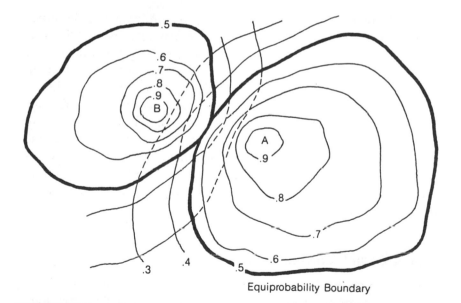

Equiprobability Boundary

Figure 16   Equiprobability boundaries.

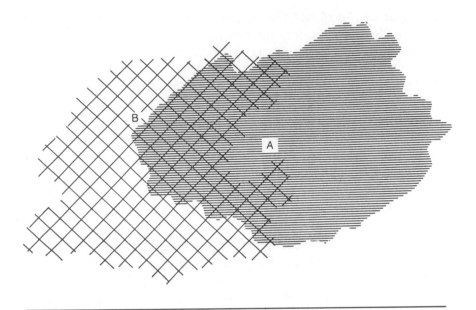

Figure 17   Nonboundary service area.

Neither of these approaches is inherently preferable to the other. The nonboundary approach best describes reality, but it does not provide a mechanism for allocating specific geographic areas to a facility. On the other hand, the boundary approach, if used in the equiprobability sense, does not identify the total area from which a facility's patients are derived. If a boundary is drawn at the outer fringe of the area from which a facility obtains its patients, the description of that area is complicated by the fact that many patients inside it will cross the boundary and use other facilities. In the process of conducting service-area boundary studies, the market analyst may first use the nonboundary approach and then place boundaries on that service area to identify major subareas.

Patient Origin/Market-Share Analysis

Whenever possible, service areas should be established on the basis of patient-origin data, since they directly reflect the geographic area from which a patient load is derived. For market-share analysis of inpatient services, hospitals may use admission or discharge data; the latter is preferred because it is more complete and more likely to be accurate. Using a facility's own data provides a crude indicator of market penetration, but without similiar data on competitors, the analysis will be incomplete (see the section on Competitor Intelligence in this Chapter, pp. 215-220).

Market-share analysis can be conducted using two complementary approaches, which are based on two different perspectives: that of the market (community) and that of the health organization (service sponsor).

1. *Relevance Index*: The first approach—relevance—seeks to identify the degree to which a community depends on a facility. The relevance index can also be called a market-share analysis, according to Folland.[5] The data required to complete a relevance index involve a communitywide patient origin study. The first step in the process is to construct a hospital discharge matrix similiar to that shown in Table 12. The matrix arrays hospitals in the columns and tracts in the rows, with each cell indicating the number of discharges from a specific hospital to a specific census tract. For example, according to Table 12, there were 50 discharges from hospital B to tract 3.

The relevance index indicates the percentage of all discharges from a specific hospital to a certain tract. Using data from tract 3 and hospital B, the relevance index can be calculated as follows:

$$R = \frac{D}{TT} = \frac{50}{100} = 0.5(100) = 50\%$$

where

$\quad$ R $\;=$ Relevance index
$\quad$ D $\;=$ Discharges from hospital B to tract 3
$\quad$ TT $=$ Total discharges from tract 3

2. *Commitment Index*: Both the relevance and commitment indexes show a relationship between a specific geographic area (e.g.,

---

[5] Sherman T. Folland. "Predicting Hospital Market Shares." *Inquiry*, 20(1):34–44, Spring 1983.

TABLE 12   Hospital Discharges by Census Tract (Sample Community, 1989)

Tract	Hospital A	B	C	Total
1	40	40	10	90
2	70	60	30	160
3	30	D 50	20	TT 100
4	60	30	40	130
5	100	20	50	170
Total	300	HT 200	150	650

census tract, ZIP Code) and a specific hospital or health organization. Both analyses rely on communitywide patient origin data.   The commitment index is calculated as follows:

$$C = \frac{D}{HT} = \frac{50}{200} - 0.25(100) = 25\%$$

where

   C = Commitment index
   D = Discharges from hospital B to tract 3
   HT = Total discharges from hospital B

The commitment index of 0.25 indicates that one-fourth of hospital B's discharges were to tract 3; in other words, hospital B derives 25 percent of its patient load from that tract.

With these two indexes, a market analyst could conclude that residents of census tract 3 are fairly dependent on hospital B for inpatient services, but that hospital B is not so dependent on census tract 3. Table 13 shows a complete set of relevance and commitment indexes for this example.

TABLE 13   Relevance (R) and Commitment (C) Indexes (Sample Community, 1989)

Hospital

Tract	A		B		C		Total
	R	C	R	C	R	C	
	Percentages		Percentages		Percentages		Total Percentages
1	44	13	44	20	12	7	100
2	43	24	38	30	19	20	100
3	30	10	50	25	20	13	100
4	46	20	23	15	31	27	100
5	59	33	12	10	29	33	100
Total		100		100		100	

The relevance index has its highest utility from a market-wide perspective. This index, however, can be calculated only when a full set of discharges for all facilities or provider organizations is available, or when a systematic and reliable sample of discharges is available for all providers.

In contrast, the commitment index can be used by a single facility or health care provider to calculate its market dependence on specific geographic subareas. The market analyst will find this a particularly useful approach in conducting marketing activities and planning market strategies.

Other Methods of Service-Area Definition

A number of other approaches have been used to develop service areas. The following examples are illustrative.

1. *Health Service Areas*: The National Health Planning and Resources Development Act of 1974, Public Law 93-641, established the concept of health service areas. The geographic regions are designated by the governor of a state and the Secretary of Health and Human Services and are based on population, availability of resources, and other factors necessary to provide health services for residents. The underlying notion is that each service area is a relatively independent medical trade area that provides most specialized and routine health services to residents of the area. Most health service areas are multicounty and conform to political boundaries. In California, for example, 14 health service areas comprise from 750,000 to 2 million residents. Although P.L. 93-641 has been phased out, a number of states continue to use health service areas for a variety of planning and regulatory functions.

2. *Regional Model*: Patient-origin data may be used to define service areas, based on levels of care provided by organizations within the larger region. Anthony Rourke,[6] in one of his Nebraska studies,

---

[6] Anthony Rourke. Personal communication.

proposed three service areas: *base service areas,* which are served by hospitals that meet most routine inpatient needs; *peripheral service areas,* which are served by hospitals with more specialized services that are not always available in base-level hospitals; and *regional service areas,* which are served by hospitals with highly specialized facilities and advanced levels of care.

3. *Catchment Area*: In mental health planning, the concept of a "catchment area" has evolved. Since no universal definition of a community has been developed, mental health authorities adopted a range of population size—from 75,000 to 200,000—to define a community. This normative notion is intended to equalize access to mental health facilities and services by all within the catchment area and across a region composed of several catchment areas. The concept largely ignores political boundaries and assumes that mental health problems are fairly evenly distributed among all population groups. Because of the looseness of this definition, it has been applied in a variety of ways and to a variety of services. For example, Illinois based its catchment areas on the distances from mental health hospitals, whereas Pennsylvania's areas conform strictly to county boundaries. In Arizona, catchment areas are based on both geographic area and distance from a mental health center.

The catchment area concept has many problems. Census data are based on political boundaries; where these are ignored by catchment areas, population analysis is problematic. Population shifts require an adjustment of boundaries. Population density is another problem; what should be done when the population is very sparse or very dense? For example, 75,000 people could be spread so widely that one community mental health center would not be accessible to everyone in the catchment area.

4. *Census Tract Allocation*: In a competitive marketplace, one approach to service-area definition is to designate census tracts to particular providers as the basic units for defining each facility's service area. Thus, if four hospitals received patients from a single census tract, the responsibility for that entire census tract would be assigned to whichever hospital received the highest proportion of patients. This approach is simplistic, but can provide a graphic overview of how facilities share a market. Obviously, caution is needed in generalizing from this method.

5. *Patient-flow Matrix*: The patient-flow matrix proposed by Morrill and Earickson[7] is a highly sophisticated approach. It assumes that use of the nearest hospital is an ideal, and then measures the deviations from this standard. Their Chicago study clearly shows, first, that the service areas, as normally defined, are gross misrepresentations of the facts. For example, 35–40 percent of all patients crossed boundaries to use a facility other than the hospital that was most convenient. Second, service areas cut across normal community and political boundaries, making population forecasting difficult. Recent developments in small-area data, beginning with the 1970 census, now make it easier to define service areas on the basis of patient origin. Few communities, however, have the geographic base file necessary to convert ordinary maps into locational grids and then to plot residential addresses on these grids.

6. *Retail Gravitation*: An approach that works well in areas of low-population density is the application of Reilly's law of retail gravitation.[8] This technique identifies the breaking point between service locations on the bases of the distance between locations and the size or capacity of the services involved. The boundary point is identified as follows:

$$B = \frac{M}{1 + \sqrt{S}}$$

where

B = Boundary between facilities X and Y in miles from Y
M = Miles between X and Y
S = Size or capacity of X divided by the size or capacity of Y

This technique merely identifies the breaking point between facilties X and Y and does not circumscribe a complete boundary

[7] Richard L. Morrill and Robert Earickson. "Locational Efficiency of Chicago Hospitals: An Experimental Model. *Health Service Research, 4*(2):128–141, Summer 1969.

[8] Laurence S. Klugman. "The Law of Retail Gravitation (Reilly's Law) Applied to Eastern Shore Hospital Service Areas." Philadelphia, Pa., Health Planning Research Services, 1975. Mimeographed.

around either. It thus provides useful information with a minimum of data for low-density population areas.

7. *Travel-Time Zones*: One of the simplest approaches to delineating service areas is to set travel-time standards for specific services and then to establish boundaries around a facility based on these standards. This approach differs from the others in that it is based on a description of what should exist within a community rather than what actually does exist. Travel criteria may be established by the use of market research, for example, as specified acceptable travel time by consumers to reach a particular service or facility. For public health facilities and services, travel time criteria may be established by policy consistent with the accessibility and availability criteria, for example, that a Board of Health may establish for a given community.[9]

8. *Geopolitical Boundaries*: Poland and Lembecke[10] apply a method similar to that described in item 4, in that they use census tracts, townships, or minor civil divisions as the basic units of analysis and then allocate these to various facilities. The allocation is done by computing the percentage of total admissions from a geopolitical unit that went to each facility and then drawing a single continuous equiprobability line around each facility. If the facility under study has a clear majority of the patients from a certain geopolitical unit, the boundary line is drawn through that unit on the basis of transportation networks and population centers. This technique avoids some of the inaccuracies identified in the approach outlined in item 4.

9. *Relevance Index for Geopolitical Areas*: The approach defined by Griffith[11] is based on relevance indexes and uses the census tract, township, or minor civil division as the unit of analysis. A relevance index is computed for each facility, and the service area

---

[9] Robert Marrinson. "Hospital Service Areas: Time Replaces Space." *Hospitals*, 38(2):52–54, January 1964.

[10] E. Poland and P. A. Lembecke. "Delineation of Hospital Service Districts: A Fundamental Requirement in Hospital Planning." Kansas City, Mo., Community Services, 1962. Mimeographed.

[11] John R. Griffith. *Quantitative Techniques for Hospital Planning and Control.* Lexington, Mass., Lexington Books, D. C. Heath and Co., 1972, p. 75.

for a given facility is determined by plotting its location on a map and shading the various units, based on the relevance index. An arbitrary definition of relevance could be made, such as high relevance equals 75 percent or more, moderate relevance equals 40–74 percent, and low relevance equals less than 40 percent. The concept is quite flexible and can utilize the ideas of primary and secondary service areas. In addition, the total population being served by the facility can be computed by multiplying the relevance index for each unit by the total population of the unit and summing the products of all the units. This approach is one of the most useful for a service-area analysis.

This list of methods is by no means exhaustive, but it does represent the approaches that can be taken to determine service areas. The availability of data frequently will determine which method can be used, but the planner should use the relevance index approach whenever possible, because it most clearly defines the service-area concept.

Facility/Service Location Analysis

The market analyst's concern with geography and space also is based on the need to evaluate the location of new health services. Since accessibility is one of the major criteria for evaluating the location of new health services, this discussion will deal primarily with accessibility criteria.

Accessibility can be broken down into four major components, with each affecting the desirability of a location for a given health service. Often, the decision to locate a health service at a given point is a function of trade-offs among these four aspects of accessibility.

1. *Spatial accessibility* is measured in terms of physical distances. The distance a patient is willing to travel for service depends on the urban or rural setting and the degree of specialization of the service involved. Health care consumers are more willing to travel great distances for specialized services than for routine services. Individuals in urban areas tend to be indifferent to distances up to

approximately two miles, while individuals in rural areas tend to be more sensitive to the distance factor.[12]

2. *Temporal accessibility* often is measured in terms of travel time. This factor seems to have a greater effect on outpatient and primary care than on specialized ambulatory or hospital care; however, it may affect the choice of a hospital when more than one facility is available.[13] Another temporal factor—waiting time—may be as important a factor as travel time in the selection of a facility for services such as obstetrics.[14]

3. *Social accessibility* is measured in terms of the population characteristics that may affect the use of a given facility. For example, sex, religion, race, and social status have been shown to affect accessibility to given facilities.[15] These factors, however, are at best difficult to measure, and few generalizations can be drawn as to how they affect the location of health services. Market research can identify consumer preferences of specific market segments, delineated by various social factors, and these consumer wants may be programmed into the facility location determination.

4. *Financial accessibility* may be affected by a facility's rates, provisions for free care, and third-party payer agreements. As Health Maintenance Organizations (HMOs) and Preferred Provider Organizations (PPOs) selectively channel more patients to "preferred providers," the impact of contracts will influence financial accessibility. Government-funded patients are being channeled into selected facilities in a number of states, and the Health Care Financing Administration is promoting Medicare HMOs. Medicare PPOs may be established in the next three years; five pilot projects were initiated in 1989. The more a service population depends on a limited number of

---

[12] J. E. Weiss, M. R. Greenlick, and J. F. Jones. "Determinants of Medical Care Utilization: The Impact of Spatial Factors." *Inquiry,* 8(4):50–57, December 1971.

[13] M. S. Blumberg. "The Effects of Size and Specialism on Utilization of Urban Hospitals." *Hospitals,* 39(10):43–47, May 16, 1965.

[14] James Studnicki. "An Analysis of the Spatial Behavior of Obstetrical Patients in Baltimore City." Doctoral dissertation. Baltimore, Md., Johns Hopkins University, 1972.

[15] Health Planning Research Services, Inc. "A Guide for Evaluating the Location of a Health Service." Fort Washington, Pa., 1976. Mimeographed.

sources of financing for care, the more these considerations become important in deciding where to locate a facility.

The above factors are important in locating health facilities, but no uniform theory describes how they should be applied in a location decision. One methodology that attempts to take accessibility into consideration was developed by Health Planning Research Services, Inc. of Phildadelphia. This model consists of a five-step procedure based on temporal and spatial accessibility:[16]

Step 1: Determine the service areas of present facilities or services, based on travel-time standards. This step establishes the percentage of the population within the acceptable travel time of each service or facility.

Step 2: Determine the best location for a new service—"best" being the point that will minimize the average travel time or distance for the residents of the area under consideration.

Step 3: Determine the service area for a new facility or service located at the "best" location. This is accomplished by using the travel-time standards established in step 1.

Step 4: Determine the impact of the proposed facility or service on the aggregate travel time of the total population or the target market segment from a defined geopolitical area. Aggregate travel time is defined as the total amount of time a population would travel if each individual made one trip to the nearest service site.

Step 5: Determine the impact of the proposed facility or service on the total aggregate travel distance of the population, defined as the total distance traveled if each individual in the population made one trip to the nearest service or facility location.

This methodology has proved useful in rural and suburban settings but tends to break down in urban areas because of the close proximity of facilities and service settings.

Although this discussion has focused on accessibility as the major factor in determining facility and service locations, other market

---

[16] Ibid.

factors must also be considered. Facility location often is affected by such factors as zoning; availability of desirable sites; political and legal constraints; availability of ancillary services (e.g., sewerage, water, power); cost of available land; and environmental, physical, and aesthetic factors.[17]

MARKET ANALYSIS

For market planning purposes, it is essential to define who is a potential customer of the health organization's services. To define the market, the organization must define its *market offer*. Kotler and Andreasen[18] define a market as "the set of actual and potential consumers of a market offer." The term *consumers* includes buyers, clients, adopters, users, and responders. In the health care market, consumers may be individuals, families, groups, organizations, employers, third parties, governmental agencies, insurance plans, and managed-care organizations such as Health Maintenance Organizations and Preferred Provider Organizations. Even physicians, as the purchasing agents on behalf of individuals and families, may be considered health care consumers.

The concept of *market offer* is simply a term of reference, which could include a tangible good, service, program, idea, or anything that might be offered to a group of responders. Complicating the definition of a market offer for a health service is that "health" is an intangible product.

According to marketing expert Theodore Levitt,[19] the marketing of services is different from the marketing of goods, in that goods are tangible—they can be seen, tasted, touched, and tested. Often this can occur before a purchase decision has been made. A service such as health care is an intangible product that can seldom be experienced

---

[17] A discussion of specific site factors can be found in O. B. Hardy and L. P. Lammers, *Hospitals: The Planning and Design Process,* Germantown, Md., Aspen Publishers, 1977, Chap. 8.

[18] Philip Kotler and Alan R. Andreasen. *Strategic Marketing for Nonprofit Organizations.* 3rd Edition. Englewood Cliffs, N.J., Prentice-Hall, 1987, pp. 236–237.

[19] Theodore Levitt. "Marketing Intangible Products and Product Intangibles." In: *The Marketing Imagination.* New York, Free Press, 1983, pp. 94–97.

or tested in advance. When prospective customers cannot taste, test, feel, smell, or watch the product in operation in advance, what they are asked to purchase is, simply, a promise of satisfaction. Thus, a market offer of a health service is an implicit promise to the patient (consumer) of an improved state of health as a result of the service or treatment. Also assumed in the market offer is that the provider, at least, will do no harm to the patient, for example, the physicians' Hippocratic Oath. Consumer satisfaction with the market offer will occur when the patient's expectations for an improved or restored state of health occur.

According to Kotler and Andreason,[20] consumers in the market for something have three characteristics: an interest in the product or service, the ability to transact if they wish to receive the product or service, and access to the product or service when they wish to purchase it.

The potential market is the set of consumers who profess some level of interest in a defined market offer. Consumer interest is insufficient to define a market. As price is attached to the offer, potential consumers must have the economic ability to afford the purchase. It is axiomatic in market behavior that the higher the price, the fewer the consumers. The size of a market is a function of both the interest level and the ability to transact. Market size is further affected by access to the product or service. The market offer is contingent on the time and place that the product or service will be available to consumers. Access factors make the market smaller. The market that remains is the available market, defined as the consumers who have interest, ability to transact, and access to a particular market offer.

Three additional characteristics define a market. The first is qualification. In some market offers, the organization may establish some restrictions regarding whom they will transact with. For a hospital emergency room service, for example, qualified consumers will be those with an urgent need for medical attention or with an acute medical emergency. Nonqualified consumers seeking medical

---

[20] Philip Kotler and Alan R. Andreasen. *Strategic Marketing for Nonprofit Organizations*, p. 237.

attention for a nonurgent condition may be referred to a community physician or ambulatory-care center.

The second characteristic, which will further refine the definition of a market, is the concept of the served market. This is the segment of the qualified available market that the organization attempts to attract and serve. To continue the illustration of the market for emergency room services, the served market would be those consumers whose need for urgent or emergency medical services meets the definition of the hospital's license for level of emergency care; for example, Level I—basic emergency, Level IV—trauma, and so on.

The third characteristic narrows the definition to those consumers who respond to the product offer and are actually served—the penetrated market. Figure 18 integrates the preceding discussion of markets. In the illustration, the ratio of the served market is 1:10; that is, only 10 percent of the potential market is qualified, available, and the preferred market that the organization attempts to serve. Of those in the served market, half the consumers in the illustration actually respond to the market offer and are served. Thus, the penetrated market is 5 percent of the potential market.

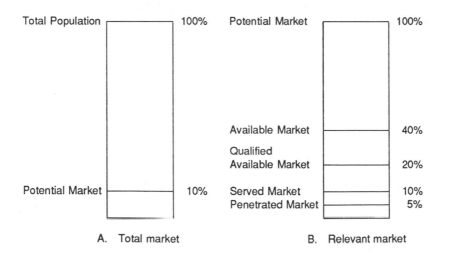

SOURCE: Adapted from Philip Kotler and Alan R. Andreason, *Strategic Marketing for Nonprofit Organizations,* 3rd Edition, Englewood Cliffs, N.J., Prentice-Hall, 1987.

Figure 18 Levels of market definition.

Estimating Market Demand

Constructing estimates of market demand requires a sequence of analyses that selectively focus the marketing program and resources on that segment of the market which is qualified, available, and that the organization prefers. Further, it is necessary to estimate the share of the served market that the organization will actually penetrate by calculating the market share of the organization and its competitors.

Total market demand is not a fixed number. It reflects a number of conditions that are continuously in flux, such as the state of the economy, level of personal disposable income, consumer knowledge and awareness, level of promotional investment, product features, consumer incentives, distribution and availability of the product, price, and product alternatives.

1. Market minimum may be stated as the minimum level of the served market; that is, those consumers who are qualified, available, and actually consume the product or service without any promotional marketing investment. This base level of demand will occur without any demand-stimulating expenditures by the organization.

2. Market maximum may be considered the level of the served and penetrated market that is the maximum which may be stimulated by marketing expenditures of the organization. This is a theoretical level beyond which additional marketing costs or promotion yield little additional demand.

3. Marketing sensitivity of demand is the distance between the minimum and maximum market levels.

4. Expansible market demand is that segment of the potential market that is quite sensitive to marketing expenditures and relatively expansible with promotion.

5. Nonexpansible market demand is that portion of the potential market that is relatively unaffected by marketing expenditures; for example, emergency room users who will come to the hospital for treatment of serious injuries or trauma regardless of the level of promotional investment.

Defining markets with these concepts sharpens the marketing focus of the organization and improves the marketing return on investment.

The health organization operating in a nonexpansible market can take that market's size (the level of primary demand) for granted and focus its marketing and promotion on attracting a desired market share (level of selective demand).

Developing Market Forecasts

The market forecast is the estimated level of market demand resulting from the organization's marketing expenditure in the service area. This is seldom a precise number. Estimates can vary widely, depending on the assumptions that are factored into the forecast equation. Market analysts should prepare a range of estimates that reflect varying levels of demand as the assumptions are manipulated.

The most common of the market forecast techniques is the chain ratio method. This method is calculated by multiplying a base number, for example, service area population, by a succession of percentages that lead to an estimate of the served and penetrated market. The percentages reflect various assumptions about consumers' market interest, availability, ability to transact, meet qualifications, and who will select the organization's product or service over alternatives offered by competitors. For example, hospital A is developing an "express care" center adjacent to the hospital's emergency room (ER) to provide routine health services to those ER patients whose need for health care is urgent but who do not require full emergency medical care. The market potential has been estimated by the chain ratio method as follows:

Total number of residents of service area population	1,000,000	
Percentage who require emergency care	$\times .10 = 100,000$	
Average emergency room visits by those needing emergency or urgency care	$\times 2.5 = 250,000$	
Hospital A's market share of regional demand for emergency care	$\times .20 = 50,000$	
Percentage demanding emergency care whose needs could be met by express care	$\times .50 = 25,000$	
Percentage willing to accept express care as a lower cost alternative to emergency care	$\times .90 = 22,500$	
Percentage able to pay or covered by insurance for express-care services	$\times .75 = 16,875$	

This chain of numbers shows the market potential for those who may use the new express-care service to be 16,875 visits per year. The revenue potential that may be realized through a market offer for express care may be calculated by using the following formula by Kotler and Andreasen[21]:

$$R = NQP$$

where:

    R =   total potential revenue
    N =   number of buyers in the specified market who might buy under the given assumptions
    Q =   quantity purchased by an average buyer
    P =   price of an average unit

Thus, if there are 16,875 potential users of express care at a market offer of $50 per visit (a discount of 50 percent from the hospital's price of $100 for an emergency room visit), and 25 percent of express-care consumers also purchase an ancillary service (lab test or X ray) at $25 per unit, the total potential revenue would be $949,218, derived as follows:

Potential market, estimated visits/year = 16,875 × $50
  per visit   = $843,750
Plus purchase of ancillary service by potential market
  × .25 = 4,218 × $25 per ancillary service   = $105,468
    Total revenue potential/year   = $949,218

Estimating Segment Market Demand

Marketing strategy begins with the selection of a target segment. The target market consists of those individuals or organizations who are most likely to purchase services. The process through which a market is studied and broken down into groups, for selecting one or more target markets, involves strategic choices. Market segmentation,

---

[21] Ibid., p. 243.

according to Eugene Johnson et al.[22] is the process of dividing the service market into separate subsets, or segments, of buyers. This enables the health organization to concentrate its marketing efforts on a distinct subset of the market it prefers to serve, or to develop different marketing approaches for each market segment. In some ways, service providers have a unique advantage, because each service can be tailored to the precise needs and expectations of an individual customer.

The most frequently used bases for segmenting markets are demographic, geographic, psychographic, and purchaser-volume characteristics:

1. *Demographic segmentation* subdivides a market on the basis of age, sex, income, occupation, marital status, education, health status, or other demographic variables. Preferred market segments for hospitals and health care organizations may include women, the aged, upper income, chronically ill, and the like.

2. *Geographic segmentation* subdivides a market into different locations. It may vary considerably for different services. Providers offering cardiac surgery may market to a region defined as all consumers within two hours travel time of the hospital, while other services, such as emergency care, may be marketed to a much more limited service area.

3. *Psychographic segmentation* subdivides a market using combinations of consumer variables such as life-styles, attitudes, values, and expectations. Health organizations may offer an "executive woman" health promotion program targeted at working women with personal incomes in excess of $25,000 per year who are concerned with fitness and health enhancement, or market a "new-family health program" to families married or living together for less than five years.

4. *Volume segmentation* subdivides a market based on service usage. Purchasing patterns and preferences of heavy, medium, and light users are analyzed. For each volume segment, the health organization will identify what distinctive market advantage it may

---

[22] Eugene M. Johnson, Eberhard E. Scheuing, and Kathleen A. Gaida. *Profitable Service Marketing*. Homewood, Ill., Dow Jones Irwin, 1986, pp. 118–119.

have with each class of customer, and focus its market strategies to the target segments' needs, for example, rapid return-to-work emergency medical service for small- and medium-sized employers referring employees for work-related injuries.

The purpose of market analysis is to identify preferred market segments and to approach them using an array of marketing strategies, which fall into three basic categories:

1. *Undifferentiated marketing* uses the same marketing approach for all consumers; for example, billboard advertising, which attests that "hospital A cares about its patients." This approach may raise the level of consumer awareness of the health organization, but it will probably be inadequate to convince many consumers to use its services unless the market offer is made more specific and is focused on the needs and wants of a target market segment.

2. *Concentrated marketing* directs the organization's services and marketing efforts toward a single market segment. Focusing on a key market segment may be the most efficient use of limited marketing resources; for example, hospital A concentrates its marketing efforts on the elderly through enrollment in a senior membership plan, provision of senior discounts, free screening programs, and mobile health services to retirement communities and senior centers.

3. *Differentiated marketing* is a more complex strategy for developing different services and marketing approaches for the separate market segments that the organization prefers to serve; for example, a home health agency may focus its routine health services to the chronically ill, target homemaker services to seniors living alone, and provide high-tech in-home services to AIDS patients.

The market analyst may use one or more of the following methods to estimate market segments:

1. *Sales volume distribution*: To forecast the demand of a particular market segment, the market analyst may conduct studies of demand distribution by the target market segment; for example, women of childbearing age. In this manner, the analyst can calculate use rates based on past years' demand for the service(s) under analysis.

Factoring out the service-use experience of the target market segment from the universe of all users of the service provides a basis on which to predict future demand, using the chain ratio approach. Ideally, the analyst will have at least three years of experience to analyze, and the data will be current at least to the past year. Rapidly changing market conditions and reimbursement policies in the U.S. health industry have made data older than three years of less value for predicting future patterns.

Charting the geographic location of past users is a helpful visual aid to analysis, using hand methods (e.g., map pins) or computer-aided mapping with available microcomputer software. The analyst should use caution to not overstate the results of this limited analysis in forecasting future demand. Variations in demand could be the result of past marketing or advertising, be driven differentially by location of key physician offices, or fail to reflect the impact of new competitors. These and other factors may be incorporated into the equation, using the chain ratio approach.

2. *Single-factor analysis*: In this approach, the market analyst attempts to identify a single factor that reflects the market behavior of the target segment, for example, education. The health organization would then distribute its marketing effort in those geographic areas having higher concentrations of the desired characteristic. Identifying the single factor that is most closely associated with the higher demand can be accomplished by using techniques of multivariate analysis. Alternatively, or as a complementary approach, market research with individuals (e.g., household surveys) or small groups (e.g., focus groups) may provide the indicator the analyst seeks.

3. *Multifactor analysis*: Reliance on a single factor for market strategy is risky. Using multivariate analysis on the database, the market analyst may use two or more factors to derive use patterns for market forecasting, for example, education and income. The multifactor analysis may be adjusted in a number of ways; for example, some factors may be weighted instead of taking a simple average. When factors do not lend themselves to expression as a percent in the chain ratio approach, these may be converted using a scale (e.g., 1–10 points) and then used to weight the factors. The goal of multifactor analysis is to construct an index that effectively describes present use patterns, which may be used to determine

the market potential of different geographic areas or population subgroups for various health services. The indicators can also be adjusted for distance, using travel time or political boundaries as surrogate variables for access.

Estimating Market Share

Beyond estimating potential demand, the health organization will want to know the total number of services that are being provided (total market demand) in the defined service area. In today's competitive environment, such data are not always easy to obtain (see Chapter 9, Information Systems and Data Sources).

The organization must attempt to estimate the total services that are being provided in the defined market area by all competitors. These may be obtained from competitors directly, a trade association, or a state agency to which all competitors report sales and use. When standardized data on all competitors are not available, these must be estimated by using various techniques of competitor intelligence (as discussed in the following section on Market Research).

Comparing the organization's volume with that of competitors should reflect past experience (for example, increases or declines) relative to competitors, using the most current data that are obtainable. Health market analysts and planners need to calculate their organization's share of the total market, the share of the served market, and the share of the market relative to the leading competitor or top three competitors.

MARKET RESEARCH

Health organizations have made relatively little use of original market research in the past. This attitude is changing. Rapidly shifting market conditions, rising competition, and increasing risk in the business environment have combined to increase the value of market research in health planning.

The following approaches are illustrative of market research techniques that are available to the health planner and market analyst:

1. *Consumer opinion survey*: This traditional technique has been updated with modern methods of telecommunication and computerization. The telephone survey is perhaps the most effective method for eliciting consumer opinion where questions are relatively unstructured, and is quite efficient in the conduct of short-structured interviews. Even "robot surveyors" are now using computerized telephone calls, where interviewees respond to questions using their touch-tone telephones. Mail surveys yield relatively low returns (3–15 percent response rate is commonplace) but at low cost. The response rate on mail surveys may be improved by using incentives for interviewees, or by endorsement by outside organizations, for example, trade associations, Chambers of Commerce.

Market researchers understand that consumer behavior is a complex phenomenon. Tapping into that behavior with multivariate analysis and models of behavior can yield deeper insights from consumer opinion surveys. Some researchers use paired comparisons of attitudes to rank the most important factors associated with consumer behavior.

2. *Panel studies*: Health care's "Framingham Study," now ongoing for more than 20 years, is an example of a panel study that can yield market insights. The VALS survey by SRI International has now been in continuous existence for more than 15 years. Researchers who wish to monitor the behavior of a target market over time can use several measures to analyze and predict future market performance. Databases such as VALS can be used for comparison with a local panel of consumers, for example, a sample from the hospital's service area, by matching the local panel with the national panel for key demographic characteristics, and comparing attitudes and behavior.

3. *Experimentation*: Survey research is handicapped by its reliance on consumer opinion, which may or may not be related to the underlying factors that influence consumption decisions. Health organizations can make more creative use of experimentation to determine consumer behavior. Experimental opportunities exist across the wide range of services and products supplied by the health organization. For example, an organization interested in testing the effect of incentives could conduct a market direct mail campaign for a service such as an ambulatory-care center. Using an experimental approach, different incentives could be tested, for example, discount

coupons, free initial visits, or free repeat visits, while a control group would receive only the direct mail promotional materials with no incentives.

4. *Focus group interviews*: Using groups of 8–12 consumers who are usually (but not always) homogeneous, researchers facilitate a group discussion of a specific set of issues. Although the results of focus group discussions are not generalizable to the entire market segment they represent, the results are often a candid insight into consumer perceptions and expectations regarding a service, product, or organization. Focus groups are useful in testing product concepts, proposed media campaigns, packaging, incentives, convenience, and other consumer factors regarding existing or new services/products. The results of focus group discussions can be used in generating lists of questions or factors to consider in more complex opinion surveys or research programs.

5. *Sampling approaches*: Kotler and Andreasen[23] suggest several approaches for low-cost sampling to obtain useful data. Convenience sampling studies people coming and going in the organization, for example, patients, family members, service delivery personnel. These groups have more information about the health organization and may be biased in their opinions, but it may be argued that they are also groups that are part of the organization's target market, from whom insights would be very valuable.

Snowball sampling uses participants in current opinion surveys to suggest "others like them" who could be contacted. This second group might be expected to match the primary group in many characteristics, but would probably have relatively little information about the organization that might bias their opinions.

Piggybacking takes advantage of another organization's research investment and piggybacks additional questions. Several national research organizations, such as SRI International, Louis Harris, the National Opinion Research Center of Lincoln, Nebraska, and others, regularly conduct omnibus studies to which local questions may

---

[23] Philip Kotler and Alan R. Andreasen. *Strategic Marketing for Nonprofit Organizations*, pp. 228–229.

be added. Volunteers and students provide other resources for conducting market research.

COMPETITOR INTELLIGENCE

The entire field of competitive strategy, a popular subject in today's business press and health industry journals, assumes that firms have all the facts about their competitors in hand. Unfortunately, this assumption is way off the mark, in health care as well as in private industry. There are few sources to which a market analyst or health care strategist can turn to scrutinize a competitor's income statement, distribution channels, or marketing strategies. Sometimes the most difficult part of competitor analysis is collecting accurate and reliable intelligence.

In the past 10 years, the health industry has been deregulated as one-third of the states have eliminated certificates of need, and the level of competition in many health care markets has become intense. As competition has risen, the routine disclosure of data to competitors, which was once commonplace, has been markedly limited. Most hospitals and health organizations today consider their data and strategic plans to be proprietary. Few hospitals and health organizations would now make a major strategic move without considering its impact on competitors, yet information on competitors is often scant.

Corporate Intelligence Gathering

Competitor intelligence is defined by Fuld[24] as "highly specific and timely information about a corporation." While the term *intelligence* conjures up images of corporate espionage, an estimated 95 percent of information on competitors is available in the public arena.

Intelligence gathering has roots in a number of very different yet complementary disciplines, including sales prospecting, library science, statistics, accounting, sleuthing, and puzzle-solving. Never

---

[24] Leonard M. Fuld. *Competitor Intelligence: How to Get It; How to Use It.* New York, Wiley, 1985, pp. 9–10.

underestimate the contribution of common sense and ingenuity to competitor intelligence. For example, counting the parking spaces in the parking lot of a competitor's new ambulatory surgery facility can yield a rough estimate of expected patient flow.

Puzzle-solving implies the ability to take what on the surface appear to be unrelated pieces of information and fit them together to form a complete picture. For instance, the following facts come to light:

1. A vendor reports to hospital A that a competing equipment manufacturer has taken an order from hospital B for magnetic resonance imaging (MRI) equipment to be delivered in the coming 6–12 months.

2. From the medical staff of hospital A comes a copy of a prospectus being circulated to community physicians on staffs of both hospitals A and B to participate in a limited partnership to acquire and operate an MRI facility by hospital B.

3. Hospital A's real estate broker makes calls to several commercial real estate brokerages in town and discovers that hospital B has taken an option to lease space in a new office building.

4. The department manager of hospital A's radiology department brings in a help-wanted ad for a manager of a new freestanding MRI facility; although the ad provides only a post office box, the mail address is in a large city, which is the corporate headquarters of hospital B's parent company.

These random pieces of information become intelligence when collected and analyzed. Clearly hospital B is developing a freestanding MRI facility as a joint venture with its medical staff. The prospective location of the new imaging facility is known, and the target date when the new facility will open can be forecast. Now hospital A can develop a strategic response before hospital B can open its facility and while there is time to explore alternatives, for example, a joint venture between the two hospitals or with a competing facility.

Many sources of information for competitor intelligence are available to health organizations, hospitals, and health systems (as discussed in Chapter 9) from public governmental sources, industry associations, market analysts, and the media. Competitor intelligence is not limited to the process of sifting through public reports and online databases. There are a number of more creative approaches to competitor intelligence, including:

1. *In-house experts*: Those who work for the health organization in the area of interest may be the most informed—and most accessible—expert sources of industry trends and competitor intelligence. These include department managers, physicians, and staff specialists. For many hospitals, physicians with privileges in competitor facilities are excellent sources of information on competitor performance and plans. Department managers maintain awareness of competitor activities through professional associations, peer contacts, and hiring employees who formerly worked for competitors. Former employees of competitors are also informed sources who should be consulted. Remember that intelligence gathering is built on many small and often unrelated pieces of information. These in-house experts may not have the "big picture," but they can contribute many pieces of the intelligence puzzle.

2. *Financial sources*: Except for states in which uniform financial accounting is required, obtaining financial information about competitors is a difficult process. A national database of Medicare cost reports is now commercially available through Health Care Investment Analysts (HCIA) in Baltimore, Maryland. (See Chapter 9). HCIA can produce customized reports on competitor financial performance.

Financial information may also be obtained from credit reports, financial ratios, and expert interviews. Credit reports concentrate on payment record and debt, not on income or operating expenses, and are designed for purchasing agents, not researchers. Credit reports, however, may provide useful information on areas such as sales and net worth, reports of financial difficulty, length of payment to vendors, and court cases outstanding. Firms such as Dun & Bradstreet and TRW offer credit information.

Financial ratios are the tools of bankers and financial analysts. When the market analyst has limited pieces of financial information, standard industry ratios provide a formula for filling in the missing information. Standard financial ratios for the health industry are well established. A health organization's accounting firm or financial adviser can provide key ratios of interest to the market analyst, with advice on adjustments to ratios; for example, in a rate-regulated state, to reflect unique state or local market conditions. The limitation of ratios is that they are designed to reflect industry averages and will only approximate the behavior of smaller, larger, or otherwise unique competitors, for example, a children's hospital. Financial experts can provide the shading and qualifications to the dry world of financial ratios. For each financial ratio, specialists can provide additional information. Access to these experts can be facilitated by the health organization's chief financial officer, purchasing agent, and business office manager. These inside experts have industry contacts with outside experts, including bond underwriters, bankers, financial analysts, purchasing agents, suppliers, contractors, insurers, and trade associations. Interviewing the experts is a valuable adjunct to competitor financial analysis. Outside experts can suggest modifications of ratios to more accurately rate the financial strengths and weaknesses of competitors.

3. *Yellow Pages/city directories*: The *Yellow Pages* and city directories are two potent corporate intelligence sources. Each can reveal a health organization in a new light, as it presents itself to the market. Do not neglect *Yellow Pages* in outlying areas. Many health organizations are now advertising in markets that are more than one hour or 50 miles from their home base location. Ads are designed to encourage self-referrals by patients seeking alternative service sources and often include "800" toll-free telephone numbers. Advertisements in the *Yellow Pages* more frequently include specialized services and qualifications of competitors. Use the cross-index to ensure that the listing of competitors is complete. Market analysts should check physician listings as well. Physicians are making widespread use of the *Yellow Pages* as one of the few professionally appropriate vehicles for marketing. Physicians and medical groups may be presenting themselves as "institutes" or "health centers" specializing in the care of particular diseases or customers (segment marketing). Look also in "business to business" directories in those areas where they are available. Competitors may be advertising under health-related categories to volume purchasers, employers, insurers, and third-party administrators (TPAs). Business-to-business directories will cover a larger trade area, 50 miles instead of 35, for example. *Yellow Pages* are also available online. The Electronic Yellow Pages are available from the information firm Market Data Retrieval. City directories,

the cross-directories, list individuals and firms by location, and can be used to fill in information about competitors, for example, businesses neighboring the location of a competitor's diagnostic imaging facility. All of a competitor's varied businesses and service locations will be found together in the alphabetical directory.

4. *Visual sightings*: "Eyeballing" a competitor's facility can provide important competitive information. The number of parking spaces in a a competitor's urgent-care center may be factored into a ratio of parking spaces to users, to estimate demand and the capacity of the new facility. A day spent counting patients coming in and out of a competitor's facility can provide a rough estimate of use. Three days spent taking license plate numbers in the physician parking lot, and charting the time that cars were left in the parking lot, can provide valuable information on key physicians' involvement with competitors. Real estate signs on a competitor's new medical office building will often provide a description of the total square feet. A call to a real estate broker can provide more information. A visual tour of a competitor's facility may provide information on use and demand, waiting time for service, and activity. A walking tour of a competitor's facility can provide visual confirmation of whether the facility appears to be neglected, renewed, or used at capacity. Often, equipment can be eyeballed and noted. Aerial photography can provide a visual overview of competitor facilities to complement the street-level view. The aerial view can identify competitor space constraints and opportunities on the competitors' campuses. Mapping the competitor's off-campus locations, both support and service, can provide insights into how the competitor defines its market and future expansion plans.

5. *Literature review*: The professional literature and trade publications can often provide information about new programs and advanced practices of competitors. Information on new programs or management innovations is often telegraphed by articles written by the staff of competitor facilities. The same holds true for the medical literature, which may announce research findings on new treatments or tests of new equipment in the competitor's facility.

6. *Professional conferences/seminars/trade shows*: Annual meetings, conferences, and seminars can be sources of information on new programs and advanced practices of competitors. Management

or medical staff from the competitor facility may participate in seminars or conferences, in which they may provide specific information on new services, advanced medical practices, or management innovations. Even when these educational programs are conducted out-of-state, tape recordings or written proceedings are often available.

7. *Help-wanted ads*: Information on the status of competitors' work forces and programs is regularly available in the help-wanted classified ads that competitors place in the local media, as well as ads for managers or technical specialists that are advertised in professional journals. These can be tracked by the health organization's human resources management department.

An intelligence file should be developed and maintained for each competitor in the health organization's market area. A comprehensive assessment of competitors should be periodically conducted as background for strategic and product-line planning.

SUMMARY

Health care has become a highly competitive industry. Health policymaking must cope with an era of limited resoures. Health planning today reflects this evolving market environment. The development of sound strategy and public policy must be based on a fine-grain analysis of market behavior. The heart of health planning is market analysis. Market strategy must be developed in the context of broader macroenvironmental factors. Market assessment is a complex and sophisticated process today, as the focus of health planning shifts from beds to product lines. Definition of the target markets for each service and product is the challenge of market analysis, using all the modern tools of planning and research. Supplementing traditional approaches of population-based planning, the tools of market research and competitor analysis can provide new insights into market behavior. All the information derived from the process of market assessment is the background against which the health organization can develop effective market strategies. In a competitive health industry, it will be important to position the organization and its services in ways that are tailored to satisfy the expectations of health care consumers—patients, physicians, and major purchasers.

CHAPTER 8

DECISION ANALYSIS

Decision analysis methods are tools that assist planners with quantifying and qualifying uncertainty. Most organizational decisions are made under conditions of uncertainty. Strategic planning is uncertainty compounded, since the alternatives are based on a scaffolding of opinions, assumptions, and forecasts. The role of the planner in strategic decision making is to illuminate future implications of choices that are made in the present.

The evolution of the health industry in the past decade is a saga of choices made under uncertainty. There have been winners and losers. Two California health care companies provide a case in point. Three attorneys, who purchased a distressed hospital in Southern California in the early 1970s, expanded their holdings into National Medical Enterprises (NME), a Fortune 500 company with assets worth hundreds of millions of dollars in acute hospitals, acute psychiatry, and long-term care. At approximately the same time, Fred Wasserman, a Ph.D. faculty member at the University of California in Los Angeles (UCLA), parlayed his knowledge of the Health Maintenance Organization (HMO) concept into the nation's second largest HMO, Maxicare, and then saw his company fall victim to over-expansion, with the stock value plummeting from $15 to $1 in one year. Both companies, launched in Southern California during the same era, expanded nationally, but one succeeded and one failed. NME saw the decline of acute hospitals coming; it sold hospitals, cut losing divisions, and focused on high-profit speciality

221

niches like psychiatry. Maxicare expanded too fast; it purchased two competitors in less than a year, then could not service the huge debt load for the acquisitions. Both companies made "bet-your-company" decisions under conditions of high uncertainty, but the success of NME contrasts with Maxicare. The case illustrations underscore the necessity for decision analysis when making strategic choices.

ROLE OF DECISION ANALYSIS IN HEALTH PLANNING

Different models of the future provide an enhanced understanding of the consequences of making decisions today so as to achieve an objective in succeeding months or years. The role of decision analysis is to clarify the implications of choosing from among alternative strategic paths to gain the organization's objective.

In the decision-making process, various methods of decision analysis are used to overcome the following problems:

1. Quantitative factors are usually preferred by decision makers, but data are seldom fresh or complete; decision analysis is often necessary to supplement quantitative information with qualitative data and opinions.

2. Competing stakeholders have their own goals, which are often conflicting; decision analysis can identify and clarify the goals of important interested parties to the decision.

3. Formal analysis makes explicit all the critical variables that are involved in strategic decisions, making them available for critique and modification.

4. Uncertainty is present in all decisions; the role of decision analysis is to define the relative uncertainty that is involved in key assumptions and critical variables.

DECISION ANALYSIS APPROACHES

Rational Decision Making

The term *rational,* suggest Hartle and Halperin, presupposes a decision process that is dominated by logical reasoning. Conclusions are deduced from evidence and inferences made, based on facts not emotions.[1] Rationalism is inherently logical, orderly, and objective, making decisions that are based on observed data and comprehensive information.

Lindblom[2] outlines the rational decision-making process. Faced with a given problem, rational persons

1. First clarify their goals, values, or objectives, and then rank or otherwise organize them in their minds.
2. They then list all important possible ways of, and policies for, achieving their goals.
3. They investigate all the important consequences that would follow from each of the alternative policies.
4. At which point, they are in a position to compare the consequences of each policy with their goals.
5. Finally, they choose the policy with consequences that most closely match their goals.

The rational model is familiar, accepted, and widely used across disciplines and problem sets. Decisions made rationally are comparable to past and concurrent decisions that were reached by using the same model. The emphasis on efficiency and economy have made the rational model the dominant decision-making pattern for large organizations.

Despite its popularity and widespread application, the rational decision-making process has some significant limitations. As critiqued by Lutrin and Settle,[3] "rational" decision makers suffer from:

---

[1] Terry W. Hartle and Michael J. Halperin. "Rational and Incremental Decision Making: An Exposition and Critique with Illustrations." In: Michael J. White et al. *Managing Public Systems: Analytic Techniques for Public Administration.* North Scituate, Mass., Duxbury Press, 1980, p. 125.

[2] Charles Lindblom. *The Policy-Making Process.* Englewood Cliffs, N.J., Prentice-Hall, 1968, p. 13.

[3] Carl E. Lutrin and Allen K. Settle. *American Public Administration: Concepts and Cases.* Palo Alto, Calif., Mayfield Publishing, 1967, p. 95.

1. An unwillingness or inability to make decisions
2. A tendency to make snap decisions on the basis of incomplete or superficial evidence
3. Accepting the most readily available short-range solutions
4. Making false analogies between old and new experiences
5. An over-reliance on past experience
6. Relying on preconceived notions
7. "Group think"

The shortcomings of the rational model are evident in Lutrin and Settle's critical assessment of the rational decision-making process. Even identification of the problem depends heavily on the conceptual framework of the decision makers. The world view of the organization and dominant mind-set of its senior management often restrict the definition of the problem to familiar territory. The failure of U.S. corporations in the automobile, electronics, and copier industries in the 1970s to recognize the threat of foreign competition until their market share eroded badly is a case in point.

Articulation and ranking of goals are hardly objective processes, even when quantified criteria are used. Both the selection and weighting of the decision screens are influenced by the dominant values of the decision makers. Individual as well as organizational values flavor the process. As Lutrin and Settle note,[4] "there is not one set of goals, [but] there are as many as there are actors in the decision process."

Assuming that the first two steps in the rational model are carried out as objectively and logically as possible, the rational development of strategies and alternatives is limited by time, resources, and imagination. There is seldom time for in-depth consideration of more than a few alternatives. Decision makers are capable of absorbing and using only limited amounts of information. Thus, more complex decision matrices might be a waste of the planner's time. Finally, the imagination of the decision makers places limits on the range of alternatives that can be considered. Few planners, for example, would suggest that a children's hospital should consider an alternative future

---

[4] Ibid., p. 127.

without children, even though a declining number of young children in the 1990s is widely forecast by demographers.

Selection and implementation of strategies, the final stage of the rational decision model, is only partly a rational process. Organizational politics, private agendas, personal ambitions, interpersonal and interorganizational conflicts, turf wars, personal biases, and the unpredictable are all part of the decision milieu.

Despite its limitations, the rational model continues to dominate organizational decision making and strategy. Planners and market analysts are thoroughly trained in the rational process. Professional journals and associations showcase examples of the rational model at work. The rational decision process is, and will continue to be, the most widely used organizational process for problem solving and strategy formulation.

Systems Analysis

The systems approach, described in Chapter 1, is an extension and elaboration of the rational decision model. Systems thinking ensures a systematic examination of the relevant factors in making organizational decisions. In the planning context, systems thinking provides a conceptual framework within which to articulate goals, array data, identify possible decision choices, and assess probabilities of successful implementation.

Managers (and planners) seldom devote the time required to understand the complex systemic relationships that make up the structure of their organization and their marketplace. Kiefer and Senge[5] of the Massachusetts Institute of Technology are advocates of systems thinking. They define a system as the web of interrelationships between elements that work together for some purpose. Kiefer and Senge observe that systems theorists have discovered a number of common properties across a wide range of social and biological systems. One of these is the tendency of a system to resist attempts

---

[5] Charles F. Kiefer and Peter M. Senge. "Metanoic Organizations: Experiments in Organizational Innovation." In: *Systems Thinking and New Management Style Program.* Cambridge, Mass., Massachusetts Institute of Technology, Alfred B. Sloan School of Management, 1986, pp. 8–9.

to change its performance, even though changes would be "for the better." At the root of this problem is a systems quality called compensating feedback; that is, efforts to increase performance are fully compensated for by the system as a whole. Even though there may be a short-term improvement, it will be localized, and the overall system will remain unchanged.

The second characteristic of systems, according to Kiefer and Senge,[6] that is not understood by rational decision making is the concept of leverage points. Systems theorists consider organizations as being highly complex, with thousands of interconnected and compensating relationships that, over time, bring the organization into a stabilizing equilibrium, or homeostasis. The practical effect of this interconnectedness is that problems are complex, not simple, in their causes. Simplicity is the solution to these complex problems, but changes must be focused on the key leverage points that are at the vortex of the situation. Often, the leverage points may be found far from the symptoms, which will require more thoughtful, time-consuming, and complex analysis than many organizations will tolerate. The search for leverage points draws planners and managers into a more systemic view of the organization, which differs fundamentally from the symptom-response orientation of the rational model.

The systems approach has its own limitations. Armstrong[7] advocates two cautions when using the systems approach in long-range forecasting: "First, one should examine objectives before considering ways of solving a problem; and, second, one should begin by describing the system in general terms before proceeding to the specific." These ideas are illustrated in Figure 19. The arrows indicate time priorities and the boxes indicate the separate steps of the approach. Thus, the first step is to identify the system's goals, and the last step is to develop an operational program. The approach moves from the conceptual to the operational levels, and from goals to means.

---

[6] Ibid., pp. 9–10.
[7] J. Scott Armstrong. *Long Range Forecasting: From Crystal Ball to Computer.* 2nd Edition. New York, Wiley, 1985, p. 14.

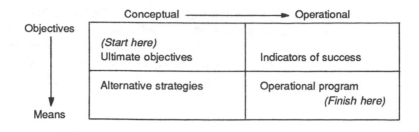

Figure 19 The systems approach.

As previously stated, the first step in the systems approach is to identify the ultimate goals. This analysis should start at the highest conceptual level. No consideration should be given to alternative strategies during the initial phase, Armstrong warns. Planners should set up a separate time period for this analysis and write a separate report on goals. A word of advice: review the goals to ensure that they do not imply strategies. The identification of goals may be the most important step in decision analysis. If this step is ignored or done too quickly, the planner risks moving to strategies prematurely without clearly understanding the real goals to be reached.

One technique for identifying goals is the stakeholder analysis. The first step in a stakeholder analysis is to identify all the groups or individuals who may be affected by a change in the system. Brainstorming can assist in identifying stakeholders. Expert consultants will know who should be factored into the analysis. Finally, publicizing that changes are being considered may surface stakeholders who previously were unaware or uninvolved in the decision process. With a list of interest groups in hand, the planner can identify the goals of each segment. Survey research and the use of key informants from among stakeholders can accelerate this step in decision analysis.

Defined goals provide a basis for establishing explicit success indicators. Procedures must be developed to measure how changes in the system will affect each of the goals. It is desirable to find measures that can be quantified, and better yet, accurately quantified.

Planners should prepare multiple strategies for meeting the goals. This is true even when the planning assignment is to assess the probablity of success in implementing strategy X. Decision makers should also be exposed to alternatives Y and Z before deciding on strategy X. Use of experts can speed the identification of potential strategies. Experts can further assist by ranking the options, using various decision criteria (based on the goals). Ideally, the alternative strategies should differ substantially. This becomes more difficult when dealing with narrowly focused problems. The risk of limited strategic choices is worsened when all expertise comes from specialists in the problem area. Specialization is a double-edged sword. Strategies advanced by specialists will be highly relevant, but they may lack innovation.

Selecting from among alternatives begins with reducing potential strategies to a manageable number. This can be done by rating the alternative strategies against each other, using the indicators of success as criteria. Decision makers can set minimum acceptable levels of success as the threshold criteria. This approach is known as *satisficing*. Subjective unit weighting scales can be used as a group of decision makers screens the alternatives, namely, a rating scale of 0–10. More promising strategies can be illustrated with scenarios (see Chapter 10), which can be presented to decision makers for their reaction.

Further screening may then follow, using the same procedures as described above. Since it is more difficult to make choices at this stage of decision making, key indicators should be translated into a common denominator, for example, dollars. This requires the various goals of stakeholders to be assessed, essentially by using a cost-benefit analysis. If a single alternative is not preferred, the organization can always pursue multiple strategies, at least for a time, with one or more strategies serving as contingency plans for the dominant strategy.

TECHNIQUES OF DECISION ANALYSIS

Cost-Benefit Analysis

One of the most powerful tools for strategic health planning is cost-benefit analysis. Simply stated, suggest Thomas and Chapman, the process of cost-benefit analysis is to sum all the benefits that can be enumerated as resulting from a decision and then to subtract them from all the costs.[8] These costs should include both the direct and opportunity costs of the investment. Planners should also factor indirect costs into the analysis. These can be significant from a stakeholder's point of view, for example, the cost of transportation to gain access to a service. Costs must also include any losses that are attributable to the decision. The difference between benefits and costs is net benefits, which must be evaluated in competition with net gains from other uses of resources, for example, compounded capital at current or projected rates of interest.

Collecting data is one of the most difficult phases of cost-benefit analysis. Three types of data include:

1. *Source data:* Ideally, source data can be obtained directly from the project or organizational subunit for which a decision or plan is being considered. Alternatively, source data may be obtained from similiar projects conducted by the organization, comparable sponsors, or other outside sources. A thorough literature search can reveal valuable data on costs and benefits. Interviews with experts, convening of expert panels, and site visits to comparable projects can yield relevant information. Data may be developed through survey research, for example, surveying or interviewing a national sample of comparable projects.

2. *Pilot studies:* Where possible, the organization may initiate the development of one or more alternatives on a pilot basis, to evaluate the concept or project on a small scale. These data are then extrapolated to the scale of the final project to provide decision makers with a sense of the potential benefits and costs. As a caution, pilot studies should be used with restraint in cost-benefit analysis. The "learning curve" may disadvantage a small, new project, while a longer term effort could potentially overcome the limitations of a start-up. Conversely, a "honeymoon" effect could suggest a promising future for a project or concept that might not be sustainable over time. Pilot studies are most useful when they are conducted at multiple sites

---

[8] Henry B. Thomas and Jeffrey I. Chapman. "Cost-Benefit Analysis: Theory and Use." In: Michael J. White et al. *Managing Public Systems: Analytic Techniques for Public Administration.* North Scituate, Mass., Duxbury Press, 1980, p. 292.

by various sponsors. Single pilot efforts should be used with care in generalizing to large-scale applications.

3. *Simulation:* These studies, either computer-based or mechanical, can provide valuable insights into the potential costs and benefits of a strategy or project. They are much less costly to the organization than a pilot project but do not provide the hands-on experience of a real-world enterprise. A simulation study models the experience of a real test of the concept. Simulation allows planners and decision makers to change base assumptions and to see the effects.

Cost-benefit analysis assumes that an individual or organization that is willing to invest capital gives up potential present gains to achieve a higher return over time. If benefits are simply added up year by year, the concept of present value is ignored. Simply stated, individuals and organizations tend to prefer present benefits over future benefits. This preference reflects both an emotional quality and an economic reality. Money placed at interest will result in capital growth over time. Thus, an investment that will be worth $1,000 a year from now may be worth $950 today, if the organization could invest the $950 at 5 percent tax-free interest for a year. The formula for computing the present value of any income (or cost) stream received over N periods of time can be calculated with the equation

$$PV = \sum_{i=1}^{N} \frac{C_1}{(1+r)i}$$

where

C_1 = the consumption benefits in period i
r = discount rate

To calculate the present value of a project that lasts N years, it is necessary to first determine the discounted value of the benefit and cost for each year and then to add up the values. The general decision principle of cost-benefit analysis is that decision makers will favor the alternative in which the present value of benefits exceeds the present value of costs.

Payoff Matrix

One of the simplest techniques of decision analysis is the classic payoff matrix, which, according to Bunn,[9] consists of a list of possible actions that could be taken, a list of the possible outcomes that could occur, and a straightforward evaluation of each decision-outcome pairing.

This is represented as a payoff matrix

	a_1	a_2	. . .	a_m
0_1	y_{11}	y_{12}		y_{1m}
0_2	y_{21}	y_{22}		y_{2m}
.				
.				
.				
0_n	y_{n1}	y_{n2}		y_{nm}

where

a_j is the decision variable, which can take m discrete values, indexed by j. Therefore, the list of possible actions is $(a_1, a_2 \ldots a_m)$. 0_i is the outcome variable, which can take discrete n values, indexed by i. Therefore, the list of possible outcomes is $(0_1, 0_2. \ldots 0_n)$.

The payoff matrix as a decision model considers only two factors at a time, and there are no rules as to how the outcomes might be determined. Outcome data could be based on pilot projects, literature reviews, expert opinions, or sample studies. Payoff matrices do not provide for any representation of intricate action-outcome relationships. The method works well with factors that can be represented by money. It does much less well when representing qualitative factors, such as consumer satisfaction. Even with a simple payoff matrix, the problem of selecting the optimal action is not always obvious. Choices involving relative risk can be enhanced by assessing the probabilities of various outcomes.

---

[9] Derek A. Bunn. *Applied Decision Analysis*. New York, McGraw-Hill, 1984, pp. 16–17.

Minimax and Maximax

As Bunn[10] notes, the analyst can apply decision rules to narrow the choices. For example, the analyst can search for outcome dominance to eliminate choices that are clearly inferior to other alternatives. If a decision maker prefers more to less, then actions that yield larger outcomes will always be preferred to actions that result in less. Dominance testing can prune the number of choices for analysis, but will still leave a payoff matrix to analyze.

Maximin is a decision rule that focuses on those actions which result in the worst possible (minimum) payoff. The action for which the worst payoff is highest is then selected. Thus, the decision maker maximizes the minimum payoff. The maximin rule targets "worst-case" scenarios.

At the other extreme, the maximax decision rule looks at the best of the possible outcomes. The decision maker searches the payoff matrix for the action that yields the largest possible payoff. The danger is that actions associated with highest yields (payoff) often carry the greatest risks (losses).

Risk Analysis

Today's health care organizations are learning the value of risk analysis. In the cost-reimbursement era (1965–1983), hospitals were low-risk organizations from a financial or entrepreneurial perspective. Since the advent of prospective payment systems (PPS) and the emergence of a pro-competitive environment, hospitals and health organizations began to initiate diversification ventures that exposed them to substantially more business risk. After experiencing some early disappointments, many health organizations have begun to more systematically analyze the risks to which they might be exposed through business development and joint ventures.

Assessing risk is becoming relatively commonplace among health planners and health care analysts. Risk analysis is now a major field of inquiry, complementing other forms of decision analysis; it can be complex. In the previous section, minimax and maximax focus

---

[10] Ibid., pp. 32–33.

only on the two extremes. Other measures that distribute payoffs, such as means and modes, do not factor risk adequately. Consider the following choices, where both A and B have the same expected value and would be equally probable:

Option A: Receive $5 with probability 1/2
Lose $5 with probability 1/2

Option B: Receive $5,000 with probability 1/2
Lose $5,000 with probility 1/2

Most analysts would consider option B to be more risky, even though both A and B have the same probability.

As Bunn notes, while most analysts focus on financial risk, there are important types of risk other than high losses that also are of interest to decision makers. Some risk analysis focuses on the probability of undesirable events, while other forms of risk assessment attempt to quantify the degree of undesirability with an event that could conceivably occur. The former is typical of financial analysis, where risk is often presented as a payoff probability distribution.

Other risks abound for analysis. For example, political risk assessments could be undertaken to evaluate the probability of favorable or unfavorable regulation of health care providers in a presidential election year. This locus of risk analysis is similiar to public policy analysis, which attempts to quantify the uncertainty and impact of a change in public policy or regulation. Here, the risk to be evaluated could be the treatment of capital by Medicare, or the likelihood of a reimbursement increase of X percent, depending on the outcome of an election. Risk in the insurance industry typically refers to the maximum amount the company could lose on a particular policy or category of policies.

Risk analysis provides a companion measure—the riskiness of an action—that is evaluated concurrently with another criterion, such as expected value. Decision analysts prefer to develop these factors independently and to combine them when comparing projects or alternatives with different expected payoffs and risks. For example, analysts may screen investment opportunities using the approach of mean-variance dominance. Given the following five options with payoff means and variances:

Option	X_i	si_2
a_1	6	1
a_2	7	2
a_3	8	2
a_4	7	1.5
a_5	10	3

Action a_3 dominates a_2 *with its higher payoff, and a_1 dominates a_4.* Thus, the decision maker is left with the options of a_1, a_3, and a_5, which cannot be further reduced by the dominance approach. This still leaves a choice to be made, but with fewer favorable alternatives. Now the trade-offs are based on the preferences of the decision makers and their tolerance of higher levels of risk in exchange for greater rewards.

Decision Trees

A decision tree, as defined by Myrtle,[11] is a graphic method of expressing, in sequential order, the action choices that are available to a decision maker and the options that are determined by chance. Decision trees are symbolic of human reasoning. The approach graphically depicts the interrelationships between actions and events, some based on rational choices and others determined by chance. In displaying the alternatives, decision trees are a decision enabler. A decision tree can depict the uncertainty involved in the action choices, the risks involved in selecting one alternative over another, and the payoff expectations.

Schlaifer[12] suggests the following process for diagramming a decision tree:

1. The decision maker must show all the action options from which he wishes to choose. The diagram must also show all chance events,

---

[11] Robert C. Myrtle. "Decision-Trees: A Method for Analyzing Sequential Action Choices." In: Michael J. White et al. *Managing Public Systems: Analytic Techniques for Public Administration.* North Scituate, Mass., Duxbury Press, 1980, p. 187.
[12] Robert Schlaifer. *Analysis of Decisions Under Uncertainty.* New York, McGraw Hill Book Co., 1969, as cited in Myrtle, Ibid., p. 202.

present or future, that may substantially affect present or future choices.

2. The decision events must be both mutually exclusive and collectively exhaustive. No more than one action option can be chosen from a given set of options, and the diagrammed choices can leave out no additional options.

3. The events diagrammed must reflect correctly the information that will and will not be available at the time the decision maker actually has to make a choice.

4. The time period of analysis must be specified.

For example, a patient who has been diagnosed as needing cardiac bypass surgery can choose between seeking surgery at a local community hospital or at an academic medical center. The decision tree outlines a simple illustration of alternative choices and estimated satisfaction (see Figure 20).

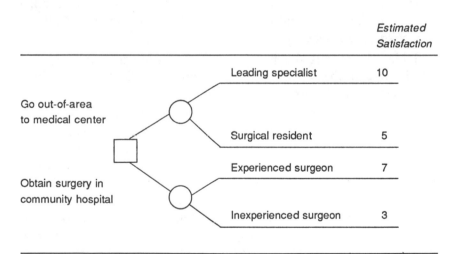

Figure 20   Decision tree for physician selection.

The four characteristics of a decision tree are graphically represented: Choice points are represented by boxes; chance alternatives are depicted by circles; probabilities are assigned to each chance alternative; and tree displays depict both choice and chance options.

TABLE 14   Outcome Probabilities and Utilities for Physician Selection

	Probability of Outcome	Value of Outcome
Out-of-Area Medical Center		
Leading specialist	0.5	10
Surgical resident	0.5	5
Community Hospital		
Experienced surgeon	0.8	7
Inexperienced surgeon	0.2	3

SOURCE: Adapted from Robert C. Myrtle. "Decision Trees: A Method for Analyzing Sequential Action Choices." In: Michael J. White et al. *Managing Public Systems: Analytic Techniques for Public Administration.* North Scituate, Mass., Duxbury Press, 1980, p. 187.

The expected value of an outcome can be determined when the final or intermediate outcome can be quantified. It can then be multiplied by the probability of that outcome, which is the product of all the probabilities leading up to it.

Table 14 presents the probabilities of getting a certain type of physician and the values that a consumer might assign to these outcomes for the illustration shown in Figure 20.

On an expected-value basis, the consumer would be better off deciding to seek an experienced surgeon in his/her local community hospital. There are other criteria that could be applied in this illustration, but in decision analysis, the expected-value criterion is usually the most important to decision makers. More complicated problems may need dozens, even hundreds of branches, to inform decision makers of the implications of pursuing various alternatives. To avoid unnecessary complexity, the planner should identify those major strategies and critical chance events that depict the use of this approach. This results in pruning the decision tree to a discrete number of alternatives that decision makers can rationally compare.

One more concept is useful in analyzing problems by using decision trees. Rollback, according to Myrtle,[13] is moving backward through

_____

[13] Robert C. Myrtle. "Decision Trees", p. 191.

the decision tree from the most distant point in time to the present by averaging monetary values at chance modes and choosing the most favorable course of action at each decision mode.

TOOLS FOR DECISION ANALYSIS: MICROCOMPUTERS, SOFTWARE, AND DATABASES

We are in a new era—the information age. To cope with the information explosion, planners and analysts have access to a broad arsenal of tools and databases. Microcomputers, software, and databases are being packaged for planners as decision-support sytems that automate and simplify many of the more tedious aspects of transforming data into information. One innovative package, the OptionFinder, facilitates real-time voting by a group of decision makers, using digital keypads linked to a microcomputer.

Microcomputers are revolutionizing strategic planning. Computers with a "footprint" of barely two square feet provide the power and capacity of a minicomputer that was state-of-the-art only 10 years ago. The proliferation of microcomputers is now being integrated with electronic mail and local area networks, where all occupants of the hospital's executive suite may share a powerful micro- or minicomputer. This facilitates the sharing of databases and models, as well as software, by as many as 18–30 users, supported by a high-power microcomputer. Considering the decreasing cost of the hardware, an entire executive suite can be computer-equipped for $15,000–$25,000. With microcomputers in every office, planning is no longer a staff function conducted only by specialists. Today, any executive or middle manager can conduct a broad range of planning studies or ask strategic "what if" questions using a desktop computer.

Commercial data services now provide a wealth of demographic information that is customized to the needs and market definitions of users (see Chapter 9). Online health industry databases offer specialized data sets to health organizations that track use, cost data, and financial information. Quality data may be next. Dr. Paul Ellwood[14]

---

[14] Paul M. Ellwood. "Shattuck Lecture—Outcomes Management, a Technology of Patient Experience." *New England Journal of Medicine*, *318*(23):1549–1556, June 9, 1988.

of InterStudy in Excelsior, Minnesota forecasts development in the 1990s of a national database on the "outcomes" of health care. Such a database could ultimately include every hospital admission, physician visit, and ambulatory-care service.

Public sector databases offer a cost-effective alternative to commercial online data, which can be expensive. Computerized data is available from governmental agencies such as the National Center for Health Statistics, the Centers for Disease Control, the National Institute of Mental Health, state health departments, and other agencies with legislative mandates to maintain databases, for example, rate review commissions. These public sector data are often available for only the cost of reproduction. Bibliographic information can be obtained from the National Library of Medicine. With microcomputers becoming widely available, public data can be obtained on diskette or downloaded by modem directly into the microcomputer.

DECISION SUPPORT SYSTEMS

Planning in today's health organization will be simpler and faster, thanks to newly available decision-support systems that were developed specifically for health care applications. Where once planners had to custom-tailor every planning question by using a computer programmer, today's executives and analysts can ask the same questions with only a few keystrokes on their personal computers. The answers and the newly created specialized data sets will be electronically stored for future consideration. Users will be able to retrieve that information with an ease that would astonish anyone who remembers health care planning and management before the advent of microcomputers.

Some examples of decision-support systems that may become commonplace in health care analysis in the future are:

1. *OptionFinder* (Option Technologies, Mendota Heights, Minn.): In the hands of inventors Flexner and Wheatley,[13] what had been a

---

[13] Kimbal L. Wheatley and William A. Flexner, "Research Tool Changes the Way Marketers View Data," *Healthcare Marketing Report,* February 27, 1987; see also Donald E. L. Johnson, "OptionFinder Increases Focus Groups' Productivity," *Health Care Strategic Management,* March 1988, pp. 2–4.

research tool became a decision-support system. The OptionFinder marries the market research technology of computer-linked keypads with decision software and on-screen displays of decision data. It uses a four-step process to facilitate group decision making:

a. *Brainstorming:* A group of people—focus group, planning team, executive team—use formal brainstorming techniques to generate a list of items or ideas relevant to their purpose.

b. *Data entry:* The list is entered into a portable computer, where the OptionFinder software generates a systematic set of questions about the list, which are projected onto a large-screen monitor. Group discussion clarifies the meaning of questions prior to the rating and ranking phase.

c. *Voting:* The voting takes place on individual, handheld keypads linked to the computer. Participants register their opinions using a preset rating scale, for example, 1–7. The OptionFinder organizes the votes of the group into graphics, which are promptly fed back using the projection system.

d. *Discussion/Decision:* In a process much like the Delphi technique, participants interpret the meanings of the collective ratings and rankings that are projected on the monitor. Since each participant can be coded by multiple characteristics, the votes can be analyzed by groups of participants—managers, medical staff, trustees. The discussion focuses on the group's opinion, seeking consensus and probing disagreement. After discussion, and sometimes clarification of terms, a second round of voting can be conducted. This usually results in consensus and a ranking of alternatives.

OptionFinder has been used with consumer focus groups, board-level decisions, management retreats, strategic planning, product-line analysis, and new-venture screening. The system prints out charts of group ratings, as well as the votes of individual participants, that compare individual and group ratings.

For health planning, strategy formulation, and marketing, the OptionFinder simplifies and visualizes decision making. One advantage of the system is that it democratizes decision making and is less vulnerable to dominance by one individual or clique; complex issues are simplified. OptionFinder can analyze three attributes and up to eight variations simultaneously, with 50 or more participants online. The cost ranges from $6,000–$15,000, depending on the equipment selected, which includes the software license and operator manual, plus add-ons such as the computer, keypads, and projection system.

2. *Healthcare Business Planner/Market Model III* (Baxter, Management Services Division, Deerfield, Ill.): Baxter, the nation's largest supplier to hospitals, has developed several business analysis and market assessment software packages. Designed for hospitals and health systems, the Healthcare Business Planner can be applied to a variety of situations, including inpatient, outpatient, or department programs; new or existing services; single-site or multisite programs; on- or off-campus activities; wholly or jointly owned programs; and for-profit or nonprofit enterprises.

The heart of the Healthcare Business Planner is a computer software package that supports a process of business analysis. The tools and techniques of market and financial analysis are described in an accompanying manual. Prepackaged data-collection formats organize information for analysis. Common analysis procedures are automated in the software with macros—the formulas that are built into the software—requiring only a few keystrokes by the planner or market analyst. Complementary software programs from Baxter extend the range of analysis applications for the Business Planner, including the Market Model III and HealthMatch.

Market Model III software is designed for market-share analysis and demand projections that can also incorporate data from Health-Match, a computerized physician referral system. Data from the physician referral system regarding physician activity are input for a set of analyses by the Market Model or Business Planner. Market Model III integrates demographic, socioeconomic, case mix, and hospitalization rate databases to support planning analyses, projections, and "what-if" analyses of admissions, inpatient days, and market share.

A primary advantage of using prepackaged software is consistency of application across a hospital or multihospital system. St. Agnes Medical Center was an early adopter of the Baxter business planning software. The hospital uses the business planning model to organize departmental planning and budgeting. Basically, each hospital department and service unit is considered a strategic business unit, developing its own business plan using the Business Planner. Consistent application of the business planning software allows the hospital's senior management to compare capital requests and budgets across the board. Proposed new ventures are analyzed with the same software that is used for existing programs.

In a multihospital environment, the Healthcare Business Planner has been adopted by the Adventist Health System. Hinsdale Hospital, a system member, was a test site for developing the business planning software. Now 14 of the system's 73 facilities use the program. Systemwide adoption of the Business Planner and Market Model III will allow the Adventist's corporate planning office to coordinate planning and compare capital and strategic plans.

3. *MarketPlanner* (The Sachs Group, Evanston, Ill.): Market-Planner is a microbased computer planning and marketing information system for health care organizations. The database for Market-Planner includes 1980 census data and 5-year demographic projections, inpatient hospitalization rates by DRG, a cartographic database for creating maps, a medical staff database, and data from the hospital's most recent year of patient records. The software integrates these databases, performs statistical analyses, and generates maps, tables, and graphs for such analyses as market-share assessment by product line or DRG, market trends and impact on hospital performance, identification of targets for growth and development, segmenting the market by demographic or patient variables, physician practice analysis, patient origin analysis, payer mix patterns by market segment and geography, projections of market share with use rate models, product-line analysis and market strategy, and revenue by product line.

The most recent version of the MarketPlanner (version 1.22) includes expanded capacity for large data sets; the use of a hand-held computer "mouse" device for menu selection and graphics without using keyboard commands; multiple fonts and colors; "windowing" multiple-image capability for graphics; direct user import of ASCII and DIF formats, and other software such as dBase and Lotus; and enhanced projections editing.

FAILURE ANALYSIS: ANTICIPATING THE WORST

Hospitals are risky businesses! This was not always so. There was a time when a hospital administrator had no more fear of failing than a bank president. Both health care and banking were risk-adverse businesses that took few chances and were the epitome of the prudently managed enterprise in a safe market climate, but this is no longer true. A 1986 Touche-Ross survey of hospital CEOs found that nearly 50 percent feared their institutions would not survive the next five years.

Failure analysis is a tool borrowed from the Department of Defense. Think of it as contingency planning for worst-case situations. Robert Boyle, a senior executive of the Virginia Mason Medical Center, used failure analysis to identify key risk factors in determining hospital strategic failures. Boyle took advantage of his fellowship as a Maffley Scholar, selected by the Healthcare Forum of San Francisco, to study important issues in health care management.

TABLE 15   Major Early Warning Signs of Failure

Early Warning Signals	Overall Rank in Importance	Percent Selecting
Organizational Factors		
Lack of physician commitment	1	27.7
Planning Factors		
Insufficient business volume	2	17.8
Lack of consumer demand	3	14.9
Disagreement on goals	5	13.9
Leaders' unrealistic expectations	6	11.9
Lack of effective marketing	7	10.9
Management Factors		
Ineffective leadership	4	14.9
Political Factors	0	0.0

SOURCE: Robert L. Boyle, June Strickland, and Karen Endresen. "Analysis of 'Failure' and Implications for the Industry." Presented at Healthcare Forum Annual Convention, Anaheim, Calif., April 1988.

Assisted by June Strickland, Ph.D., of Virginia Mason, and Karen Endresen, President of Endresen Research in Seattle, Washington, Boyle identified the most frequent early warning signs of failure (see Table 15).

Which "macrotrends" may put a hospital in greatest danger? Boyle's survey identified a number of significant concerns industry-wide that may contribute to hospital failure (see Table 16).

TABLE 16 Industry-wide Concerns Contributing to Failure

Contributing Factors	% Reporting a Major Contributor	% Reporting not a Major Contributor	Mean Rating (1–5)
Reimbursement constraints	43.6	4.5	4.0
Ineffective administrator/ physician relationships	35.5	6.5	3.9
Limited financial resources	35.3	4.5	3.9
Competitive forces	34.4	5.2	3.9
Absence of teamwork	25.8	6.5	3.5
Governance/organization constraints	22.7	9.7	3.3
Inappropriate or unrelated diversification	22.6	13.5	3.4
Inadequate customer service	21.4	9.7	3.5
Lack of customer demand	20.1	11.7	3.3
Inadequate quality of care/ service	19.0	11.8	3.1
Internal climate problems	17.3	6.4	3.5
Human resources shortages	7.7	8.4	3.1

SOFTWARE FOR THE "HUMAN COMPUTER"

Imagine that strategic thinking is a technology. Decision Process International (DPI), a multinational management consulting firm whose healthcare practice is based in Nicasio, California, has refined strategic planning to a science. The computers that drive the analysis are the senior executives of the client corporations. DPI's planning framework focuses attention on nine critical strategic areas that drive any enterprise. Each of the nine lead in a different strategic direction.

The management challenge is to select the one that best fits the nature of its business. The nine categories are illustrated in Table 17.

TABLE 17   Driving Forces: What Companies Do Best

Driving Forces	Business Examples
Products/services	Automobiles
Market/user	Hospital supply
Production capacity	Printing, hotels
Technology	Pharmaceuticals
Sales/marketing	Retail
Distribution	Communications, utilities
Natural resources	Energy, mining
Size/growth	Insurance
Return/profit	Banking

The DPI process of strategic thinking forces an organization to sharpen its self-concept. This defines the firm's products and services scope, its customers, and its markets. Each driving force has a repertoire of appropriate strategies. The process is generic but the results are unique, with companies as varied as 3M and Marriott.

In a multiday strategic planning retreat, one hospital realized that its driving force was *capacity*—not *products/services*. This hospital, for the past five years, had worked hard to redefine itself as market-driven, but it was still struggling to complete the transformation. The hospital was never comfortable with its new market-oriented philosophy, and was disappointed with the limited payoff from marketing investments. With capacity as its organizing self-concept, the hospital defined a set of marketing and operational strategies that were designed to keep it running at high levels of utilization with a profitable payer/customer mix.

VITALITY/VIABILITY ASSESSMENT

How can a hospital tell whether trouble lies ahead? Consultants Wanda Jones and John Mayerhoffer of the San Francisco-based H.O.M. Group have developed a Vitality/Viability Assessment. The assessment protocol uses a set of 40-plus critical success factors in four groups:

1. *Environment:* National fiscal policy, Medicare reimbursement
2. *Region:* Growth, payer stability, provider concentration, competitor strategies
3. *Organization:* Information systems, management style and fit, service mix
4. *Resources:* Cash, access to capital, contracting, debt

The result is a picture of an organization that can be summarized by placement on a five-level scale, from hospitals so strong that they will have every expectation of continuing to those whose hopes of remaining an acute facility should be limited.

The game is not where a hospital lies on the scale. Most hospitals are somewhere in the middle. For those boards and CEOs, the real question is, "Where are we most vulnerable?" The focal point of the Vitality/Viability Assessment is to identify where the hospital should place its main efforts at strengthening the organization to survive the future.

This is not a self-assessment tool. External assessment provides an objective report. In an arms-length process, the consultants do the examination directly and render a confidential report to the client CEO and board. This prevents any misunderstandings or watering-down problems to the level of consensus. No denial, no misunderstandings, no false hopes.

The assessment can be done either with internal awareness and participation in interviews and data collection, or externally, so that the organization is protected from any concern that might reach vulnerability with employees, medical staff, or the press. Subjective factors can only be understood by internal interviews. External data provide comparisons with the competition. Some hospitals in a high-sensitivity situation may start with the external assessment and conduct the internal review in a second phase. Results are provided in a written report and a HyperCard-based model projection from the computer.

Think of the Vitality/Viability Assessment as a business health checkup; this kind of preventive medicine could save a CEO's job.

Think of a Vitality/Viability Assessment as a "corporate physical" to test the market pulse and financial health of a hospital or health system. Multihospital systems will likely adopt this approach to screen for problems in their subunits. The medical analogy would be preventive health screening. It makes good sense to identify potential problem situations before they become full-blown crises.

STRATEGY SELECTION

Selection and implementation of strategies, the final stage of the rational decision model, is only partly a *rational* process. Organizational politics, private agendas, personal ambitions, interpersonal and interorganizational conflicts, turf wars, personal biases, and the unpredictable are all part of the decision milieu.

This is the opportunity for decision analysis. Test alternatives in the computer before entering the market. Project scenarios with varied assumptions about key factors. Double the time planned and the resources needed. Use consultants as a cross-check against "groupthink" by the management group or hospital board. Site visit other organizations that have implemented similiar strategies. Get the real story from those in the trenches. Go back to the computer and run the scenarios again. Make the most of the opportunity for decision analysis.

Market analysts and planners also need a bias for action. Don't agonize over the decision—the paralysis of analysis—but complete the analysis in a compact time frame with as wide a margin for input as possible. There is danger in delay, but there is also a narrowing margin for moving into a window of opportunity. The high turnover of hospital planners and marketers in the late 1980s reflects their executives' impatience with inaction and lack of results.

Despite its limitations, the rational model continues to dominate organizational decision making and strategy. Planners and market analysts are deeply trained in the rational process. Professional journals and associations showcase examples of the rational model at work. The rational decision process is, and will continue to be, the most widely used organizational process for problem-solving and strategy formulation.

SUMMARY

Decision analysis provides planners with a set of tools for product-line management, facilities planning, market strategy, priority setting, and evaluation of new business ventures. Many methods and techniques developed in private industry have been adapted to the health industry. The purpose of decision analysis is to assist decision makers in making strategic and business choices under conditions of uncertainty. Decision analysis can also contribute an assessment of the level of risk associated with strategic choices and new ventures. The proliferation of powerful microcomputers has made decision analysis tools widely available to health planners and market analysts. New business and market analysis software, which is designed specifically for health care applications, is available. Through computer networking, a hospital's executive management team or a multihospital system can share databases and analysis software. Online databases make available national and regional data for planning comparisons and market forecasting. As the information revolution continues to expand health care databases, new and more powerful decision analysis tools and expert systems will become available in the 1990s.

CHAPTER 9

INFORMATION SYSTEMS AND DATA SOURCES

The essence of the health planning process is the presentation of information that illuminates alternative choices for decision makers. It makes little difference whether choices relate to new business development or to health policy. The responsibility of the planner/analyst is to illuminate the consequences of choosing among alternatives.

Data are the essential ingredients in the planning decision matrix. Implementation of the various planning methods, discussed in Chapters 6 and 7, depends almost totally on the availability of data. The purpose of this chapter is to acquaint planners with data sources and systems that will provide them with a basis for evaluating alternatives and estimating the implications of strategies.

THE NEED FOR DATA

Planning theory illustrates very clearly the need for data. For example, theorists Davidoff and Rciner[1] cite three types of planning choices: choosing goals, choosing methods for attaining goals, and choosing revisions to strategies based on evaluation. They recognize that all choices ultimately are based on good judgment, which, in turn, depends on the rigorous analysis of information that makes the purpose and impacts of the choices very clear.

---

[1] Paul Davidoff and T. A. Reiner. "A Choice Theory of Planning." *Journal of the American Institute of Planners,* 28(3):103–115, May 1962.

Hauser[2] aptly describes the need for data in a decision-making context in *Social Statistics in Use*. He states that "Statistics are quantitative facts collected, aggregated, and analyzed to provide intelligence to facilitate understanding, and to serve as a foundation for the formulation of policy, development, and management of programs." What Hauser describes as the application of statistics is, in fact, the essence of the planning process.

Good data are hardly an academic concern. In the competitive environment of modern health care, the business risks are higher and the margin for strategic error is narrower. Hospitals and health organizations operate at substantial risk today. Better market strategy yields better marketing outcomes. Sound market choices and operational decisions are informed by data. Public policymakers are equally constrained in their program and budget choices. In an era of tight budgets and limited resources, decisions must be grounded in the latest and best information available.

INFORMATION SYSTEMS/DECISION SUPPORT SYSTEMS

Today's health information/decision support systems are generations advanced from the room-size computers of the 1950s that once calculated hospital bed needs for government subsidy under the Hill-Burton Program. Microcomputers, with a greater capacity than the calculating leviathans of the past, now fit easily on a planner's desktop.

Planning decisions are ultimately made by minds, not machines. The possibilities for equipment range from pencils to computers, but the edge is shifting to advanced technology. Computers depend on programs—software—to carry out assigned functions. The user of an information system should be aware of not only the benefits but also the potential problems that can arise from choices involving software. A particular concern should be the amount of programming effort that is required to extract useful information from available files. Each request for information can be treated as a unique problem, to be dealt with by a special set of procedures developed by a trained

---

[2] Philip M. Hauser. *Social Statistics in Use.* New York, Sage, 1975, p. 1.

programmer. This process can be very expensive and time-consuming but can yield the precise information the user wants. Off-the-shelf decision support systems, such as Lotus 1-2-3 and VisiCalc, provide sets of programs that can be stored within a microcomputer. A few simple instructions from the user will incorporate these instructions into a general processing program and produce results that are more-or-less tailored to the needs of the user. The advantage here is that the programmer's costly effort is eliminated, as well as the time required to prepare a unique set of instructions. The trade-off may be that the output is only approximately what users would like to have, rather than a product tailored to fit their precise needs. In most cases, however, the general-purpose software will provide decision makers with adequate results and can often make the information immediately available.

Three recent trends have greatly expanded the options available for state-of-the-art information systems: decentralization and miniaturization of equipment, differentiation of software, and diffusion of knowledge.

1. *Decentralization of hardware* has been the result of dramatic reductions in the size and cost of various pieces of equipment. The most apparent example is the microcomputer, a device that can cost as little as $1,000–$2,000 and yet have the computational capacity of the mainframe computers of 20 years ago. This capacity is housed in a device that is approximately the size of an electric typewriter and thus fits easily into an office environment. Today's microcomputers may be work stations or mainframe systems, networked with mini-computers or otherwise linked with powerful microcomputers in an office or across the country. Laptop models weighing less than 12 pounds now may be equipped with up to 40 megabytes of hard-disk storage—enough data capacity to analyze the financial results of a large multihospital system.

2. *Differentiation of software* simply means that it is now feasible for the user to choose from a wide variety of products those decision support systems that are most suited to the analyst's needs (see Chapter 8). Moreover, these products are designed to meet the needs of nonexperts. The software is *user-friendly*. Complex formulas created by the user can be routinized as *macros* (macro instructions),

replacing the need for customized routines that once could be created only by expert programmers.

3. *Diffusion of knowledge* has emerged concurrently with the advent of user-friendly software and hardware. Planners and market analysts are trained in computer analysis. It is part of every university curriculum and a required component of many graduate programs in health administration. *Computer literacy* is advancing through the ranks of health care executives, with a widespread diffusion of knowledge about the operation of computers, for a synergistic effect. Not only is the equipment easier to use, but the number of people in the general population who have adequate knowledge to operate a computer is increasing geometrically.

The consequence is the evolution of a new form of information system called the *decision support system* (DSS). The function of a DSS is to help decision makers deal with complex situations that cannot be routinized and delegated to lower level employees. In effect, a DSS permits the partial automation of the decision-making processes of analysis and optimization that were described earlier as information system functions.

Certain important characteristics of the DSS distinguish it from the management information system (MIS). The decision support system increases ease of access to the database and provides greater flexibility in the use of data. It is a personal tool under the direct control of the users. It is evolutionary, becoming more sophisticated and more focused as its users gain experience.[3] Decision support systems contain four components:

1. *Database Manager:* The first of these four components is a database management system that allows the manager to select and organize facts from a comprehensive database containing both organizational and environmental information.

---

[3] Jacob W. Ulvila and Rex V. Brown, "Decision Analysis Comes of Age," *Harvard Business Review, 60*(5):130–141, September–October 1982; Efraim Turban, "Decision Support Systems in Hospitals," *Health Care Management Review, 7*(3):35–42, Summer 1982; Richard M. Denise, "Technology for the Executive Thinker," *Datamation, 29*(6):206–216, June 1983.

2. *Statistical Analysis Programs:* The second component is a set of statistical analysis programs that can be used to convert the data into information.

3. *Decision Models:* The third component is a system that allows the decision maker to create models to predict the outcome of decisions under a variety of conditions. Currently, these models are limited to quantitative analyses, either deterministic or probabilistic. In the future, however, as the branch of artificial intelligence called *expert systems* develops, it will become easier to incorporate nonnumeric factors into these models.

4. *Verbal/Graphic Display:* Finally, the DSS includes a capability to create verbal, numeric, and graphic displays of the results of modeling and analysis.

Of equal importance is the capability of the DSS to work in an interactive mode with the decision maker. With the decision support system, the decision maker should be able to ask "what if" questions and obtain virtually instantaneous responses.

Since the database, data sources, analysts, and decision makers are unlikely to be located proximately, an information system must provide the means by which data can be communicated from one functional area to another (e.g., from the place where analyses are prepared to the location of the decision maker). When the DSS is being used, communication will often include the transfer of selected data from computer files stored in mainframes or minicomputers to personal microcomputers for modeling and analysis. It may also involve the transmission of results between executive work stations. Furthermore, provision must be made for the transfer of data between sites within a function (e.g., when errors are detected during the validation function, the erroneous data must be transmitted to the data source, which then returns the revised data for reentry into the system). After years of development, local area network (LAN) systems are coming to market, which will link dozens, even hundreds, of microcomputers into an interactive network. More powerful microbased LANs can support 12–36 microcomputers that share data and software. This is advancing the day of the "paperless office," where electronic mail and digital record storage are commonplace.

INFORMATION SYSTEM FUNCTIONS

An information system must perform seven generic functions:

1. *Data Collection:* The first of these is data collection. The system designer must take particular care to ensure that the methods selected for data collection minimize the opportunity for errors to creep into the system.

2. *Data Validation:* The importance of this function is indicated by a term commonly used in the data processing industry: GIGO, meaning *garbage in, garbage out.* This term implies that the product of an information system can be no better than the quality of the information introduced into the database. Thus, it is important that action be taken to detect and correct errors before they are permitted to enter the system. When secondary data are used (i.e., those collected by another agency or organization), a transaction validation function, although important, is insufficient, because it merely analyzes individual items of data that were entered for compatibility with the system and, therefore, can overlook significant deficiencies. Consequently, there also must be an analysis or evaluation of the method by which the data were collected.

3. *Data Operation:* Once the new data are ascertained to be as correct and error-free as possible, they must be added to the files as additional records or corrections to existing ones. For example, if a file contains records based on experience, such as hospital discharges, a data transaction might either add or amend a record, depending on whether the person concerned had a previous hospital admission.

4. *Data Storage:* After a data transaction has been completed, the amended data must be stored in a safe and accessible place until they are needed. From the decision maker's point of view, storage-cost considerations must be weighed against the important characteristics of an information system: responsiveness, flexibility, and comprehensiveness. For instance, in an automated system, reels of magnetic tape are the least costly means of storing data, but the use of such a medium makes the data far less accessible than immediate-access storage, such as a personal computer disk file.

5. *Data Transformation:* Generally, decision makers will have little interest in the entire content of a single file. Rather, they will require a subset of records or a set of specific items from all records

for analysis, or a combination of material from several files for a complete analysis. For instance, they might wish to combine data from both inpatient statistics and ambulatory-care files to compute customer commitment in the primary and secondary service areas.

6. *Information Retrieval:* Once the data have been transformed into an appropriate configuration, the next step is to convert them into information, that is, to develop answers to specific questions. This is the point at which the decision maker has a great deal at stake. In the process of strategic planning, it is common practice to create many data tabulations that will provide general descriptions of the items of interest. Most often, the strategic plan is the repository of generic data such as small-area population forecasts. These tables, however, seldom can be used as direct answers to the questions confronting decision makers. Consequently, a great deal of manual manipulation of the data displayed in the tables is necessary to arrive at the information needed. Still, this method has been widely used because it is considered a relatively inexpensive way of providing information to multiple users. An alternative that considers the cost to the user, as well as to the provider, is to strip out most extraneous tables from the strategic plan, leaving the data in storage until the decision maker has a specific problem, then to extract the relevant material and arrange it in the most suitable manner for that problem. This option is more feasible with an automated system than with a manual system. Ways in which the data can be organized to respond to questions include listings of individual records, cross tabulations, scatter diagrams, and statistical summaries. Database management software designed to develop this kind of information is widely available.

7. *Information Presentation:* This is the last step in getting information to the decision maker. A nontrivial choice involved in information presentation is whether to use a printed format or a graphic format such as a chart, graph, or map. Many believe that graphics convey a much more effective message than a printed page does. Once again, the choice usually involves a trade-off based on cost factors.

DATABASE DESIGN DECISIONS

Few planners and market analysts can afford all the data they want, or use all the data they have. Just as inevitably, the format of the data is seldom available in the way the user/decision maker wants it. In constructing a planning database, most decisions involve trade-offs between desirable characteristics and increased costs. Thus, an overall strategy is required at the beginning of the design process even though the system may be developed on an incremental basis. If this advanced planning has been done, some characteristics can be upgraded later. For example, responsiveness and flexibility can be improved by going from a few fixed programs to a general-purpose statistical system. To achieve this, however, the core database must initially be designed to be compatible with later system additions. Specific operating characteristics that should be considered include:

1. *Responsiveness:* This represents the time lag between the initiation of a request for information and its receipt by the user.

2. *Flexibility:* Flexibility in database design involves two major considerations: the structure of the information produced (it should be as close as possible to the needs of the user) and the level of aggregation. Data can be grouped, for instance, in a highly aggregate form, which can conserve storage space and thus reduce costs. Once the data are aggregated, however, it is virtually impossible to dis-aggregate them for an analysis that requires a different organization of the information.

As an example, storing data on persons in the age groups 0–14, 15–45, 45–65, and over 65 would probably be quite satisfactory for hospital use information. On the other hand, if the planner then wanted to use the data for a market study of the need for substance abuse treatment programs for adolescents, it might be desirable to compile data on persons in the age group 12–20. If the data have been stored in summary form for the age groups previously described, a re-analysis based on school years would be virtually impossible; if, however, the data were stored either in single-year groups or as individual records for each person involved, then the aggregation in a different arrangement would be completely feasible.

3. *Comprehensiveness:* This relates to how much data the system should include, whether it be the minimum essential information or additional items that might be useful at some point in the future.

4. *Accuracy:* Concern for accuracy involves data validity (i.e., are there any errors in the recorded information?) and data completeness (i.e., has the system succeeded in gathering all the information that is eligible for inclusion in the file?). Although it is unlikely that any file will ever be 100 percent accurate, the degree of accuracy that is necessary to satisfy the purposes of the decision makers must be determined. Since many decision makers seem to believe that nothing less than perfect information is acceptable, it is important for database designers to emphasize to users the impossibility of achieving this objective, as well as the extraordinarily high costs of even approaching that level of accuracy.

5. *Timeliness:* Timeliness relates to how current information must be and how frequently it should be updated. Data can be changed continuously to reflect the most current situation, but this is well beyond the requirements of any planning decision—although there will be great pressure on decision makers to have very current statistics, especially in situations where data are being used in an adversary situation (e.g., a disputed application for a certificate of need). Cost-benefit questions must be answered when aiming to achieve a very high level of timeliness.

6. *Compatibility:* Because different files will frequently be used together to provide information, they must be compatible. For instance, when calculating incidence or prevalence rates, numerator and denominator data should be from the same time period; also, when two files contain comparable elements, definitions of data elements should be the same.

7. *Consistency:* File data should be consistent over both time and space. In other words, comparisons should be possible between historical and current data and between political jurisdictions or geographic areas.

8. *Linkages:* When data are to be combined from different files, a common element in the records of each file is essential. For instance, an analysis of hospital activity by different medical specialists might require the use of both personnel and hospital discharge files. In this instance, a number would be needed to identify individual physicians both within the personnel file and for each of the hospital discharges for which the physician was responsible.

A common type of linkage is *geocoding,* in which individuals, organizations, and transactions are linked to a specific area about which the decision makers have a certain amount of information.

9. *Security:* A discussion of linkages raises the question of security for two reasons. First, operators and users of information systems have both moral and legal obligations to protect the privacy of individuals about whom information has been collected. Second, linkages make it possible to use data in ways that were not anticipated when the affected persons reported information about themselves (e.g., employee requests for treatment of drug abuse by employee assistance programs).

10. *Costs:* Information is a commodity. Therefore, decisions on database and systems design can be informed by cost-benefit analysis to answer questions such as, does increased accuracy or inclusion of additional data result in improvements in decision making (i.e., reducing financial risk), and are those benefits worth more than the costs involved?

DATA ANALYSIS

Data are of little value in and of themselves. To be useful, they must be transformed into information, a process that requires an explicit or implicit model. Some of these models are described in Chapters 7, 8, and 10. In this chapter, first, a generic model is presented that reflects the relationship between health services and health status. Next, a more specific flow model, which indicates the series of decisions that must be made to plan health services, is outlined.

Figure 21 shows that desired outcomes, goals, or objectives are affected by a set of planning variables that the analyst can influence, as well as by a set of nonmanipulable variables that are beyond the control of the organization but that have a significant influence on goal achievement. Planners should not be discouraged by all those nonmanipulable factors that are outside the control of the planner and their organization. From a systems perspective, both sets of variables are related and open to change. Frequently, the desired outcomes will feed back to the nonmanipulable variables and change them in significant ways. Also, implementation of programs

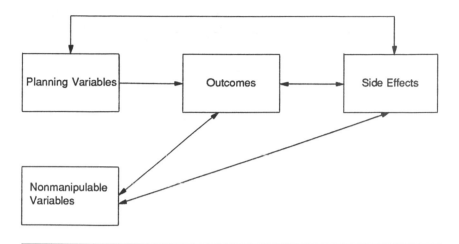

Figure 21   **A generic model reflecting the relationships between variables and goals.**

affecting planning variables will often produce both primary and secondary side effects arising from changes in the goal status. In turn, these side effects may feed back to change the goal status and the nonmanipulable variables.

This is clearer in Figure 22 where health terms have been substituted for the abstractions in Figure 21. The diagram shows that the goal—in this case, increasing market share—is the product of cardiac care, which the planner can vary, and competing services, over which the planner has virtually no influence. It also shows the feedback from the goal to the nonmanipulable variables and side effects, for example, as market share expands, not only do competitors lose shares in the market, but related services are also affected. More specifically, to expand on the example, planning that results in the recruitment of a *superstar* heart surgeon may improve the hospital's cardiac surgery use, as well as boost the demand for related services such as cardiac catheterization and balloon angioplasty.

In Figure 23, the planning process begins with population data for the entire region. Next, those market segments that are to be served must be determined. Measures of potential demand, based on incidence and prevalence rates, must be determined for each market

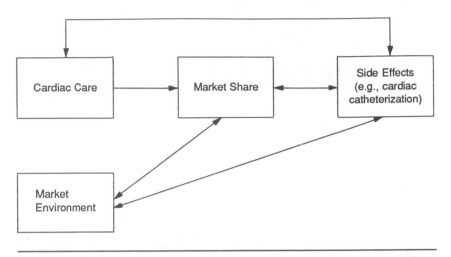

Figure 22 A model reflecting the relationships between health services and market share.

segment. This information (use rates) is combined with data on the size of market segments within the service area defined by the planner. The result is the quantity of potential services needed in the service area. The potential demand is then compared with actual use data, where available.

The next level of analysis is to determine the market share of the planner's organization, as well as that of other significant competitors in the same service area. The organizational demand is determined by combining the existing market share and the additional market share that the planner intends to capture. Knowing the organizational demand, this can then be translated into resource requirements for the service that is the focus of the analysis. Finally, the resource requirements can be compared with the population distribution of the target market segments to determine the optimum location(s) of the service.

This flow model incorporates a number of models described in Chapter 7 (e.g., the model for estimating the number of acute-care beds required) and develops data that will provide useful inputs for other models (e.g., the cost-benefit model and the priority-setting

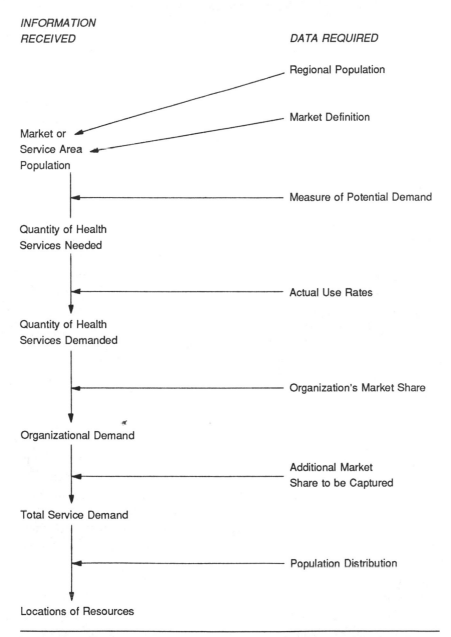

Figure 23 Flow model indicating the decisions involved in planning health services.

model). It also implies the need for micro data to analyze the market segments.

MICRO DATA

Analyses of groups of people, whether they are residents of a geographic area, members of an age cohort, or whatever, inevitably require some form of average measure to represent the group as a whole. This is a widely accepted practice with which all health planners and market analysts are familiar. Perhaps they are too familiar with this compromise between group and individual data, because the differences between groups with a similiar average is often overlooked. In fact, the reason that there are differences between groups is that there are differences *within* groups. Unfortunately, these differences are often obscured in the process of computing an average. For instance, if there were two groups of five people each, and each group had an average age of 40 years, the actual ages might be as follows:

Group A	Group B
30	10
30	10
40	10
50	80
50	90

It should be evident that the health needs of these two groups would be markedly different despite their identical average age. The solution is to reduce the size of the groups analyzed to the maximum practical extent so as to reduce the variability around the average measure. This is done by dividing populations of interest into small, homogeneous segments. For example, it is assumed that there is some similarity among people residing within a census tract. Another way to increase the homogeneity of a population's subgroups is to divide the population along age and sex lines. In certain cases, ethnic or racial grouping may be more functional (e.g., distinguishing blacks from other groups when analyzing the incidence of sickle-cell anemia).

As market planning, segmenting, and targeting get more precise, there is great interest in acquiring data that would be sufficiently detailed to permit analyses of different population subgroups. Unfortunately, the more detailed a file, the more expensive this is likely to be. In the past, most files of this kind were available only from governmental agencies because of the large investment required to establish and maintain them. Corporations often have such data (e.g., telephone companies), which they have extracted from government files, but because of the effort and expense of developing the data, these data are often treated as proprietary information. Government is no longer the only source of population data. Census data are now obtainable through commercial databases such as Donnelley Marketing Information Services, a subsidiary of Dun & Bradstreet. The level of information can be targeted quite specifically to client-defined market areas, if necessary, down the census tract.

DATA SOURCES

A perennial problem for all health planners and market analysts is the location of specific sources of data that will permit them to analyze the environment to identify opportunities and threats that should be addressed in the strategic plan or the marketing plan. Even analysis of the internal environment is often problematic. Assessing organizational strengths and weaknesses is often frustrated by inadequate and inconsistent data. Mastering the diversity of data sources is one of the primary attributes of the experienced planner.

National Data Sources

At the national level, an enormous amount of data is gathered by the Federal Government, trade associations, professional organizations, and special-interest groups.

In the Federal Government, statistical systems that are of particular interest to health planners are operated by the National Center for Health Statistics (NCHS) and the National Institute of Mental Health (NIMH). The Bureau of the Census in the U.S. Department of Commerce is the primary source of data on population and housing as an environmental factor. The Health Care Financing Administration

(HCFA) conducts a continuing research program; it publishes annual statistics on health care expenditures, Medicare/Medicaid program expenditures, and health statistics on the elderly and poor who are served by those federal programs. HCFA's *Medicare Cost Reports,* submitted by individual hospitals annually, are one of the major sources of national data on costs and the use of health care by the elderly.[4] The Department of Commerce tracks the national economy and publishes monthly reports on the gross national product and the medical care component of consumer expenditures.

A variety of private organizations operate data collection systems that are uniform across the country.[5] The Health Insurance Association of America (HIAA) collects insurance coverage and related data and publishes it annually. The American Hospital Association performs annual hospital surveys. Data on physicians are collected by the American Medical Association and more than a hundred other health professions that track and report on their members annually.

National Center for Health Statistics

The National Center for Health Statistics (NCHS) is revising its existing health care surveys to collect data in new settings, such as hospices and home health agencies. NCHS is attempting to make it easier to combine findings from different surveys. One result is that it will collect data annually in each health care setting and track patients to see what happens after they are cared for. Over a five-year period, the National Health Care Survey will replace existing surveys of health care providers. Because of new diagnostic and surgical techniques, the old surveys no longer include all health care providers.

The five components of the new National Health Care Survey will include:

---

[4] The content of this data system is explained fully in Alpha Center for Health Planning, *A Planner's Guide to the Medicare Statistical System,* Washington, D.C., American Association for Health Planning, 1981.

[5] For an excellent description of the potential of cost-related systems for providing a large amount of the data required for planning, see Terry W. Rothermel, "Forecasting Resurrected," *Harvard Business Review, 60*(2):146, March–April 1982.

1. *Hospital and Surgical Care Component:* In 1988, the first component became operational. The new Hospital and Surgical Care Component is an improved version of the National Hospital Discharge Survey, the principal source of uniform national data on hospital patient characteristics, payment sources, length of stay, diagnosis, surgical treatment, and patterns of care. The new component will also cover outpatient surgery units and freestanding surgicenters, although the latter will not be covered until the early 1990s.

2. *Ambulatory Care Component:* The second part of the National Health Care Survey became operational in 1989. It is an improvement on the National Ambulatory Care Medical Care Survey, which currently collects information on medical care from a sample of office-based physicians. The latter survey was conducted annually between 1974 and 1981, and periodically since then. Beginning in 1990, the new Ambulatory Care Component will be continuous, including, by 1991, physicians working in hospital outpatient clinics and emergency rooms. This component will also cover ambulatory care that is provided in other settings, such as urgent-care centers (freestanding emergency clinics) and health clinics.

3. *Long-Term Care Component:* The new Long-Term Care Component will improve on the National Nursing Home Survey, conducted infrequently since 1963 and most recently in 1985. The new component will also cover home health agencies and hospices, because these providers are becoming increasingly important to health care as the population ages. Home health agencies will be sampled in 1991, and residents of nursing homes in 1992. There will be annual data collection thereafter.

4. *Health Provider Component:* The Health Provider Component will expand on the National Master Facility Inventory. Conducted periodically since 1963, this survey produces a comprehensive list of inpatient facilities that provide medical, nursing, personal, or custodial care. The new survey will also include providers of ambulatory acute care and community-based long-term care.

5. *Patient Follow-On:* The fifth part of the National Health Care Survey is brand new. It will ask patients or their families about the outcome of a patient's care and whether the patient had any follow-up care. The goal is to gather data for assessing the quality, use, and

financing of health care. The first longitudinal data will be gathered from nursing home residents, tracking them for 12 to 18 months, to see how they continue to use hospitals and nursing homes.

The new survey will produce reports that will allow planners to compare statistics on health care use with data on people's actual health. Data on all five components will be compiled annually, greatly enhancing comparability over the episodic surveys that were conducted in the past by NCHS. For the first time, NCHS data will be provided on a small-area basis; such data are unavailable from the current survey series. Finally, the new survey will be organized by subject, for example, long-term care, including—but not limited to—nursing homes. These improvements in the national health database will be enormously valuable to health planners and market analysts, and they are long overdue.

COMPETITOR INTELLIGENCE DATA SOURCES

There are literally hundreds of sources of information on competitors and industry trends in the public domain. Among the most useful of these basic sources are public filings to federal, state, and local governments. Publicly traded companies must report detailed accounts of their performance annually to the federal Securities and Exchange Commission (SEC). Most common of these reports are the 10-K (annual financial report), 10-Q (quarterly financial filing), proxy (special event report given to stockholders to vote on), prospectus (for new companies first issuing stock), 13-D (major stock acquisition of 5 percent or more of the company's stock), and other required reports. Facilities certified by Medicare are required to submit annual reports that are quite informative.

State corporate filings are much less revealing, often providing little more than the firm's name, address, and list of officers. Some states require considerably more information, including financial performance data.

Health insurance plans and HMOs are required to submit extensive financial reports in many states. A few states currently regulate PPOs, but more will likely follow the pattern of HMO regulation in the future.

Hospitals in most states are required to file extensive reports with state health departments; these reports are in the public domain and provide the most common source of competitor intelligence in the health industry.

Certain other health facilities and services are also required to submit annual reports, such as nursing homes, outpatient clinics, psychiatric facilities, and some specialized services, for example, cardiac surgery. Other related facilities, such as personal-care homes, are licensed by state departments of welfare or social services and are required to file annual reports; they are also subjected to state surveys.

State securities offices act as state SECs, requiring each company offering a certain amount of stock within the state to file a prospectus. This can be a useful source of information on new health enterprises that are to be capitalized as a syndicated limited partnership, for example, a medical office building or a diagnostic imaging facility.

State licensing agencies conduct periodic surveys of health facilities. Their reports are public information.

At the local level, health facilities are required to file applications for zoning changes and building permits, which can provide significant information about the programs and services to be provided in the proposed facilities.

Some localities may require environmental impact studies of proposed health facilities. These reports are available at public hearings while the proposed facilities are in official review and on request from local building authorities.

Access to SEC reports and filings can be readily provided, within hours if needed, by specialized information services. In Washington, D.C., and in each state capital, there are a number of private copying services and information brokers who can assist in obtaining and copying desired governmental reports.

DATABASES FOR DECISION ANALYSIS

Health planners can now gain online access to computerized databases for decision analysis. A number of these information sources have been identified in Chapter 7. Examples of these computerized databases include:

1. *Health Planning Data:* Systemetrics of Santa Barbara, California is a prominent supplier of health planning data through on-line database services. Its customers pay an annual fee, plus on-line charges, to access the company's national database. One key to Systemetrics's success is the capability of incorporating a hospital's data into the Systemetrics database. This allows hospital planners to analyze their data in the context of regional averages and with data from peer-group facilities. The Systemetrics database is designed for product-line analysis, demand forecasting, and market-share analysis. Not all analysis and "what if" scenarios are run on-line. Systemetrics users can download a data set that they have just created and manipulate it at their convenience.

2. *Health Care Claims Data:* MedTrends Indicators is an example of a new category of databases covering private insurance claims. The databases will give hospitals and health care purchasers new insights into the cost and use patterns of America's privately insured health customers.

MedTrends Indicators is available through a consortium of claims review companies, MedStat Systems of Ann Arbor, Michigan. Claims data have not been publicly available in the past. MedStat's databases track medical and surgical claims in 45 cities, representing some $5 billion in health care expenditures. Primary customers are expected to be insurance companies and employers, who will use the data to evaluate the impact of changes in health benefit coverage.

Another health claims database being marketed is the Health Expense Manager. Three claims review organizations are pooling their data to provide claims information on 120,000 insureds. They are Iris Health Information Systems Corporation of New Haven, Connecticut, Health Economics and Market Analysis of Springfield, Illinois, and Resource Information System of Naperville, Illinois. The data were extracted from a broader pool of claims for 12 million insureds, administered by 350 claims administrators. The database allows payers to track health care costs, demographics, and use patterns for insured groups.

MedTrends ranks seven indexes of health plan performance and makes comparisons with industry norms on these factors: cost of benefits, inpatient costs, outpatient costs, per diem hospitalization costs, hospital use rates, employee out-of-pocket expenses, and case-mix severity on inpatient services.

Data on Health Maintenance Organizations is also of interest to hospitals and health care buyers. HMO use and cost data will be made available by MedStat, which is building a database from 140 HMOs, with the cooperation of General Motors (GM) and the United Auto Workers (UAW). MedStat will target three dozen HMOs that provide 80 percent of the care to GM/UAW members, to monitor the cost, use, and quality of care in the HMOs.

3. *Financial Data:* Two new databases showcase the range of financial data that is now becoming available for healthcare facilities.

a. *Health Care Investment Analysts* (HCIA) is a Baltimore, Maryland-based firm founded by economists and researchers from the Johns Hopkins University. Its database contains information on more than 4,500 hospitals—every short-term general hospital in the United States with more than 50 beds. Data include fiscal years 1984–1987, and are updated frequently. This is a database for competitor analysis. While providing detailed use data and departmental summaries of profitability, the databases also include the complete financial statements of the hospital. The hospital-specific database is complemented by supplementary information on county and metropolitan area demographics, HMO and PPO enrollment, and state-level Medicaid and regulatory programs.

In addition to hospital strategists, HCIA's databases are frequently tapped by investment banks, bond insurers, mutual funds, equipment leasing companies, accounting firms, research groups, and even business coalitions of major employers. Individual hospital and comparative peer-group data are available via personal computer and modem. HCIA collaborates with the accounting firm Deloitte, Haskins, and Sells to make available the *Hospital Industry Sourcebook,* an annual compendium of detailed cross-comparisons of more than 100 peer groups, as well as an analysis of historical and projected health care trends.

b. *Para, Limited* of Pasadena, California is a West Coast source of detailed financial and strategic market data in the health field.

Financial and market comparisons are the heart of Para, Limited's approach. Its financial comparison/demographic data resource program allows clients to evaluate their hospitals, competitors, and peers on a quarterly and year-to-date basis. The information base is driven by annual and periodic reports to California's Office of Statewide Health Planning under the state's uniform hospital accounting and disclosure law.

Para provides more than market assessment; this is also a market analysis service. Para's clients receive semiannual analyses of patient origin, a summary and detailed case mix, and an extensive series of financial reports. Color maps graphically profile the hospital's regional and local market share by key service clusters, including medicine, surgery, psychiatry, substance abuse, women's services, pediatric and newborn services, oncology, orthopedics, and plastic surgery. Para's ProMax program assists hospitals in maximizing the profit potential of their market share and case mix.

4. *Consumer Research:* Between now and the end of the century, the U.S. consumer market will experience extensive changes. The youth market will be shrinking as the older market grows. According to one market research source, people in their middle years will account for nearly 75 percent of the total growth in consumer spending.

The Consumer Research Center is a nonprofit spin-off of the widely respected Conference Board, which represents big business on policy and management issues. Based in New York, the Consumer Research Center produces a series of reports on consumer attitudes and demographics, including:

a. An annual consumer survey, based on 60,000 households, on population and purchasing power

b. A marketers guide to discretionary income of the "upscale" market

c. A U.S. market report series on changes expected before the year 2000 in major segments of the consumer market

d. How consumers spend their money, with a detailed product-by-product report of consumer expenditures

e. A consumer market guide of 200 tables—a marketing data book

f. Special reports such as the recent "Working Woman" and "Midlife and Beyond"

g. A consumer confidence survey—a month-by-month tracking by geographical region, age, and income

h. Three monthly newsletters, including "Consumer Market Research," "Help-Wanted Advertising," and "Forecasters' Forecasts"

5. C.A.C.I. of Fairfax, Virginia is representative of demographic data vendors of microcomputer-based data files. C.A.C.I. provides the latest market demographic profile—age, income, housing, employment, and spending potential information—on computer diskette for microcomputer analysis. The company offers software that uses Lotus 1-2-3 to drive customer-defined tables and analyses. Data are available by file, for example, age by income; or by folder, for example, spending potential.

CUSTOMIZED DATABASES

If every hospital executive was a marketing genius, their hospitals' strategic planning efforts would be directed to those product lines that optimize payer mix and to the appropriate age markets that would maximize volume with a minimum of marketing expense. It will be easier to look like a marketing guru if the hospital strategist has the latest in strategic weapons—a customized database of the hospital's market service, with projections to the year 2000 by product and service line.

There is no way in today's health care market that "every hit will be a home run," but it is definitely possible to improve the success ratio and profitability of hospital plannng and marketing. The key is information—developing a macro view of how each community in a hospital's service area will change demographically, and how that change will translate into shifts in short- and long-run demand for inpatient, ambulatory, and other health services.

Geodemographic Databases

The *baseline* of a health care organization's strategy is a customized database of population and health use in its market. This economic-political assessment must forecast key market changes for the entire service area. The assessment focuses on the geodemographic forces that fuel growth and the controversial issues that surround growth potential. The intent is to identify and quantify the impact on health care delivery. Essential components of a customized local market database include not only demographic and health use data, but also residential and economic development, community infrastructure, and relevant political issues.

A second database that should contribute to strategic hospital marketing is information on population projections. A detailed series of population projections by age and sex from 1989 to the year 2000 is essential in planning for the future. These must be custom-developed small-area projections, not off-the-shelf forecasts. The projections and ensuing analysis should cover the entire age range, and should also focus on topical issues such as the aging of baby boomers, the current baby boomlet, and all senior age groups over age 65. With today's microcomputer technology and databases, population forecasts can be developed for individual ZIP Codes or entire service areas.

PRODUCT-LINE DATABASES

Demographers can now assist hospital marketers in strategically planning on a product-line basis. Product-line forecasts are designed to provide a macro view of the inpatient market between 1989 and the year 2000. Such reports examine the detailed impact of the population growth in the service area on each of the health care organization's service and product lines.

A hospital's product lines are defined by Diagnostic Related Group and ICD9 codes. Each product line is analyzed by separate age groups. Because of the strategic importance of Medicare, product-line forecasts should include a special breakout of potential patients over age 65. Product-line forecasts can be developed in depth, zeroing in on individual ZIP Codes or hospital-defined service areas.

Health organizations can now modify product-line forecasts and look at "what if" scenarios by alternating assumptions. Today's product-line forecasts accommodate adjustments in existing use rates and length of stay based on factors such as new technology and shifts in use patterns. Two examples are: payer and regulator pressure on Ceasarean sections may force a decline of 10–15 percent in the next five years, and the impact of mental health HMOs could be factored to reduce psychiatric length of stay by 15–25 percent during the same period.

The planner can use outside experts, literature reviews, medical staff opinions, micro studies, and other trend data to fine-tune the assumptions that are driving use rates imbedded in the custom database. Unique local factors, such as the Southwest's "sunbird" seasonal migration influx, can be incorporated into the rates. These factors can then be compared to the baseline forecasts, which assume current use patterns, projecting alternate scenarios of growth and change on a product-line basis.

What about competitors? Market-share forecasting is a potentially powerful strategic tool in a competitive environment. Very detailed market-share analysis can be enhanced by incorporating population forecasts on an age- and sex-adjusted basis. This can also provide a base that is suitable for day-to-day census forecasting, targeted marketing strategies, and product-line financial analyses.

PAYOFF FROM CUSTOMIZED DATABASES

The development of a customized local-market database is an investment in strategic management and marketing. Forecasts developed from a customized database provide the health care executive and market strategist with a clear understanding of the market forces affecting each hospital or health organization's future.

Effective market strategy needs to be driven by two sets of factors: health industry trends in financing, use, technology, and medical practice; and community growth and development trends, including population growth, in- and outmigration, age composition, economic development, infrastructure investment (water, sewers), and political factors.

Local Impacts Guide Decision Makers

These *macrotrends* need to be put in the local-market context to be useful. In one hospital's market area, the median age for its immediate service area was forecasted to be 62 by 1995, rising to age 65 by the year 2000. The hospital knew the percentage of elderly was high, but this forecast compelled a specialized strategy that was targeted to older consumers, since this group heavily influences the hospital's future demand.

Market-share trends in the hospital's primary market show the early impact of competitor efforts to "skim the cream" of the senior population. This hospital's focus on two centers of excellence— heart disease and cancer—aligns well with the growth of the elderly predicted by geodemographic market forecasting. But as profit margins under Medicare decline, the hospital needs to look to the future and expand two secondary centers of excellence, which will be used by a younger insured market clientele.

Niche-Oriented Market Strategy

Market strategy can be targeted to precisely the preferred segments that a hospital wishes to reach for a specific product line. One southern California chest pain center was targeted to 45–65 year old men in its service area. By using a forecasting model's capacity of 36 different age/sex groups for population analysis, and 7 distinct age groups for product-line forecasting, the potential exists for much more accurate target marketing. Fine-grain detailed analysis for financial planning of activity levels and hospital census is possible.

Shifting Assumptions Dictate Strategic Moves

As regions move from one phase of economic growth to another, a hospital's market strategy must adjust to fit changing market conditions. For example, hospital A's future looks bright: the area economy will thrive and prosper in the next five to seven years as older, heavy manufacturing gives way to light industry and R&D, led by high-tech companies. But growth may level off by the year 2000. The longer range problem is already evident. A shortage of developable land is driving land prices up, and affordable housing levels will shrink beyond the five- to seven-year growth period. Traffic congestion will also increase, local officials predict. Hospital A, with its custom database, can chart market moves years ahead of the trends and expand or shrink its services in line with market shifts.

Each service area has its unique characteristics, which are not always evident without some "shoe-leather demographic analysis" of local data sources. School and birth data show hospital B's market will be influenced by the growth of ethnic populations. Asian and Filipino populations are doubling, and minority schoolchildren exceed 40 percent. By the year 2000, this hospital's service area may be at least 50 percent minority. Ethnic marketing strategies will be an important adjunct of hospital B's strategic planning for the future.

SUMMARY

Customized forecasts based on custom databases are state-of-the-art. This information is a strategic weapon, and definitely proprietary. Hospitals once freely shared data, but this is no longer the case. Information is powerful. Today's customized forecasts represent an advancement beyond the simplistic data sets that are available from governmental agencies, private software sellers, and data brokers. Such reports are objective in perspective, representing exhaustive field work and local data analysis. There is a rich supply of databases and health-related information for planning and competitive analysis. Information services that provide online data and prepare custom databases are now readily accessible to the market analyst. In the information age, health organizations with better information will make better strategic, policy, and budget choices.

CHAPTER 10

FORECASTING

Today is the first day of the future. Strategic decisions made today will drive tomorrow's future. These decisions are based on assumptions about the future environment. Forecasting provides a more informed base for decision making, involving actions that will have their impact in the future.

The future is neither remote nor mysterious. Most of the major driving forces in tomorrow's health care economy and the wider environment are well-known to the planner and market analyst. The purpose of forecasting is to clarify and quantify the conditions of uncertainty under which all decisions about the future must be made.

There are many possible futures, but only a relative handful can be considered highly probable. These alternative futures are the primary focus of forecasting. Ideally, forecasts should provide information that will prove to be 100 percent accurate in the future. Realistically, planners and decision makers must be satisfied with information and projections that, at best, can only approximate future realities.

There are three cautions to exercise in forecasting.

1. There is no one most probable future state waiting to be discovered by the perceptive analyst. Planners should expect that the future will include multiple trends that will conflict as well as coexist. Analysts should beware of the tendency to oversimplify the future. Tomorrow's environment will be a rich mix of trends and forces—just like today.

277

2. Avoid the error of assuming that the future will be like the past. Be aware of the potential for major discontinuities with the past. These watershed events or trends can make all forecasts obsolete. For example, a federal takeover of state Medicaid programs would give 10 to 12 million additional Americans access to health insurance. This would be a distinct change of federal policy, but is definitely possible.

3. Planners should be aware of the bias built into every forecast. Forecasters impose value judgments on their assumptions. The best forecasts will make their assumptions clear. Planners must explicitly state their assumptions, for example, "HMOs will enroll 50 percent of the population by 1955, and this will reduce hospital use rates to 700 days per 1,000 population."

TYPES OF FORECASTS AND FORECASTERS

Forecasting is both an art and a science. Methods and biases are arrayed along the spectrum of types of forecasts. This typology ranges from computer models and databased extrapolations to the opinions of experts and intuitive visions. The various types of forecasts are highlighted in Figure 24.

Among forecasters, the future is a relative term. For planning purposes, forecasts may be divided into classes based on their time horizon:

Near Future: From the present to the next two to three years: Three years is the most commonly accepted planning horizon for corporate strategic planning. Some firms use the "next 1,000 days" as a way to dramatize predictions for the near future or to focus a major strategic initiative by the organization.

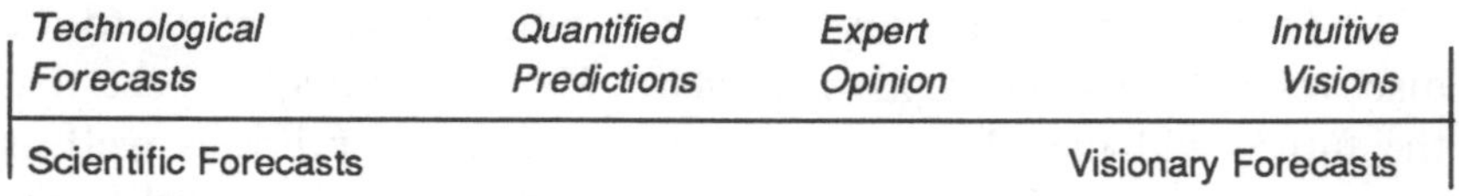

Technological Forecasts	*Quantified Predictions*	*Expert Opinion*	*Intuitive Visions*
Scientific Forecasts		Visionary Forecasts	

Figure 24   Spectrum of forecasts.

Midrange Future: Most commonly, this time frame incorporates the next 5 to 15 years and is often presented in 5-year increments. Few companies have strategic plans that extend beyond 10 years, although key trends may be forecasted for longer periods. Exceptions are public utilities and transportation planners, who often develop capital investment plans and capital needs schedules for 10 to 20 years, based on longer range forecasts.

Far Future: Public finance offices and health departments routinely develop long-range predictions of economic and demographic factors for the next 10–20 years. Often, these forecasts are developed by elaborate multifactor computer simulation models. Frequently, they are expressed as a range of predictions, based on variations in key assumptions.

In strategic planning for health organizations, projections beyond 15 to 20 years are often considered highly speculative and of limited value. Planners may underrate the value of long-range forecasts. For example, incidence rates for heart disease or cancer may be important in strategic decisions on making a major capital investment in a specialized health care institute or on building a center of excellence in a particular clinical speciality.

Planners also should not overstate the significance of forecasts in strategic decisions. Just as there are many possible futures, there are a number of probable forecasts for any market condition. Forecasts may more realistically be expressed as a range rather than a single number. Planners should educate decision makers on using a range of forecasted indicators and avoiding over-reliance on target indicators. The desire for a best projection imputes a level of precision to the forecast that may understate the complexity of the situation.

FORECASTING AND PLANNING

A chapter in Rothschild's[1] book, *Putting It All Together, A Guide to Strategic Thinking,* is entitled "Looking Backward with One Eye on

---

[1] William E. Rothschild. *Putting It All Together, a Guide to Strategic Thinking.* New York, AMACOM, 1976.

the Future." This succinctly describes the nature of most forecasting processes and the job of the health planner. Planning can be defined as making current decisions in the light of future expectations.

When discussing forecasting, the question frequently asked is, "Can the future be predicted?" Most knowledgeable authors agree that the value of forecasting far outweighs the pitfalls.[2] The following quote, attributed to Albert Olenzak,[3] Director of Corporate Planning and Economics at Sun Company, Inc., characterizes the value of forecasting:

> Forecasting might be thought of as analogous to the illumination provided by the headlights of a car driving through a snow storm at night. A bit of what lies ahead is revealed, not always clearly, so that the driver may find his way. It is not necessary for the driver to recognize every landmark and road sign, but merely to avoid danger and pick out enough detail so that he may arrive at his planned destination.

A forecast consists of two elements: content (the prediction) and rationale (the supporting data and assumptions). The specific situations or phenomena being forecasted comprise the content. Examples of forecasts are the demographics of a market, the use of a service, and the adoption of a new technology. The rationale of a forecast seeks to explain how the situation will evolve from its current state to the future state. The application of a rationale to the content results in an outcome or in the description of alternative futures.[4] For example, the content of a forecast might project that the percentage of persons over 65 years of age in a given market area will increase dramatically over a period of 10 years. The forecast rationale might go on to state that this increase will occur because of an economic decline within that market area. Such a decline would reduce job opportunities, driving out younger persons normally found in the labor force and leaving the area with a residual of elderly persons. The

---

[2] Edward Cornish. *The Study of the Future*. Washington, D.C., World Future Society, 1977, pp. 93–95. Cited in Terry W. Rothermel, "Forecasting Resurrected," *Harvard Business Review*, 60(2):147, March–April 1982.

[3] Terry W. Rothermel. "Forecasting Resurrected." *Harvard Business Review*, 60(2):146, March–April 1982.

[4] The term *alternative futures* implies that the planner is more interested in identifying reasonable alternatives than in the precise state of the future. See Willis W. Harmon, *An Incomplete Guide to the Future*, New York, W. W. Norton, 1979.

net effect of this change would be to reduce the absolute size of the population and to increase the proportion of persons over 65 years of age.

Decision makers may have a tendency to over-focus on the prediction and to neglect the underlying rationale. This common error erodes the credibility of forecasts and reduces their value. Much of the criticism of forecasting focuses on inaccuracies in the predicted outcome, but to the planner, the benefit of forecasting is frequently contained in the construction of the rationale. The assumptions imbedded in the rationale may make the most important contribution to strategic decision making.

Factoring Forecasts into the Planning Process

The planner must have a solid understanding of all reasonable alternative futures. Thus, the scope of the forecast must be comprehensive. It should contain both quantitative and qualitative data and should be based on the best available information, whether that is the average expected condition or a range of expected conditions. Parts of the forecast content frequently are combined into sets of alternative futures to be considered by the decision makers.

Planning drives forecasting, not vice versa. The process of forecasting in health planning begins with identifying the forecast content needed to illuminate key decision points in the plan. Next, the current status of critical factors relating to decision points is measured (baseline), and the basis for determining the rates of future change is laid out (forecast). Finally, the rates of change are applied to the current status to predict the future. In carrying out this process, the planner must analyze facts and data and interpret them in conjunction with qualitative judgments to determine a rationale for the forecast.

The goal of this process is to allow decision makers to plan how to bridge the gap between what Ackoff[5] calls the reference scenario and the alternative futures that the planner has forecasted. The reference scenario is the future that would most likely occur if there were no significant changes in the environment or in the behavior of the

---

[5] Russell L. Ackoff. *Creating the Corporate Future.* New York, Wiley, 1981, pp. 101–102.

planning organization. Changes predicted for the reference scenario are developed through a process of environmental assessment.

The content of the environmental assessment component of the plan generally consists of five S.T.E.E.P. components, outlined in Table 18, and presented in more detail in Chapter 6. The items listed under each component are intended to be illustrative rather than comprehensive. A brief explanation of each component follows:

Social: Provides a description of the community's population, demographic, and health status characteristics

Technology: Considers the state of technology that will prevail in health, environmental management, economic activities, and services

Economic: Includes geographic and communications information, as well as traditional economic factors

Environment: Contains a separate discussion of each major component of the physical environment, with relationships between components also described, including health resources and services

Political: Describes the decision-making individuals, organizations, and processes—both official and unofficial

The content of a forecast most appropriate for an organizational planner will include several of these elements; the political, social, and technological components are critical external variables to the organization. The planner will be concerned with linking these with market variables for the organization. For example, the forecast of demographic variables will need to be constructed in relation to those market segments that are most important to the organization. If the organization is providing services to a market with a high percentage of older adults, the forecast will need to focus on the demographics of that market segment and portray the changes that will occur within it.

Geography, political boundaries, psychographics (social, life-style), and the need/demand for services are also examples of important variables that are related to market segments. Their use is discussed in Chapter 7. Beyond the external variables concerned with the forecasting process, the planner must address internal variables such as management capacity, organizational resources, and the capacity to accept new technology. At the heart of the forecast is the set of critical variables used in marketing the services provided by the organization. In addition, the forecast must be sufficiently broad to help the planner identify potential new markets and to provide information to help the organization determine if it is meeting its social obligations to the community.

Developing the Forecast Rationale

The baseline structure of forecasts is composed of the underlying assumptions. When preparing statements about alternative futures,

TABLE 18 Outline of the Forecast Content: Specific Forecast Components

A. Social
1. Population size and composition
    a. Age, race, sex
2. Education
3. Housing
4. Ethnicity
5. Mobility
6. Health status
    a. Mortality
    b. Morbidity

B. Technological
1. Health services technology
2. Environmental management technology

C. Economic
1. Major sources of employment
2. Occupations and income
3. Natural resources
4. Transportation systems
5. Land use

D. Environmental
1. Environmental health (e.g., water quality)
    a. Current status and impact
    b. Existing programs
        (1) Criteria
        (2) Procedures
        (3) Resources
        (4) Constraints
2. Health resources
3. Health services

E. Political
1. Jurisdictions*
2. Governments
    a. Official health agencies
3. Health policy
4. Health expenditures

*The general content of this and each specific component outlined should be current status, trends and other bases for determining rates of change, and the expected future state or states.

the planner must identify the specific rationale that leads to each statement. The rationale is essential because it clarifies the result of the forecasting process. Without knowing the rationale, it is impossible for the decision maker to understand or evaluate a given forecast. For example, the decision maker may be given a forecast stating that women of childbearing age in a community will increase by 25 percent in the next five years. If there is no rationale for that forecast, the decision maker is forced to accept or reject it on intuition. When the rationale is added that this population increase will result from added jobs that will be created by a major new planned unit development in the community, the decision maker is able to evaluate whether the level of predicted change is appropriate for the circumstances involved.

Not only does the forecast rationale provide a basis for evaluating the strengths of the forecast, it also helps clarify the decision maker's expectations for the future. After studying the rationale on which a forecast is based, the planner and decision maker can more readily increase or reduce the forecasted condition, based on changes in the underlying assumptions. Approaches for quantifying and validating forecast rationale are presented in the following section on forecasting methods.

ART AND SCIENCE OF FORECASTING

Forecasting is not an exact science. At their best, forecasts combine well-grounded predictions tested by expert judgment. As previously discussed, techniques for looking at the future fall into two broad categories, the *art* and the *science* of forecasting. The first category includes *authority methods,* which rely on experts— including the forecaster as expert—to predict the future.[6] The second set of scientific or technological forecasting approaches, uses some

---

[6] See J. Scott Armstrong, *Long-Range Forecasting: From Crystal Ball to Computer,* 2nd Edition, New York, Wiley, 1985; and F. Gerard Adams, *The Business Forecasting Revolution: Nation, Industry, Firm,* New York, Oxford University Press, 1986.

quantitative approaches to identifying the current condition, rates of change, and future states, based on those rates of change.

The major difference between these two approaches is that with the authority methods, the planner does not try to create or evaluate the forecast rationale but relies on and accepts the rationale that is proposed by authorities. In contrast, the technological forecasting methods require the planner to become involved in developing and evaluating the forecast rationale. Many forecasters are not neutral in their preference for the method of approach. The technological forecasters believe that human judgment only degrades a good technologically derived forecast, while forecasters and futurists who prefer to rely on intuition discount scientific predictions as the work of narrow-minded technocrats.

Authority Methods

Much of the art of forecasting relies on the opinions of experts. Authority methods of forecasting are based on the planner's ability to identify and organize the opinions of experts. This task would be easier if there were a well-accepted definition for expert. Generally, the narrower the scope of the subject, the easier it is to identify knowledgeable observers and thought-leaders in the field, using bibliographic search methods and collegial networking. Frequent sources of experts include the professional literature, trade associations, professional associations, consulting firms, vendors and suppliers, research organizations, universities and teaching programs, and honors and awards.

The prospect of finding knowledgeable people depends on the subject matter. For example, identifying several experts or authorities in the use of diagnostic ultrasound techniques would not be difficult; however, the prospect of finding an expert in "the American way of life" is another matter. Although many individuals would claim expertise, it would be difficult to identify a single, generally accepted expert. The problem lies as much in the diffuse nature of the topic as in the number of individuals claiming expertise. In general, the more narrowly defined and/or scientific the subject matter, the more easily one can identify an expert.

There are certain characteristics that the planner must be aware of in the search for expert judgments. First, expertise does not always equate with education. In the sciences, the two are often linked, but in other spheres, that is not always the case. For example, the best expert on a local political situation is not likely to be the university political science professor but the local mayor. Second, an expert can more easily be prescriptive than descriptive about the future (i.e., generally he can identify what *should* occur more readily than what *will* occur). Third, it is sometimes difficult to persuade experts to identify the specific rationale behind their predictions. Experts with a great deal of knowledge in an area may assume that major portions of their rationale are generally accepted or well-understood assumptions. The planner must make a determined effort to clarify the rationale cited by the experts.

The advantages of using authority methods relate primarily to time and money, since these methods tend to be quick and inexpensive. In addition, they lend themselves better to qualitative than to quantitative subject matter. The main disadvantage of authority methods is that equally qualified authorities may develop very different views about the future. If a forecast uses only one expert, it is difficult to know whether that individual's views are consistent with general thinking. On the other hand, if several authorities are used, there arises the problem of resolving potentially diverse opinions.

There are a number of approaches to incorporating expert opinion into forecasts. This list is not exhaustive but represents a series of techniques that can be used by most health planners and market analysts in the health planning process:

1. *Expert Consultant:* Like an expert witness in a legal case, the use of a single individual who is highly informed in the forecast's content area can provide a window on the future from the perspective of a knowledgeable observer. The consultant can develop a position paper on the topic of interest and/or provide consultation directly to the planning process as an invited participant to the planning committee or decision makers.

2. *Expert Panel:* Convening a group of experts who can provide collective input into the forecast content provides a multiperspective to strategic decisions. Even when experts disagree, the planning

process will be illuminated by both consensus and conflict. Giving decision makers an opportunity to interact directly with a panel of experts cuts through the layers of ambiguity that sometimes cloak expert predictions.

3. *Delphi Panel:* Gathers information from a group of dispersed experts (a more detailed explanation of this technique appears on pp. 290–291).

4. *Delbecq Panel* (or nominal group process): Maximizes the input of a group of experts gathered in one place (a further discussion appears on pp. 291–292).

5. *Questionnaire:* Surveys the responses of a large group of experts to a list of questions.

6. *Permanent Panel:* Identifies and maintains a group of experts who can be used for several studies of the future.

7. *Essay Writer:* Obtains a group of experts to write essays on the forecast content (this approach is especially useful in identifying the forecast rationale).

Opinion Methods: The Art of Forecasting

Forecasting future conditions is far from an exact science. Much of the content of forecasts is based on opinion. These qualitative data are often used in developing assumptions on which quantitative forecasts can be constructed. The use of opinion in forecasting recognizes the value of experience and intuition in predicting futures.

1. *The Practice of Intuition:* Think of the future as an "ill structured problem," suggests Mendell.[7] Confronting it, the planner will be involved in the search for new patterns. If ever a Nobel prize is awarded for thinking, the British psychologist Edward de Bono will probably win it. The mind, according to de Bono,[8] acts as a "pattern-creating system. As information pours in, the mind searches

---

[7] Jay S. Mendell. "The Practice of Intuition." In: *Handbook of Future Research.* Edited by Jib Fowles. Westport, Conn., Greenwood Press, 1978, p. 149.

[8] Edward de Bono, *Lateral Thinking for Management,* New York, American Management Assn., 1971; see also _____, *New Think,* New York, Basic Books, 1967.

for and discovers patterns (concepts, abstractions, or models) that condense, organize, and give meaning to the incoming information." This patterning behavior has advantages and disadvantages. It relieves the mind of extensive conscious data manipulation and repetitious thinking if incoming information fits existing patterns. In the planning context, some incoming information is interpreted in terms of existing patterns (planning assumptions, strategies); some is used to extend and enlarge existing patterns, or to link together existing patterns; but some is filtered out if it does not fit patterns with which the planner is familiar. When new information is inconsistent with accepted assumptions, it may be ignored. Thus, de Bono argues, "Thinking about the future consists not only of creating new patterns but of getting rid of new ones."

The practice of intuition is not limited to a few gifted individuals. Developing new patterns—insights—can be enhanced by the use of idea generators. Roger von Oech,[9] author of practical guides to innovation such as *A Whack On the Side of the Head,* defines discovery as "Looking at the same thing as everyone else and thinking something different." In a subsequent work, *A Kick in the Seat of the Pants,* von Oech[10] identifies a number of useful approaches that can lead to new ideas and conceptual breakthroughs:

   a. Adopt an insight outlook
   b. Know what your objective is
   c. Look in other fields
   d. Develop lots of ideas
   e. Expect the unexpected
   f. Shift your focus
   g. Don't overlook the obvious
   h. Pay attention to the small things
   i. Look at the big picture
   j. Use obstacles to break out of ruts

There are many reasons to explain the natural tendency to stay with established patterns until forced into new ones. Individuals

---

[9] Roger von Oech. *A Whack on the Side of the Head.* Menlo Park, Calif., Creative Think, 1983, p. 7.
[10] _____. *A Kick in the Seat of the Pants.* New York, Harper & Row, 1986.

and organizations will cling to the status quo until there is too much disconfirming information to ignore. Like machines, human enterprises operate as efficiently as possible. Breaking old routines is time-consuming and inefficient. There is the fear of being wrong and the cost of taking risks. With the complexity of today's environment, specialization is another factor that limits the ability to see new patterns; von Oech[11] cautions that the planner must be aware of the problem that psychologist Abraham Maslow recognized when he stated, "People who are only good with hammers see every problem as a nail."

2. *Environmental Scanning:* When the rate of change increases, so does the need for information on the environment. Scanning in the context of forecasting simply refers to the process of gathering information on a variety of factors in the organization's environment. For forecasting purposes, the emphasis is on the search for signals of change, which suggest that old patterns are breaking down or new patterns are emerging.

Forecasters and corporations have institutionalized the practice of environmental scanning. More than a dozen Fortune 500 companies such as Allstate Insurance, Security Pacific Bank, and McDonald's have established futures research programs to conduct continuous environmental scanning. Most have a small professional staff who read and digest a broad array of books, journals, and technical reports. The purpose of these programs is to protect their sponsors from unanticipated threats and to identify future opportunities before their competitors do. One of the longest established environmental scanning programs is based at the American Council of Life Insurance (ACLI) in Washington, D.C. For more than a decade, the council used a permanent panel of scanners from some 100 insurance companies. These volunteers read a broad array of journals, from the United States and abroad, covering many fields, looking for signs and signals of change. The council's Trend Analysis Program (TAP) published a newsletter called *Straws in the Wind*. Although the network of scanners is no longer used, ACLI continues to publish periodic reports on a wide array of socioeconomic changes. The Futures Research Division of Security Pacific Bank in Los Angeles initiated

---

[11] Ibid., p. 52.

the publication of a weekly newsletter, *FutureScan,* which highlights trends from wide-ranging sources. The newsletter has a circulation of thousands of readers inside and outside the bank and is now available commercially.

3. *Delphi Method:* The ancient site of Delphi was renowned in mythology for its oracle. In more recent times, the RAND Corporation adopted the name Delphi for a procedure to obtain a reliable consensus of opinion from a group of experts by a series of questionnaires and controlled opinion feedback. Delphi is a relatively simple approach for probing uncertainty by using expert opinion without the cost or limitations of face-to-face communication.

Forecasters have found that Delphi is a communication process with a versatile range of uses: setting social priorities, exploring the pros and cons of alternative policies, evaluating budget or investment options, assessing the significance of actual or potential events, and evaluating the likehood of future conditions such as medical breakthroughs.

Linstone[12] defines the sequence of steps in conducting a Delphi analysis:

a. Formation of a team to undertake and monitor a Delphi on a given subject

b. Selection of one or more panels to participate in the exercise; customarily, the panelists are experts in the area to be investigated

c. Development of the first round of Delphi questionnaires

d. Testing the questionnaire for proper wording (e.g., ambiguities, vagueness)

e. Transmission of the first questionnaires to the panelists

f. Analysis of the first round of responses

g. Preparation of the second round of questionnaires

h. Transmission of the second round of questionnaires to the panelists

i. Analysis of the second round of responses (steps g–i are repeated so long as needed to achieve stability in the results)

j. Preparation of a report by the analysis team to present the conclusions

---

[12] Harold A. Linstone. "The Delphi Technique." In: *Handbook of Futures Research.* Edited by Jib Fowles. Westport, Conn., Greenwood Press, 1978, pp. 274–275.

The flexibility of the Delphi method makes it suitable for many planning problems. In forecasting the future of the health industry, Coile and Grossman[13] have conducted an ongoing modified Delphi survey research series for *Healthcare Forum* magazine, with corporate sponsorship from the Healthcare Forum in San Francisco and companies that include Laventhol & Horwath, the Grimmelman Group, and Citibank. Their "FutureTrack" column is based on a bimonthly Delphi survey of 20 questions to a permanent panel of 500 experts drawn from all regions and sectors of the health industry. Topics such as the future of AIDS, hospital-physician relationships, and key market indicators have been predicted using the Delphi approach.

4. *Delbecq Technique:* Also known as the *nominal group process,* the Delbecq approach is a process for communication and consensus. Unlike the Delphi method, the nominal group process uses face-to-face communication. In a typical Delbecq session, the group or panel proceeds in the following sequence:

a. Participants are given a clear statement of the task they are to accomplish.

b. Individual participants write down their ideas.

c. Following this period of idea generation, the participants, in round-robin fashion, express their ideas, which are listed on a flip chart by the Delbecq facilitator; no social interaction occurs during this step, so that all individuals will be encouraged to participate and contribute ideas to the process.

d. Each idea is then discussed to ensure that everyone clearly understands the intent of each point.

e. If a ranking of the list is desired, this is done individually, in silence, and reported in round-robin fashion; ranking often is done in two rounds to generate a final priority listing of ideas.

Like the Delphi technique, the Delbecq approach seeks to inhibit social contact at the critical point of idea generation. This allows for a

---

[13] Russell C. Coile, Jr. and Randolph M. Grossman. "Future Track: Forum's 'Panel of 300' Charts Healthcare's Next 1,000 Days." *Healthcare Forum,* January–February 1987, pp. 6–8.

broad range of viewpoints, does not prematurely limit lines of inquiry, reduces group-think, and encourages a constraint-free expression of ideas. Two key factors in making the Delbecq approach work are agreement among the participants to adhere to the rules of the process and a well-trained leader who is capable of managing the group process. The Delbecq technique has proved useful in areas other than forecasting and has demonstrated its utility in establishing priorities and setting criteria or standards.

5. *Content Analysis:* Futurist John Naisbitt[14] has popularized the technique of content analysis. Literally, this method is based on analyzing the content of the media. Staff members of the Naisbitt Group sift and measure the column inches and content of news coverage on various topics appearing in the printed media. This method of monitoring public behavior and events was developed during World War II by military intelligence, and it is used widely today in the intelligence community.

Content analysis is based on an assumption that societies, like human beings, can only handle a limited amount of information at one time. The collective store of topics and events in the media is referred to by Naisbitt as the "news hole." For economic reasons, the amount of space in a newspaper that is devoted to news is limited. When a new topic is introduced, topics of lesser or declining interest get less coverage or are dropped from the news hole. It works on the principle of forced choice in a closed system. Naisbitt notes in *Megatrends* that when environmental concerns and events such as "Earth Day" began to be noted in the national media, there was a corresponding decline in media attention to civil rights, on a one-to-one basis. Within two years, content analysis showed a crossover of media priority to environmental issues, reflecting that they had become a more important priority than civil rights.

Health organizations and market analysts can use a news clipping service to track media attention to health-related issues. Changes in the extent of coverage, as well as in the topics picked up by the media, can suggest shifting market trends and public attitudes. These signals

---

[14] John Naisbitt. *Megatrends: Ten New Directions Transforming Our Lives.* New York, Warner Books, 1982, pp. 3–4.

of change can then be explored by using other methods of futures research.

6. *Scenarios:* The most artful form of forecasting is the scenario. The primary definition of a scenario is "an outline or synopsis of a play." Like a movie screenplay, a scenario is a story about the future. Scenarios are essentially a method for communicating future conjectures. Kahn and Wiener[15] put a scenario in the context of forecasting by defining it as a "hypothetical sequence of events constructed for the purpose of focusing attention on causal processes and decision points."

By their nature, scenarios are hypothetical. They are evocative dramatizations of future conditions, based on a set of assumptions. Since a scenario is only a sketch, it should map out the key branching points in a sequence of decisions or events. These will highlight the major determinants that might cause the future to evolve from the present to one or more alternative futures. Scenarios sketch in the consequences of following a causal chain into the future. Finally, scenarios are more holistic than single-factor projections. Scenarios have an ability to present the future in a more complete and multifaceted manner. Combining social, economic, and technological trends gives decision makers a sense of the cross-impact of key changes in the future environment.

Some scenarios may be clearly visionary, reflecting the value judgments of their authors. Visionary scenarios project a preferred state of affairs. Some of the most evocative future scenarios have been visionary, such as Orwell's classic *1984.* Among the alternative futures projected by Hawken, Ogilvy, and Schwartz[16] of SRI International in *Seven Tomorrows,* the authors suggest a *transformational alternative,* in which Americans voluntarily downscale their materialism, begin to live within limited resources, and show a new respect for others and for world peace.

---

[15] Herman Kahn and Anthony J. Wiener. *The Year 2000: A Framework for Speculation on the Next Thirty-Three Years.* New York, MacMillan, 1967.
[16] Paul Hawken, James Ogilvy, and Peter Schwartz. *Seven Tomorrows: Toward a Voluntary History.* New York, Bantam Books, 1982.

Given the uncertainty of predicting future states with precision and the complexity of real-world decision making, planners are encouraged to develop multiple scenarios by varying key assumptions.

Technological Forecasting: The Scientific Methods

At the other end of the methodological spectrum from the visionary futurists are the technological forecasters. The most extreme adherents among forecasters in this school believe that factoring opinion into quantitative predictions only weakens the validity of the forecasts.

Technological methods of looking at the future always involve the three-step process of identifying the current state, identifying the rates of change, and drawing conclusions based on the two elements. These techniques tend to be especially suited to manipulating quantitative data but are by no means limited to that activity; some are also very useful in manipulating qualitative information. Martin,[17] introducing the methods of technological forecasting in the *Handbook of Futures Research,* states that the degree of success of forecasters in using technological methods depends on the extent to which (1) there are reliable patterns in past events, (2) these patterns are known to forecasters, and (3) forecasters can obtain the data that are needed to use these patterns in the generation of forecasts.

Technological forecasting assumes that there will be a predictable connection between past and future events. In those fields or market sectors where patterns of behavior are clear-cut and involve only a few variables, forecasts can be quite precise, and decision makers can rely on them with a high level of confidence. Where patterns involve numerous variables, many of which are only slightly known or for which data are limited, then the quality of the forecast will be similiarly impaired. Technological forecasting does least well during periods of high discontinuity, where old patterns are breaking down rapidly but new patterns are not yet clear. Under these conditions, only short-term forecasts are of any value, since they may approximate market events and indicators in transition during the next 6 to 18 months. Projections beyond 2 to 3 years, under conditions of high

---

[17] Joseph P. Martin. "Technological Forecasting." In: *Handbook of Futures Research.* Edited by Jib Fowles. Westport, Conn., Greenwood Press, 1978, p. 369.

uncertainty, will have only limited use unless they are expressed in ranges of relative change.

Within the category of technological forecasting, or *conjecture methods,* is a hierarchy tied to the forecast rationale: the simpler methods are limited in their rationales, whereas the more complex methods have well-developed rationales.

The major advantage of conjecture approaches is that the rationale tends to be more highly developed and better understood than that of forecasts based on opinion. The major disadvantage is that conjecture approaches are usually more expensive and more time-consuming. Following is a list of specific methods of technological forecasting that are useful to health planners and market analysts:

1. *Extrapolation–Linear:*   This approach measures the current state, makes assumptions about rates of change, and draws conclusions based on both. It seeks only to discover what will happen if the assumed rates of change are realized. Although assumptions are clearly stated, the simple projections developed by the linear extrapolation approach do not critically evaluate these assumptions. Such techniques as time series analysis fall under the category of simple projection. Linear extrapolation is most closely associated with quantitative phenomena, although it may be qualitative as well.

2. *Extrapolation–Growth Curves:*   Use of growth curves simulate the natural *lazy S* curve frequently observed with natural phenomena. The growth in performance of some technological approach to solving a problem is a frequent application of growth curve analysis. For example, when forecasting the future demand for cardiac bypass surgery, the lazy S curve fits the pattern of a slow initial growth when the procedure is in early development and testing, then rapid growth with widespread acceptance, followed by a gradual easing of the growth slope as the market is saturated and newer methods such as balloon angioplasty begin to take market share away from the defending bypass surgical method.

3. *Extrapolation–Trend Curves:*   These extrapolation methods identify the current state, seek to identify and evaluate the most probable factors affecting the rates of change, then draw appropriate conclusions based on the three elements. Trend curves chart the

long-term behavior of some condition. The use of trend curves assumes that whatever factors produced the trend will continue to produce an extension of it. In particular, if the past has seen a succession of growth curves, with each curve reaching a higher limit, the forecast assumes that the upward trend will continue within predictable limits. During the high-growth phase of a technology or market trend, predictions may be predictably exponential. The risk for the forecaster lies in predicting when the exponential growth will slow or level off, for example, when the enrollment expansion rate of HMOs fell from an annual rate of 25 percent to 12 percent between 1987 and 1988. Often, the trigger factor that may interrupt the growth trend may come from background factors such as politics, economics, or technology.

4. *Correlation Methods:* The forecaster can take advantage of correlations between the variable that is being forecasted and some other quantity that can be more readily measured or estimated. Frequently, projections of demand for health services are correlated with demographic factors. With these techniques, the forecast rationale is developed more completely and incorporates more complex sets of factors.

5. *Cross-impact Matrices:* The methods discussed above are used for forecasting single variables or factors. A problem arises when combining multiple variables, each with its own forecast, into an overall prediction. This method is not a forecasting technique. It is a means for combining forecasts and determining whether the forecasts are consistent with each other. Martin[18] outlines the technique succinctly. The basis for a cross-impact matrix is a set of events that are to occur within a specified period of time. Each event has associated with it a date when it is forecast to occur and a probability of occurrence, which may be a single date or a span of time. The events are listed in chronical sequence of occurrence and arrayed as the rows and cells of a matrix (see Figure 25).

6. *Computer Simulation:* While all of the technological forecasting methods can be carried out manually, many can be done much more efficiently and effectively with computer support. Manual methods

---

[18] Ibid., pp. 387–388.

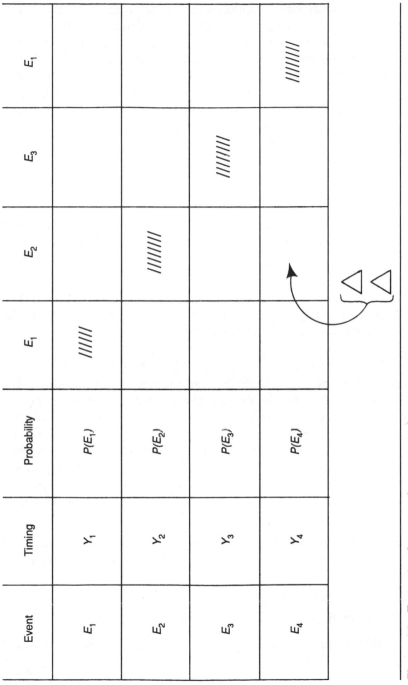

Figure 25 Example of a cross-impact matrix.

are tedious; moreover, computerization can reduce human error. Ordinary extrapolations are speedier on a computer, and cross-impact analyses even more so. Correlations can be quickly run on multiple factors. A number of existing statistical and financial software packages such as Lotus 1-2-3, Baxter's Market Model, or the Sachs Group's MarketPlanner can aid this forecasting analysis (see Chapter 8). Using a causal model is almost impossible without the aid of a computer to follow the interactions of the variables.

POPULATION FORECASTING

Today's health planners have access to extensive demographic data-bases from public and commercial sources. Nevertheless, a dis-cussion of forecasting for health planning is incomplete without an introduction to the methods of estimating and projecting small-area populations.

The methods used to create current population estimates and to develop projections of the population are frequently similiar, but the differences between them must be understood:

1. Current estimates of the population are derived by applying postcensus ratios to data derived from the most previous census. For example, the 1989 population of a city is estimated by adjusting the 1980 or 1985 census data for births, deaths, and net migration that took place between the most recent census and 1989. Birth and death data for that period are available through the Vital Registry System and can be used to calculate the current estimate for 1989. Actual migration data may be available from state governmental sources or universities, or it may be estimated by using the most recent migration data from the prior census.

2. Population projections are, technically, estimates made for future dates. Thus, the data used for a projection are predictive rather than observed.

Methods for Estimating and Projecting Populations

Five major methods that are used to estimate and project populations are:

1. *Extrapolation:* The least complex method of population projection is simple extrapolation. This can be done on an arithmetic basis, which involves equal amounts of change throughout each period, or on a geometric basis, which allows for constant rates of change. This technique should be used only for rough estimates or projections that do not consider more discrete factors, such as age or sex.

2. *Ratio method:* Another technique is known as the ratio method, which relates the total population with some regularly measured variable, (e.g., school enrollments, utility hookups, automobile registrations) that is assumed to be constantly proportional to the total population. In the ratio method, the historical relationship between two populations is used as the basis for determining the projection. For example, if a subpopulation has consistently been 25 percent of the larger population, then 25 percent of the latter's projected size is used to approximate the subpopulation's projected size. This method can be applied in a number of different ways and situations but only with populations that have been stable over a period of time.

3. *Correlation method:* The third approach, the correlation method, can be simple or multiple. It is a more sophisticated version of the ratio approach and uses statistical correlations of variables in the projective process. This approach tends to give better results than the ratio approach, since the implied relationships can be measured and tested; however, the following problems can arise when using correlation methods:

a. There is the possibility of omitting certain variables, even when using multiple regression.

b. Multicollinearity, in which independent variables also are correlated with each other, may yield an accurate outcome, but the effect attributed to each variable cannot be determined. This can be overcome by stepwise multiple regression.

c. Autocorrelation, in which the dependent variable (projected population in the latter year) is most closely correlated to its previous value (e.g., population in the first year), can be solved by differential equations.

d. Identification, in which there are two curves—such as supply and demand—either of which can shift so that neither can be identified by points of intersection between a stable curve and a moving curve, can be overcome by making one of the curves more variable than the other by adding an extra independent variable to one equation. For example, weather could be added to agricultural supply, but not to demand. This would make the supply curve sufficiently variable to show how it moves along a stable demand curve.

e. Spurious correlation or causality occurs because forecasting models frequently are based on a consistent relationship between variables without considering the causes of that relationship. Such a situation can be very misleading. Consider, for instance, a case in which emergency room (ER) use and the hospital's marketing budget are positively correlated. In reality, increased use of the ER may or may not be in any way related to hospital spending for advertising and marketing. This problem can be avoided by using a structural model that is based on a theoretical causal relationship rather than on the simple outcome of mathematical manipulations.

4. *Component method:* A fourth approach to population forecasting is the component method. This can be used to forecast total population or to measure the outcome for subgroups (e.g., age, sex, race), which can be summed to give an overall total. The component formula is simple and straightforward:

$$P_{t+1} = P_t + B - D + M$$

where:

P_{t+1} = the population after the completion of one period
P_t = the population at the beginning of the period
B = the number of births during the period
D = the number of deaths during the period
M = the net migration during the period

With this method, the death rate is assumed to be constant. No one really looks for dramatic changes in mortality rates, since most major diseases have now been controlled, and mortality rates change little from year to year. This is true, however, only for the overall population, because it may be possible to decrease the mortality rate of specific subgroups, particularly infants and children. The birthrate is not so predictable; therefore, low, medium, and high fertility rates are used to generate a range of outcomes. The migration rate is difficult to identify and often varies substantially from place to place.

Net migration can be roughly estimated by applying the residual net migration to data acquired from previous censuses. The formula for residual net migration

$$M = P_{t + 1} - (P_t + B - D)$$

assumes that the data on births and deaths are accurate; unfortunately, such an assumption is seldom completely justified.

These four population forecasting methods may be insufficient to meet the requirements for planning health services, facilities, or product-line planning. An assumption that the aggregate projections can be broken down into the same proportions as the base population is inadequate. A display of changes in individual cohorts is needed. Each cohort has special population growth and health characteristics; therefore, the projection should include adjustments for any changes in health status that may be likely to occur (e.g., a survival rate for a given cohort may change as new health programs are added, or as immigration will change household income levels).

5. *Cohort survival method:* The fifth approach to population forecasting, the cohort survival (CS) method, overcomes the limitations noted above. In addition, the sum of the cohorts yields a more accurate projection than the aggregrate projections described in the other approaches to population forecasting. Following are the steps involved in the cohort survival method:

   a. The population should be broken down into appropriate subgroups. The interval covered by each age group should be equal to periods of projection; for example, for 5-, 10-, or 20-year projections, use 5-year age groups (10–14, 45–49, ...).

   b. Multiply each subgroup by the appropriate survival rate, which is the complement of the death rate for the cohort. If the death rate is 10 per 10,000, the survival rate will be 9,990 per 10,000.

   c. Adjust each cohort for the percentage that will advance to the next cohort due to age increase during the year. The percentage depends on the width of the cohort. This should be based on the number of survivors rather than on the initial number of individuals in the cohort.

    d. Multiply female groups in the 15–44 age cohort by the appropriate birthrates to obtain the number of births.

    e. Multiply the total number of births by the proportion of male births and the proportion of female births to obtain the number of male and female births.

    f. Multiply male and female births by the appropriate survival rates.

    g. Add surviving births to the youngest cohorts.

    h. Adjust each group for net migration.

    In Table 19, column $t + 1$ (cs) illustrates the computations by the cohort survival method. Note the following for the male cohort in the 0–14 age group:

    970 of the original 1,000 survived
       70 (approximately 1/14 of 970) moved into the 15–44 age group
       50 male babies survived the 90 births to the 1,000 females in the 15–44 age group

    Column $t + 1$ (95.5%) illustrates the results that would have been obtained had the total population been decreasing at a rate of 4.5 percent over the past decade. The aggregate projection would be the same as that obtained by the cohort survival method, but when this aggregate is broken down into age groups on the basis of the age distribution at time t, it does not reveal the shifts in age and sex distribution, which are of critical importance in planning health services and estimating future demand.

Factoring for Migration

One of the continuing problems of population estimation and forecasting is measurement of net migration. Two factors should be noted: Net migration is a function of both in-migration and out-migration, and, although actual net migration may be zero, changes might have occurred in the makeup of a population. Even though a planner may find little or no net migration and no change in total numbers, the analyst should be careful to identify any major population shifts within those numbers.

TABLE 19 Example of Cohort Survival and Constant Rate Methods of Population Projections

Age Group	Mortality Rate, in percent	Number		
		t	*t + 1 (cs)*	*t + 1 (95.5%)*
Male				
0–14	3	1,000	970 – 70 + 50 = 950	955
15–44	1	1,000	70 + 990 – 30 = 1,030	955
45–64	4	1,000	30 + 960 – 50 = 940	955
65 and over	22	1,000	50 + 780 = 830	955
Total Male	8	4,000	3,750	3,820
Female				
0–14	2	1,000	980 – 80 + 40 = 940	955
15–44	0.5	1,000	80 + 995 – 35 = 1,040	955
45–64	2	1,000	35 + 980 – 50 = 965	955
65 and over	11	1,000	50 + 890 = 940	955
Total Female	4	4,000	3,885	3,820
Total Male and Female		8,000	7,635	7,640

Natality rate = 9 percent
Male:female baby ratio = 55:45

Methods of social forecasting other than population estimation and projection techniques have also been used, including a group of techniques based on economic data; these approaches typically view population migration as a function of employment. Land use also has served as the basis of population projection in a number of cases.[19]

SUMMARY

All strategic decisions are made under conditions of uncertainty. Forecasting is concerned with quantifying uncertainty about the future, which is the context for all strategic decisions.

Forecasting is not an exact science, any more than economics is. A variety of qualitative and quantitative approaches are available to the planner. Both opinion and historical data can provide balance to a quantitative forecast. Scenarios sketch the implications of alternatives for decision makers. Computer simulation allows manipulation of an array of decision factors. The best forecasts illuminate the context and consequences of decisions. Planners should remember this rule: Make and take all forecasts with a grain of salt! Forecasts are only a decision aid. Forecasting is not a substitute for judgment in the planning or decision-making processes.

---

[19] Richard Irwin. *Guide for Local Area Population Projections*. Washington, D.C., U.S. Government Printing Office, 1977. (U.S. Bureau of the Census Technical Paper No. 39)

AUTHOR INDEX

SUBJECT INDEX

Accountability concept in metapolicy, 77–78
Acquisition plans, 138–141
Actions, 23, 91
  defined, 85, 91–92
  by Federal Government, 67–69, 177–179
Actions, linkages, 85–89
  health services and resources, 88
  health status and services, 85–88
  resources and resource development plans, 89
Adaptive systems, 15
American Council of Life Insurance, 289
American Hospital Association, 264
American Medical Association, 264
Analysis, *see* Decision analysis;
  Decision analysis approaches
Averages, computation of, 262

Black box (element) of subsystems, 30–31
Bureau of the Census, 263
Business planning process, 136–143
  acquisition plans, 138–141

continuation business plans, 141–143
  start-up plans, 137–138
  see also Organizational planning
Business plans, 38–39, 47, 136–137
Business strategies, 43–47, 63
  competitive position, options of, 44–45
  cost considerations, 44, 46, 129–130
  cost leadership strategy, 43
  development of, 45–47
  differentiation strategy, 44, 129, 130, 131
  focus strategy, 44, 129–130
Business strategists, types of, 126–127
Business unit strategies, 126–136
  for declining markets, 134–135
  development approaches, 128–129
  development factors, 129–130
  environmental dependencies, 127–128
  for growing markets, 131–132
  for mature markets, 132–134
  for new markets, 131
  options, 130–135
  see also Strategic planning